BUSHWHACKERS!

BUSHWHACKERS!
THE CIVIL WAR IN NORTH CAROLINA (VOLUME II: THE MOUNTAINS)

William R. Trotter

DEDICATION
To Craig Gaskell, with love and gratitude.

BUSHWHACKERS!

The Civil War in North Carolina
The Mountains

William R. Trotter

John F. Blair, Publisher
Winston-Salem, North Carolina

This book is printed on acid-free paper.

Library of Congress Cataloging-in-Publication Data

Trotter, William R.
Bushwhackers : the mountains / William R. Trotter.
p.   cm. — (The Civil War in North Carolina ; v. 2)
Includes bibliographical references and index.
ISBN 0-89587-087-8 (pbk.)
1. North Carolina—History—Civil War, 1861–1865—Underground movements.
2. United States—History—Civil War, 1861–1865—Underground movements.
3. Guerrillas—North Carolina—History—19th century.
I. Title. II. Series: Trotter, William R. Civil War in North Carolina ; v. 2.
E470.T79 1991
973.7'4756—dc20
90-28760

TABLE OF CONTENTS

INTRODUCTION

"In the mountain war the question of allegiance was not easily resolved in the safety of homes surrounded by sympathetic neighbors, secure from far away battlefields. An allegiance was worn as a target over the heart, amid armed enemies, and loyalty could attract both dangerous friends and mortal enemies...."

-- Philip Shaw Paludin: *Victims -- A True Story of the Civil War*

Although the mountains of North Carolina would have furnished an epic backdrop for a great military campaign, let the reader be aware at once that there were no large battles fought in these mountains during the Civil War — not even a single engagement on the scale of Kings Mountain during the Revolution. And yet there was no region in the state which endured more violence over a comparable period of time. Acre for acre, there was probably more gunfighting and gratuitous cold-blooded murder in Appalachian North Carolina during the Civil War than there was in any comparable chunk of the Wild West during any four-year period you care to name.

That claim may seem extreme. But although this book cannot precisely document all of the violence that took place, it does suggest what happened in a tip-of-the-iceberg manner. A great deal of the fratricidal raiding and bushwhacking occurred between small bands of men who operated under no regular military command (or did so only sporadically), and hence there were no official reports filed on most of the violence. Of those who might have been inclined to preserve their experiences for posterity, few were literate enough to write a simple letter, never mind a detailed memoir. Many anecdotes existed for years only in the form of oral tales, passed along within the family, until some local historian happened to write them down, 30 or 50 years after the fact. But based on the few contemporary accounts that do contain any detail, it seems safe to say that for every ambush and shoot-out that did get chronicled, there were probably ten more that did not.

Albert D. Richardson, a correspondent for the *New York Tribune* who escaped from the Salisbury prison camp and eventually made his way to Federal lines in Tennessee, stayed with dozens of Unionist sympathizers in the North Carolina mountains, and he discovered an incidence of everyday violence that stunned him:

> During our whole journey we entered only one house inhabited by white Unionists, which had never been plundered by the Home Guard or Rebel guerrillas. Almost every loyal family had given to the Cause some of its nearest and dearest. We were told so frequently — "My father was killed in those woods" or, "The guerrillas shot my brother in that ravine," that, finally, these tragedies made little impression on us.

What existed in the western counties, from about mid-1862 until the war's end (and after, in some places), was a sullen, smoldering atmosphere of deprivation and anxiety, of the constant possibility of violence -- a pervasive condition somewhere between low-level guerrilla warfare and epidemic banditry. The absence of large armies and epic battles did not mean that the war could be held at arm's length, or that the inhabitants of the mountain counties could feel themselves protected from war's direct effects, if not from the inevitable grief that came from losing a loved one on a distant battlefield. The war was, on the contrary, all around them. It was characterized by a latent, lurking, sense of menace, combined with economic hardship and periodic outbursts of what can only be described as fratricidal madness.

The entire subject of guerrilla warfare in the Southern Appalachians is one that Civil War historians, on the whole, have been loathe to dirty their hands with. It is not, of course, as colorful as the great campaigns of Virginia or western Tennessee. Although there was plenty of drama in the partisan strife of that era, it was also squalid, brutal, and confusing — as confusing to research and write about, in many cases, as it was to experience. But as Karl von Clausewitz pointed out, confusion is endemic to warfare, and extreme brutality is endemic to guerrilla warfare -- particularly when social, economic, and environmental factors dictate that the fighting is to be largely a matter of neighbor against neighbor. One of my tasks, perhaps the hardest one indeed, has been to minimize that confusion without softening the ambiguities.

Researching this subject was not easy. Only three books have covered aspects of the mountain war in North Carolina. Heading that short list is Philip Shaw Paludin's *Victims -- A True Story of the Civil War*, a poetic, evocative, and meticulously researched account of the Shelton Laurel massacre. I have relied on that classic work for my own treatment of that tragic incident, as any historian who writes about it must. The other two books are Vernon H. Crow's magnificently researched but occasionally confusing account of Thomas's Legion, *Storm in the Mountains*, and Ida van Noppen's excellent but long out-of-print work, *Stoneman's Last Raid*.

For the rest of the story, the process has been that of assembling a mosaic — fragmentary references in obscure county histories, family chronicles, newspaper files, and, of course, that gigantic and formidably confusing repository of Civil War data, the *Official Records*. If little has been uncovered in the preparation of this book that was totally unknown before, at least much of the information has been assembled into a coherent narrative that was scattered and buried in obscurity until now. By putting it all between two covers, I hope I have made a worthwhile contribution to the history of those times.

The events that happened in the mountain counties of North Carolina, and their contiguous neighbors in eastern Tennessee, furnish a microcosmic view of the Civil War's effects. The fighting, the suffering, and the dying all took place on an individual scale, and there is a recognizably human profile to the drama. You can tell this much from the way the Civil War period remains alive in the generational memories and oral traditions of the mountain region. This certainly includes, but goes far beyond, the still-vivid demarcations between Republican and Democratic voting patterns in certain counties. For mountain families whose roots go back that far, the collective memories do not stop with the stories of those who fell at Gettysburg or suffered at the hands of Sherman's invaders. When they speak of the Civil War, they also speak of the dark night on a backwoods lane when great-great-grandfather was cut down by bushwhackers, or of that raw frontier morning when great-great-grandmother stood on the front porch of her cabin and watched a patrol of Thomas's Legion — full-blooded Cherokee warriors hot with youth and heritage — ride whooping through a patch of morning sunlight with fresh Unionist scalps dangling from their saddle horns.

It was a personal kind of war, up in the mountains. It produced its share of heroes and more than its share of bloody-handed villains. The fighting took place in a different dimension than the organized battles on the main fronts, where huge formations of uniformed men fired massed volleys at other huge formations of distant, faceless, uniformed men. In the mountains, there was little of that long-range, impersonal killing. In the mountains, the target in your gunsight was not a nameless figure a thousand yards away, positioned at the other end of a smoke-obscured battlefield crowded with regiments. Instead, he was an individual human being with a clear and unique face, and he was, all too many times, a man whose identity and home you had known since childhood. When you pulled the trigger on such a man, you did not leave a heap of distant bones — one more swollen, powder-blackened piece of carrion among hundreds, heaped on the same acreage. You left a dead *man* whose wife and children you probably knew by name.

The Civil War is often characterized as a "brother against brother" conflict, but that is a relatively empty cliche. In the larger campaigns that dominate most history books, the brother versus brother situation hardly ever arose. Most families fought wholly on one side or the other. How many "brothers" in New Hampshire went south and enlisted in the Confederate Army? How many "brothers" made the hazardous trek from rural Georgia to disputed Kentucky, just so they could don a blue uniform?

But there was one region where that phrase was quite often literally true: the mountains of east Tennessee and North Carolina. These regions were not only physically contiguous, but also so alike in their political and economic divisions, and so interrelated strategically, that they may well be regarded as a single theater of war.

The war in the mountains may not have been large, but it was vicious, and it took place on an all-too-human scale. There were vast regions of the mountain country that were more dangerous for an outsider who did not know the score than the areas near the front lines in northern Virginia. Someone who lived, for instance, in Ashe County, would have a pretty good idea of where it was safe to travel in the neighboring counties of Wilkes or Watauga. But if duty or business called him to Caldwell or Madison counties, he'd have to be extremely careful about who he spoke to and where he spent the night. Many men took the wrong fork in a road, went a mile too far down an unfamiliar cove, and were never heard from again.

It was this kind of war in the mountains: The killers had names, their victims had kin, and everybody owned a gun.

PART 1:

WAR COMES TO THE HIGH PLACES

From far-off conquered cities Comes a voice of stifled wail,

And the shrieks and moans of the homeless Ring out like a dirge on the gale

I've seen from the smoking village, Our mothers and daughters fly;

I've seen where the little children Sank down in the furrows to die.

-- S. Teackle Wallis, "The Guerrillas: A Southern War Song," 1864.

VOTING DAY
IN
MADISON COUNTY

May 13, 1861 was the day set aside in North Carolina for the election of delegates to the state convention on secession from the Union. Then, as now, the town of Marshall, county seat of Madison County, was squeezed between the mountains on one side and the French Broad River on the other. There wasn't much to Marshall in those days, but it was still the biggest town in Madison County. It encompassed a flyblown brick courthouse, a dilapidated wooden jail, a dozen houses, four or five stores, and a couple of hotels, the largest and most luxurious of which had four guest rooms.

The morning of May 13 had dawned misty over the banks of the French Broad, but the spring sunshine had soon burned off the fog. Beneath a taut blue sky, the sunlight sparkled on the freshly bloomed tangles of mountain laurel that grew right up to the backs of the houses on the edge of town.

Marshall was packed with people that day, from all over Madison County. There were wealthy farmers from the bottom-lands and hardscrabble hillbillies from up in the remote coves of Shelton Laurel. In fact, there were more people than usually came to Marshall for the twice-yearly sessions of Superior Court -- sessions which were as much social gatherings as legal events, in this rough part of western North Carolina.

Highly visible among the milling groups of citizens was the county sheriff, an ardent spokesman for secession. He had been elected and supported in office by the wealthier farmers and merchants of the county, nearly all of whom also favored the idea of secession.

Because secession would be one step nearer realization at the end of this day's voting, the sheriff was in an exuberant mood. And because it promised to be a long and strenuous day, the sheriff had developed an early and powerful thirst, one which several of his secessionist friends had sought to quench with a proffered jug. Carried away by the sense of occasion, the sheriff blustered up and down Marshall's main street, greeting his friends and bullying his enemies. Finally, unable to contain his excitement, he stationed himself in the center of town, waved his hat, threw back his head and bellowed: "Huzzah for Jeff Davis and the Confederacy!"

From the crowd standing near the polling place came an equally passionate cry: "Hurrah for Washington and the Union!"

Well, sir! Spotting the man who had given voice to that Unionist cry -- a rural farmer known for his Lincolnite sympathies -- the sheriff drew his pistol and advanced menacingly, and perhaps just a trifle unsteadily. The Unionist raised his hands in front of his face and backed up 10 or 15 paces, while the crowd parted and grew silent. A bystander intervened at this point, however, and the sheriff's attention was momentarily diverted.

Moments later, he observed another man standing near the polling place with a pistol butt protruding from the waistband of his trousers. "What are you doing here with your gun?" the sheriff challenged, once more drawing his own weapon and advancing. To those watching, he looked like a man determined, before the morning was over, to shoot somebody.

While he was stalking the armed voter, the sheriff spotted yet a third man in the crowd, a fellow known throughout the county for his passionate Unionist convictions, and a man with whom the sheriff had, on numerous previous occasions, exchanged heated words. This time, the urge to shoot was just too strong, and the sheriff raised his heavy cap-and-ball pistol.

His intended target, observing the big barrel swiveling in his direction, instinctively lunged to one side just as the pistol went off with a cannon-like roar. The man just as quickly regretted doing so, for the sheriff, in trying to track his victim, had ended up shooting the man's son, putting a ball clean through the boy's arm and into his rib cage.

The mood of the crowd turned ugly. The sheriff suddenly seemed to understand that he was surrounded by far more presumed enemies than his pistol had shots. He quickly retreated to a nearby house -- whose startled owner, observing the angry crowd swarming down the street behind the lawman, hastily slammed and bolted the door.

But the sheriff was over the edge now, pumped up and defiant. He ran upstairs and presented himself at the second-story window overlooking the street. He brandished his smoking revolver and called out to the crowd below, "Come up here, all you damned Black Republicans, and take a shot about with me!"

There were men in the crowd all too happy to oblige him, for, as one eyewitness later recalled in a legal deposition, "a good Deal of Liquor had been drank that day," and feelings were running high. The honor of taking up the sheriff's challenge was spontaneously accorded to the man whose son had been wounded. He fired from the street and wounded the ranting law officer.

By this time the town constable had rushed to the scene of the disturbance. He gained entrance into the house and ran upstairs to take custody of the bleeding sheriff. But he didn't realize that the wounded boy's father was right behind him, and as soon as the bedroom door was thrown open, the angry man dashed in with his pistol and finished off the sheriff at close range.

At this point, all hell broke loose in the streets of Marshall. Secessionists and Unionists argued and swung at one another. During all the hubbub, the sheriff's killer managed to escape. He fled that night to Kentucky, and by the end of the week had enlisted in the Union Army. He did not survive the war.

Some of his friends and kin who helped him escape that day, however, did live through the war, and six years later they found themselves embroiled in a lawsuit instigated by the sheriff's friends and relatives. Not even four years of wartime suffering had been able to extinguish the passions of that memorable voting day in Marshall, located in a section of western North Carolina that would come to be known as "Bloody Madison."

The vote tally in Marshall that morning, incidentally, was 28 votes for the secessionist delegates to the state convention, and 144 for the Unionist delegates.

The lines were being drawn, sides were being taken, and the first shots had already been fired in what was to be a private, personal kind of war, its violence seemingly all the more bitter because of the intimate scale on which it occurred. Before it was over, the blue and secretive valleys of Madison County would be the setting of the mountain war's most harrowing atrocity.

THE LAND AND ITS PEOPLE

The western part of North Carolina is one of nature's masterpieces. A wedge-shaped region approximately 250 miles long by 150 miles wide (about 10,000 square miles), the mountain country comprises about one-fifth of the total land area of the state. Today, this region contains approximately one-fifth of the state's population; in 1860, it was much, much less than that.

As you approach the western reaches from the central Piedmont, your eye is seduced, first, by the hazy blue foothills, an almost melodic landscape of rolling, fertile croplands and snug, well-kept farms. The farther west you travel, the higher the land rises, and the more dramatic the vistas. Distances melt into further distances, and serried undulations of vast whale-backed ridges draw the eye and the spirit deeper into the mystery of the landscape. The land's pervading sense of antiquity is now serene, now brooding and dark. In places, the terrain is raw, harsh, plunging, inimical to human endeavor, and indifferent to human frailty. In other places, the vastness is gentled and rendered into poetry by the time-worn roundness of its contours.

To the traveler who ventures to cross them, the Appalachians of North Carolina have an intensely luring quality. No matter how beautiful is the spot on which you're standing, there is always another enticement of beauty somewhere beyond, perceived but made tantalizing by that diaphanous mist that softens all distances. Each receding wave of ridges seems to beckon like a promise whispered in a dream. Whatever the hungry soul yearns for — land, peace, beauty, the slowing of Time itself — the blue-veiled coves and crystalline streams, perfumed by the dark, emerald-cold scent of balsam, fir, and mountain laurel, must surely hold it...somewhere in their depths.

The geology of western North Carolina has several distinct features. The Blue Ridge Mountains mark the eastern Continental Divide, and beyond them the lofty Great Smokies spill over into Tennessee. On the high plateau between these great mountain chains, even the valleys are 3,000 feet above sea level. Here and there, the landscape stuns the eye with formations of rugged grandeur: Grandfather Mountain (5,964 feet) with its spectacular ramparts of glistening rock; or, farther south, the incomparable Black Mountain cluster, dominated by lordly Mount Mitchell (at 6,684 feet, the highest point in eastern North America), rising from perpetually shadowed valleys carpeted with evergreen forests whose depths are almost as impenetrable as those of a tropical jungle. Unwinding northeast and southwest from the heights of the Great Smokies are the lesser Smokies, with Stone, Iron, Bald, and Unaka Mountains. The whole range is dominated, between Bryson City and Gatlinburg, Tennessee, by the towering megalithic mass of Clingman's Dome.

Cutting like vast ribs across the plateau that separates the Blue Ridge from the Smokies are the shorter, lateral chains: the Nantahalas, the Balsams, the Pisgahs, and Bald and New Found Mountains. These, too, are of a scale which dwarfs man physically yet enlarges his spirit. The Balsams alone, largest of the transverse chains, measure 50 miles in length and contain numerous mountains that rise to an average height of 6,000 feet.

The first significant wave of immigration into the western part of North Carolina started in the mid-18th century. By about 1750, Salisbury had become the gateway to the mountains. It was literally the last stop before the wilderness, the place where settlers stocked up on powder and shot, salt, farming implements, and harnesses. They had their horses freshly shod and their wagons braced for the incredibly rough trek ahead.

From Salisbury, they followed the beckoning blue undulations on the horizon. What impulses drove them? Simple pioneering restlessness, of course, but also the lure of cheap and plentiful land -- land which could be theirs for the effort of taking it and holding it. Their family names still dot the map of western North Carolina and eastern Tennessee. They had streams and towns and mountains named for them, and some passed directly from historical reality into mountain folklore: Boone; Sevier; Clingman; Alexander; Rutherford; Moore; Shelton. They came looking for that elusive place of perfect beauty that might be down the next cove, around the next bend, over the next ridge. Sooner or later most of them found such a place, and in many cases it still bears their name.

In 1745, there were less than 100 men listed on the militia rolls of the western counties. Seven years later, there were 3,000. In 1765 alone, 1,000 wagons passed through Salisbury, heading west. During the Revolutionary War, the menfolk came down from the hills and crushed the Tory movement in North Carolina, exhibiting the same bloody-minded zeal that would characterize the fratricidal fighting between their descendants in the Civil War nearly a century later.

They did a lot of fighting, as well, with the mountains' original inhabitants. The biggest single factor in the early decimation of the proud, doomed Cherokees was their belief in the promises of the British. The Cherokees took up arms on the Tory side, and it was just the excuse the American settlers needed to mount campaign after campaign against them, torching their villages and pitilessly killing their women and children, in addition to their warriors.

By the time the Revolutionary War was winding down, vast areas of the mountains had effectively been cleared of their Indian inhabitants. And the war itself fueled a second wave of white immigration. Many men who went into the hills for the first time as Indian fighters fell in love with the scenery and the tang of untrammeled freedom in the laurel-scented air. The mountains seemed to offer a sense of unlimited possibility, the very real chance to become the lord of one's own estate in a land graced by some of God's finest work as a landscape artist.

Veterans who had done good service in the war were given the chance to acquire land either free or on the most reasonable terms. And many men who had previously lived in colonies like Pennsylvania or Maryland or Rhode Island responded to the lure of the North Carolina mountains. They followed the rough valley roads down the spine of the Appalachians, and they settled where the land seemed especially to beckon them. Roots thus sunk penetrated deep, and grew quickly. Within the span of a generation or two, families that had settled in the mountains had achieved an identification with the land that, for all practical purposes, smacked of the eternal.

Mountaineer families did not live *at* a certain place; they were *part* of the place itself, as much as the rocks and streams and meadows. This continued for generation after generation, until the people and their dwelling places became symbiotic on an almost molecular level.

North Carolina's state legislature helped the westward push by enacting laws that made it easy and cheap for a man to stake his claim. The fee for filing that claim was within reach of any man who still had his service bounty in his pocket: two pounds, ten shillings, per hundred acres. A husband was entitled to claim 640 acres for himself and 100 acres apiece for his wife and children. And there was no limit to what a man might claim if he had the capital: Additional land went for a shilling an acre.

As night follows day, the settlers were followed by real estate speculators, enterprising men who purchased tracts of a million acres or more and then sold them off, at a hefty profit, in 500-acre packets. (The same kind of business is still being transacted today...but not for a shilling an acre.)

Many of the first wave of mountain settlers were from the population of poor but hardy small-time farmers in the Piedmont. Others were well-to-do gentleman-adventurers. Some were driven by the prospect of quick profit, others by the romantic lure of the faerie-blue haze that shrouded, like a maiden's veil, the emerald depths of distant valleys. They were English, and the English brought their love of law, their shrewdness at commerce, their independence of mind; they were Scotch-Irish, and the Scotch-Irish brought their fierce infatuation with liberty, along with their sometimes-contradictory streak of piety and righteousness; they were German-speaking, and the Germans brought their frugality, their old-world sophistication, and their love of culture and learning.

The stereotype that all mountain-dwelling North Carolinians were backward and isolated is a gross oversimplification. In 1760, the mountains roads were poor, to be sure, but so were the roads everywhere else in the state. Travelers who passed through the region and left written accounts of their journeys often remarked on the industry, shrewdness, and intelligence of the inhabitants. A century later, however, that was not too often the case. Travelers who penetrated beyond the scattered towns began to write in terms of the classic "hillbilly" stereotypes, describing the region's hermetic and curious customs, its tight interbreeding, poverty, ignorance of the outside world, and its tendency toward violent rather than legal settlement of disputes.

Mountain society was always, in fact, far from homogeneous. Town-dwellers tended to be at the forefront of technological, cultural, and material progress within a given locality. The adjective "elite" suggests a greater standard of luxury than these people actually enjoyed, but they were the closest thing to an aristocracy that could be found in the western counties.

Next in the socioeconomic pecking order were the prosperous farmers who held the choice bottomland acreage. They produced enough to have marketable surpluses, and they were connected to their markets by reasonably passable roads.

Finally came the majority of mountain people: those who had settled in the more isolated coves and valleys, by creeks instead of by rivers, with enough acreage to take care of their own and precious little left over for surplus. The tradition of mountaineer pride was found in its rawest and most stubborn form among these people. They did not have much, but by the Almighty, it was theirs, and it guaranteed their independence in return for their investment of sweat. It was this quality of left-aloneness which hundreds of mountaineer men, and women, would suffer and die to preserve during the coming national conflict.

From cradle to grave, the rhythms of life in the region were dictated by nature's moods and by the eternal progressions of human life itself. The division of labor was strict. The man was the provider, the woman the nurturer of the young and maintainer of the domestic realm. "Providing" was a hard, full-time job, since the land had to be cleared and rigorously tended if it was to return enough crops for the family's survival. What the land did not provide, the man had to obtain through his skills as a stalker, trapper, and marksman.

His woman tended a cabin that was probably three generations old, and their furniture, utensils, and bedding had probably been created by previous occupants whose names and deeds were enshrined in family lore. She spent her days going round and round in the same harsh, toilsome groove already worn by her predecessors. She knew of their sufferings and accomplishments, as her descendants would know of hers. Mountain women aged fast — many were dead by their mid-forties — but those who survived became as tough as hickory knots by middle age. It was that toughness that enabled many families to survive the ordeal of the war years.

By the mid-19th century, history, and the pattern of westward movement, had passed these mountain counties by. The backwoods families of 1860 were vastly more isolated from the outside world than their ancestors had been during Revolutionary days. And, ironically, as the mountain towns grew and developed, the rural mountaineers just seemed to grow more and more remote from their influence.

Outsiders might regard them as "poor whites," but it's doubtful if many of them saw themselves in that light. The land provided for them, and most were free of debt; they knew the pride of owning their own patch of the Earth. Their neighbors might be few, but when folks came together, they were mighty sociable. Honesty and hospitality were valued without question and practiced as a matter of course. If most of them could not read or write very well, if at all, they nevertheless enjoyed an oral literature that was as rich in incident, character, and human insight as most of the material that appeared between two covers. Shakespeare would have found their stories and figures of speech captivating and much more familiar to his ears than the language of the city-dwellers.

They were, in sum, a class of people industrious, honest, sensitive to and respectful of their environment, and supported throughout the course of their harsh existences both by strong inter-family connections and by a rugged, simple, religious faith. In 1860, the mountain region had more churches per capita than all the rest of North Carolina.

Self-reliance was the hallmark of these people. Their lives were

steady and regular, their isolation profound, their sense of identification with place and with kin, total. The mountaineer knew who
he was, where he belonged, and what his role was in the greater
scheme of things.

The negative side of this rough-hewn self-sufficiency was found
in such pervasive traits as narrow-mindedness and ignorance of the
world at large. Physical isolation and intellectual stasis produced,
in many mountain men, a mind-set in which brute stubbornness
was raised to the power and status of a universal truth. Emotions,
in such men, tended to be inextricably bound up with pride, and
violence of the most primitive sort was usually accompanied by
powerful convictions of self-righteousness. Most mountain men
who killed someone were armed with the belief that God Himself
was aiming their gun or directing the hand that carried their knife.
The coming of war merely added the respectability of a national
cause to a longstanding pattern of personal vengeance.

Local courts did not dispense blind, impersonal justice. Local
magistrates could call whomever they chose to sit on juries, and
superior court judges tended to pick jurors from among the local
citizens who happened to share their personal convictions of right
and wrong, regardless of all those abstract fine-print stipulations in
the law books. Reputation, kinship, and even one's address in the
county were more likely to weigh in the verdict than such niceties
as evidence. The rural mountaineers therefore had little respect for
the courts and believed that private justice, based on community
values and traditions, came much closer to what God intended. And
very likely, given the raucous and frequently drunken state of most
superior court sessions in antebellum times, the mountaineers'
Calvinistic brand of vigilantism probably came closer to true
justice, more often, than the shenanigans inside the county courthouse.

When the war broke out, therefore, there was already a longstanding tradition of personal dispensation of justice. One Union
soldier, stationed at a refugee camp in the northeastern tip of
Alabama, where hundreds of civilians from the Appalachians came
looking for food and shelter after being burned or starved out of
their homes by Confederate guerrillas, remembered how the
womenfolk inculcated a thirst for vengeance in their children: "I

heard them repeat over and over to their children the names of men which they were never to forget, and whom they were to kill when they had sufficient strength to hold a rifle."[1]

THE ROOTS OF CLASS WARFARE

By 1860, the political subdivision of western North Carolina into counties had taken on a crazy-quilt appearance as the original, enormous, counties seemed to calve-off smaller counties, their borders all folded and wrinkled, following the terrain.

At the start of the 19th century, the entire western part of the state had been divided into just six counties: Ashe, Buncombe, Wilkes, Burke, Surry, and Rutherford. Then, new counties were carved out of land that had once belonged to the dispossessed Cherokees: Haywood in 1808, Yancey in 1833, and Henderson in 1838. Rutherford and Burke yielded parts of their land to form McDowell, in 1842; Madison County — destined to become the most disputed and fought-over part of the mountains — was created from Buncombe and Yancey in 1851. Haywood calved Macon County in 1828, Cherokee County came into being in 1839, and in 1851, Haywood and Macon contributed some land to form Jackson County.

In the northwestern part of the region, parts of Burke and Wilkes went into the formation of Caldwell County, in 1841; portions of Wilkes, Ashe, Caldwell, and Yancey all combined to form Watauga County in 1849. The last western county to be formed before the war was sparsely populated Mitchell County, created from segments of Burke, Watauga, Caldwell, and McDowell.

Real roads were few and far between and many tended to follow the course of shallow streams whenever practical. Ox carts were the main means of transporting goods in any quantity for any consider-able distance — a brute vehicle to cope with a brutal landscape.

Carriages could be found only in towns, and in most places they could be driven only for short distances beyond the town limits. Individual travel for long distances was by horse or mule.

The French Broad Turnpike was the main "highway" connecting Asheville with Knoxville, Tennessee. It was surely the best-kept and most commodious road across the mountains, but even it was impassable for long stretches every season, due to flooding, rock slides, fallen timber, and washed-out bridges. There was a road through Saluda Gap which furnished a fairly reliable connection with Georgia and South Carolina; it was used during the war by Cherokee refugees fleeing the starvation in their home counties. Wilkesboro was, to use modern terminology, a hub destination, with roads radiating north to Virginia, west to Tennessee, and down toward Morganton.

Even by 1861, there was not a single foot of railroad track in the mountains proper. The Western Carolina Railroad stopped just east of Morganton, and the telegraph lines did not penetrate much farther. Even Asheville, by far the most cosmopolitan little town in the region, had no telegraph line. For that matter, there were only three banks in the entire region: in Murphy, Morganton, and Asheville.

Since there were no rail connections west of Morganton, cattle, hogs, and horses were simply driven in herds over the existing roads to markets in South Carolina, Georgia, Tennessee, and Virginia. Any man wealthy enough to have that many surplus animals to sell probably also had slaves to drive them, rather like cowboys. There was a fairly good market for western-bred cattle. They would be herded into southwestern Virginia, fattened up by their buyers, and then sent on to the butcher shops of Richmond or Baltimore. Other wares exported from the region included butter, linseed oil, leather goods, feathers, and some tobacco. These products tended to flow in a southerly direction to the markets of Columbia, South Carolina, or sometimes even as far as Charleston.

So life in the mountains, by 1860, remained overwhelmingly rural in nature. According to the census for that year, there were only 192 manufacturing operations in the entire western third of North Carolina, and they were minuscule, averaging not more than a half-dozen employees each. Everyone else, beyond the confines of the towns, farmed the land. They took what the land, and their stern but sturdy God, gave them -- whether it came as prosperity or as hardship.

But the statistics do not tell the whole story. The deeper you look beyond them, the more you come to realize that the range of situations, attitudes, even of sophistication, to be found in the western counties was broader and more varied, by far, than the region's own folklore might lead you to believe. For every clan of moonshine-brewing primitives, there was also a prosperous farmer near a main road who kept in touch with what was going on beyond those violet-shaded valleys. It was these well-to-do farmers, men who had a certain amount of spare time and ambition to fill it, who furnished the towns with their law officers, judges, doctors, preachers, merchants, and militia commanders. These people were no more isolated from the outside world than the citizens of most towns in the Piedmont or coastal regions. Travelers passed through, newspapers were read, courts were held, and politicians campaigned. The outside world and its issues were known and discussed, and people cultivated values which were dramatically different from (and often opposed to) those which obtained among the more isolated rural families.

Whatever their ethnic backgrounds, the early waves of settlers brought into the mountains a sense of class identity that would stick with them, shape mountain affairs for generations to come, and contribute in no small way to the divided allegiances of the Civil War period. The class of well-to-do settlers bought up all the good bottomlands along the rivers -- those long, dark-loamed ribbons of prime soil, heavy with corn and tobacco, that remain, even today, the most desirable farmlands in the region. They also tended to buy up the choicest parcels of mountain land, either to build their own homes upon, or to hold for speculative purposes. Later settlers, not poor people but those of modest means, bought their parcels from the prosperous landlords, unless they could find suitable unclaimed land which could be purchased from the state.

At the bottom of the economic ladder were the poorest and most numerous settlers, the families that trekked in on foot, toting on the back of one spavined mule all of their worldly goods: a musket, a hoe, a pot, a skillet, an axe, an auger, a hand mill for grinding corn, a few sacks of seed, and a thumb-creased family Bible. Thousands of such people came to the mountains during the first century of settlement. They pushed deeper and deeper into the secret folds of the terrain until they found land that belonged to nobody, and that's where they put down their roots. For two or three generations, they lived in severe isolation from the outside world, working small low-yield plots of land. Eventually the game was exterminated, the soil exhausted, and the original handful of families had bred (and probably a bit inbred, as well) into a clan too numerous for the land to adequately sustain. When that pattern was established, there came into being the hardscrabble hillbilly subculture that became immutably entrenched in its own way of doing things. They lived in a virtual world apart from the prosperous bottomland farmers and the middle-class mountain people who dwelt near the main roads.

In fact, the ingredients were present for an unorthodox but essentially sound Marxist interpretation of the conflict which was to come. There are clearly discernible elements of economic class struggle operating just below the surface of the more obvious causes of disunity.

It is no historical accident that the two areas of North Carolina which harbored the most intense Unionist activity during the Civil War were the Randolph County area of the Piedmont, and the mountains. Both sections had decidedly different economic priorities than those found in areas of the state dominated by the planter aristocracy. In the counties which were heavily secessionist, the economy was as stagnant as the economies of the Deep South states, where investment money was poured into only two commodities: more slaves, and more land for the slaves to work.

But the western region of North Carolina was poised, in 1860, on the brink of a period of growth and development not dissimilar to that which occurred in the Northeast at the start of the Industrial Revolution. The war aborted that economic revolution, but the ingredients for it were lined up nevertheless: bold individual entrepreneurs with capital to invest; constantly improving transportation; abundant natural resources, particularly water power for cheap energy; technological changes that could increase production; new markets opening up for goods produced in the region;

and, back in the hills, a plentiful supply of cheap labor.

In the western counties, the prospects were excellent for a diversified and expanding economic base, one that more closely resembled the New England economy than the economies of Georgia or South Carolina. The few scattered pockets of industrialization which existed in the mountains in 1860 looked to the technologically advanced North for their inspiration, not to the labor-intensive systems of the Deep South. If the movement toward secession was fueled by the economic interests of the planter class, the Unionism of the mountain counties was an instinctive reaction spawned in part by the desire to protect that nascent, very different, economy whose seeds had already been planted in the region.

An entire economy based on slave labor cannot remain profitable unless the land is productive enough for slave labor to be used in a cost-effective manner. There were few places in western North Carolina where such conditions existed. The average farm consisted of a cabin, a barn, an outhouse, and a few acres of arable meadow. Nearly everything that was grown was consumed on the place. The accumulation of capital, and the possibility of its reinvestment, was therefore marginal or nonexistent. Seventy percent of the inhabitants of the western counties owned no slaves at all, and the remainder owned, by plantation standards, rather small numbers. In 1860, the slave population in North Carolina 9.5 slaves per square mile. In the mountain counties, it was about 4.5 per square mile.

Beyond those figures, one must examine the peculiarities of slavery in the mountain region to gain a better understanding of the economic and social distinctions that had such drastic consequences when the war broke out. It is one thing to say that relatively few Negro servants dwelt in the highland counties. But a closer examination reveals that the small numbers of slaves ("small" relative to the eastern counties, at any rate) do not reflect a wholly accurate picture of how important the "peculiar institution" of slavery was to the wealthier class of mountain citizens.

Certainly, the mountains were an atypical environment for the slavery system. That system, so the conventional wisdom goes, functioned effectively only in regions where there was a long growing season, lots of acreage, and large-scale cash-crop farming.

None of those conditions were found in the mountain counties. But that doesn't mean that the institution of slavery in the mountains was insignificant. It was, in fact, far more important than the numbers would indicate. Although slave-owners in the mountains were relatively few in number, their impact on the structure of antebellum Appalachia was profound. For them, slavery was important. And that fact alone allied them closely to the flatland aristocrats who led the secessionist movement.

Indeed, the demographics show that the generalizations commonly accepted about slavery are not wholly accurate. In Madison and Watauga counties (both of which, not coincidentally, would be hotbeds of Unionist activity during the war), the slave population was indeed negligible: 3.6 percent and 2 percent, respectively. But over in Burke County, slaves made up 25 percent of the population, and in Caldwell County, 20 percent. On the western side of the Blue Ridge, the year-round slave population of Buncombe and Henderson counties was only 13 to 15 per cent, but in the summer months, when wealthy planters from South Carolina moved to the highlands to escape the heat and bugs on the coast, the Negro population may well have doubled. Taken all together, the 15 western counties, in 1860, had an average slave population of just over 10 percent.

Furthermore, in areas which had significant concentrations of slaves, the Negroes were often a major factor in the economic and social climate. The men who owned slaves tended to be not only wealthy, but also prominent and active, frequently engaged in a wide variety of economic pursuits, deriving some of their capital from sources other than farming.

The small patchwork farms out in the coves and hollows generally produced only enough food for home, or at best strictly local, consumption. To employ slaves in this type of agriculture was economically absurd: they would eat nearly as much as they could produce. To the yeoman farmers out in the hills, a good mule was worth more than two strong field hands.

An eyewitness description of this economic pattern was written in 1853 by Frederic Law Olmstead in a book of travel reminiscences: "Of the people who get their living entirely from agriculture, few own Negroes; the slaveholders being chiefly professional men, shopkeepers, and men in office, who are also land owners and give a divided attention to farming."[1]

In other words, the slaveholders tended to be part-time gentleman farmers who derived most of their income from commercial activities: hotel-keeping, real estate speculation, and mining. Among the largest slaveholders, there seems to have been an inordinate number of lawyers. Such prominent families as the Averys of Burke County and the Loves of Haywood County fairly bristled with members of the bar. The second-largest slaveholder in all of the western counties was an attorney named Nicolas Woodfin in Asheville, who owned 122 Negroes. Another, even better-known Asheville lawyer -- Zebulon Vance, later to become the wartime governor -- owned six slaves, according to the 1860 census. His brother, Robert B. Vance, who would later serve as commander-in-chief of Confederate forces in the mountains, owned seven. And all of these men, in addition to their legal careers, manifested a bold entrepreneurial spirit, branching out into real estate, transportation, and mercantile schemes of various sorts. The capital they acquired from their dealings was quite often reinvested in slaves.

Typical of this pattern was John Happoldt of Morganton, who, in addition to practicing medicine, managed a general store and a successful tourist hotel. By 1850, he had reinvested a sizable part of his profits by acquiring a dozen slaves. The only man in Ashe County with more than 30 slaves, George Bowers, managed a store, ran a popular hotel, and was in charge of the local post office.

This correlation between large numbers of slaves and diversity of business activities appears too often to be a coincidence. It is a pattern which follows rather closely the evolution of the regional economy.

Obviously, to men such as Bowers, slaves were a form of liquid asset. Just as obviously, the slaves would not have been purchased if there had not been profitable tasks for them to perform. These jobs included, but were seldom confined to, agricultural labor. William Holland Thomas, for instance — a man of remarkable enlightenment where the Cherokees were concerned — had no compunction at all about accumulating some 50-odd slaves to work in his stores, his shoe shop, his tannery, his blacksmithy, and his

27

wagon factory.

In the last two antebellum decades, even the budding tourist industry contributed to slavery. In fact, the institution suited this business quite well. Hotel owners acquired capital, then invested it in Negroes who were promptly put to work in the hotels; the symmetry was perfect. The resort industry in Hendersonville, Asheville, and Flat Rock was more developed by the mid-1850s than is generally realized today. Flat Rock hosted so many low-country planters during the summer months that it came to be known as "Little Charleston."

Negro servants were kept busy at all these locations as waiters, maids, grooms, maitre d's, and bathing attendants. A British traveler to Asheville (a man with the marvelous Monty Pythonesque name of George Featherstonehaugh) wrote in his diary, "What a merry race of people the negroes are...all well dressed and well fed, and more merry, noisy, and impudent than any servants I have ever seen."[2]

Another major business for the wealthy slaveholders was, of course, land speculation — a business that exploded right after the inconvenient Cherokees were evicted from some of the choicer terrain in 1838. Land was a major outlet for surplus capital. If it was too steep to be farmed, some other rich man could build a summer house on it, or it could be worked for timber, or used for grazing animals, or, in some places, mining.

Since cash-crop farming was not a large-scale activity, many of the mountain slaves employed in rural locations spent much of their time as shepherds and cowboys. Pork, lamb, and beef were all marketed, more often to purchasers in Virginia and South Carolina than to nearer markets east of the Blue Ridge (the road connections were better along the north-south axis of the ranges). During "bacon season" one of the slaves' most important jobs was to round up the hogs from the mountain pastures where they roamed, and then herd them to the plantation markets beyond the mountains.

William Thomas put some of his servants to work hauling wagonloads of iron from his Cherokee County ironworks to Athens, Georgia. In Athens, the iron was bartered for merchandise, which was then loaded onto the same wagons and brought back to

Thomas's chain of stores in Cherokee and Jackson counties. Burke County had a plug tobacco factory staffed almost entirely by Negroes. And the father of Governor David L. Swain maintained a hat factory in Asheville operated wholly by black servants.

But the nonagricultural activity that involved the most slaves was mining. Gold had been discovered in the late 1820s in Burke and Rutherford counties, precipitating a mini-gold rush that lasted until the mid-1830s. By 1833, Burke County had 5,000 slaves, at least half of them involved in mining operations. Many of the mines were thoroughly integrated, with "poor whites" and indentured blacks working side by side, apparently without any significant racial friction.

Some idea of the diversity of tasks assigned to the slaves can be gleaned from ledgers that once belonged to prominent western citizens. William Lenoir of Caldwell County, for example, used slave labor to run a gristmill, a sawmill, a forge which produced marketable ironmongery, and a small textile plant that turned out several grades of products, from coarse cloth used to make bagging to fine linen-textured fabric for the Lenoir family's own use. Lenoir also kept his male Negroes busy constructing and repairing roads that connected his widely scattered real estate holdings.

Even those relatively few wealthy citizens who did concentrate on farming managed to find plenty of additional tasks for their slaves to perform. James Greenlee of McDowell County used his slaves as brickmakers, cobblers, carpenters, blacksmiths, tanners, and house servants. They built roads, fences, a dam, and all manner of outbuildings, including their own sleeping quarters. When he had a surplus of idle hands, Greenlee hired them out to other mountain capitalists for work on mining or construction projects that required extra labor. He even worked out a profitable arrangement with McDowell County officials, hiring out a number of his slaves for county road work.

The courthouses in Watauga, Henderson, Macon, and Cherokee counties were all constructed by crews of slaves hired from private masters. The first church to be erected in Jefferson (Ashe County) was built by subcontracted slave labor. Hundreds of slaves would have been hired from dozens of masters to work on the proposed railroad link between Morganton and Asheville, but the war interrupted that project.

For the wealthier class of mountain citizens, therefore, slavery was every bit as entrenched as it was in the plantation states of the Deep South. So while it is true that the slave population in the mountains was relatively small, the system itself was vigorously maintained. It is reasonable to assume that these affluent gentlemen would not have continued to invest in slaves if it were not reliably profitable for them.

And while it is true that the day-to-day lot of Negroes was healthier, more interesting, and far less brutal in the mountains than in the lowlands, they were still, when all was said and done, chattel property. They were bought, sold, traded, and invested as property, and it would be wrong to assume that their masters' attitude was other than superficially more humane than the attitude of the stereotyped planter with his white linen suit and thin cigar. One contemporary traveler through the western counties recorded a fragment of conversation which shows what the prevailing attitude toward Negroes was really like. A farmer, comparing the marketability of slaves to that of livestock, casually stated that "a nigger that wouldn't bring over $300 seven years ago, will fetch $1,000, quick, this year; but now hogs, they ain't worth so much as they used to be...."[3]

One historian who probed deeply into the facts of mountain slavery summed up the situation this way: "Slave labor in the North Carolina mountains was far less crucial to the Appalachian economy than was the case in most areas of the South. Yet, the future of the system was as much at the forefront of the secessionist crisis there as elsewhere. Enough Western North Carolinians, particularly those in positions of leadership and influence, had sufficient vested interests in slavery to make it a predominant consideration in the decision to leave or to remain with the Union early in 1861."[4]

The often-cited isolation of the mountain counties from the rest of antebellum Southern society was true only with regard to the majority of small-scale yeoman farmers. The community leaders — the men whose names would in time appear as colonels and captains of the various Confederate units raised in the mountains — shared the same interests and attitudes as other slaveholders, wherever they lived. These men engaged in a wide variety of enterprises, often with considerable help from slave labor, and they were actually quite strongly connected to the world beyond the mountains. The institution of slavery, although demographically marginal in the mountains, did in fact exercise a profound influence on the shape of events in that region, both before and during the war.

'WHEN THE WAR COME ALONG, I FELT MIGHTY SOUTHERN.'

The temper of feeling in the mountains regarding the issues at stake in the presidential election of 1860 can be sampled from a letter written by the Reverend J. Buston of Asheville, dated June 8, 1860: "...the disunion mania [is] a practical blindness and...a scheme against God and man...A sectionalized politician on the slavery question, pro or con, is my abomination, object of my implacable disgust. We want breadth, patriotism, moderation, honesty, and my opinion is...that we won't find any of these things at large in either the Democratic or Republican parties."[1]

Pro-Union feeling ran high in the mountain counties during the weeks leading up to the election of 1860. Unionist rallies were held in at least nine counties, including one in Wilkesboro which attracted 5,000 people (Zebulon Vance was one of the speakers) and another in Salisbury that was described in contemporary newspapers as "the largest gathering held in North Carolina since...1840."[2] Declarations of principle were issued by those who attended these gatherings; typical of these statements, and of the overwhelming sentiment of the populace in general, was this one, put out by the Whigs of Wilkes County:

We...are decidedly in favor of the Union of these States as they now

33

exist and are determined to oppose all efforts come from what source
they may, that either does [sic] or tends to weaken the bonds of Union
under which we live; and that we pledge ourselves to maintain the
Union and Constitution as they now exist as long as they afford the
protection to our lives and property that they do.[3]

As the actual day of the election drew near, most of the western
newspapers cautioned their readers to restrain their passions, urging
them not to assume that a Lincoln victory meant automatic dissolution of the Union. But time, and the rushing momentum of events,
was not on the side of the Unionists. The tone of the entire debate,
statewide, was becoming more and more emotional.

Despite the relative importance of the mountain men who were
slaveholders, the majority of the region's inhabitants simply could
not see how the survival of the slavery system, or secession itself,
could improve their lot. At a meeting in Rowan County in January
1861, a vote was taken by secret ballot on the question of secession. Not a single person, of the two hundred or so who attended,
voted in favor of leaving the Union. When reporting these dramatic
results, the Salisbury newspaper, *The Carolina Watchman*, declared the vote an accurate reflection of how people felt about the
issue: "This is the sentiment of almost every portion of the
County."

Private correspondence between men of the western counties
was filled with similar expressions of feeling. As one Madison
County citizen wrote to Zebulon Vance: "Madison County is
three-fourths Union. I saw a man from Cherokee today and he says
that they are all Union...in his county."[4]

To defend slavery or the "rights" of the planter aristocracy, not
one mountain man in a hundred would have shouldered a musket
for the Confederacy. Politicians from the mountain districts did not
always have an easy time in the legislative jungles of Raleigh; their
colleagues sometimes labeled them "Southern Yankees" because
of their differing priorities. Politically, there had been, for decades,
an undercurrent of tension between representatives of the mountain
region and those from the dominant eastern counties. The western
legislators were always in the forefront of any movements to open
up that area with better roads and rail connections, and the eastern
establishment was always reluctant to fund such projects. That was

one reason, maybe the main reason, why the railroad stopped at Morganton, and also why Asheville had no telegraph connection with the outside world. The mountaineers could continue their subsistence farming, but the secessionists were opposed to any measure which might increase the economic clout of anyone who did not agree with their priorities.

It should not be surprising, therefore, that the average yeoman farmer from the highland counties was utterly indifferent to the burning issues around which the secessionist movement coalesced during the 1850s. He simply didn't give a hoot-owl's damn whether people in Kansas owned slaves or not.

On the first occasion when a plebiscite was held regarding the matter of holding a secession convention, on February 26, 1861, North Carolinians defeated the proposition. Ironically, Zebulon Vance and other prominent Unionists were unhappy with those results. Their strategy had been to force the issue of a secession convention as early as possible, while, statewide, the Unionist politicians held enough power to probably defeat the secessionists.

In the mountains, the February voting broke down this way. West of the Blue Ridge, only three out of ten counties voted in favor of the secession convention, and only two of those voted in favor of secessionist delegates; east of the Blue Ridge, results were more evenly balanced, with five counties voting against the convention and six voting in favor of it.

Newspapers in the region reflected the political thinking of the more affluent class of people by and for whom the newspapers were published -- and whom the newspapers, in turn, were most likely to influence. The *Asheville News* and the *Shelby Eagle* were important platforms for the secessionists, while the two most important Whig papers, the *Asheville Spectator* and the *Hendersonville Times*, advocated continuance of the Union.

Even during the turbulent debates at the statewide secession convention that was eventually held in May 1861, about six months after South Carolina had seceded, some of the strongest voices heard in opposition were those of the mountain delegates. One delegate was heard to bellow above the noise, "Let South Carolina nullify, revolute, secess and be damned! North Carolina don't need to follow her lead!"

But like most other North Carolinians, the mountaineers drew the line at the prospect of armed intervention by the Lincoln administration. When Lincoln called for troops, thousands of mountain men enlisted in the Confederate Army. As one old-timer told an interviewer, half a century later, "When the war come along, I felt mighty Southern."[5] Confederate recruiting agents did their part, too, whipping up emotions by appealing, whenever they could, to the image of the "bold, independent mountaineers" who fought the British at Kings Mountain during the Revolution.

You can perceive the shifting attitude in the changed editorial tone of the state's newspapers. An editorial in the March 5, 1861, issue of the Salisbury paper read:

> ...Another point: that of coercion of the seceding states, as a means of bringing them back into the Union. The triumph of Union men here, if they have triumphed, does not affect this question; but believing there is no constitutional power in the government for such a measure and that it would be mischievous in its effects for reasons independent of its unauthorized character, the Union men of North Carolina are not less opposed to this doctrine because they have condemned the actions of the seceding states....[6]

After Lincoln's inaugural address was published throughout the state, Union men in the western counties found their influence shrinking daily. They were swimming against a tide that was gathering force with every passing week. The most that pro-Union politicians and newspapers could do now was to urge patience, clear-headedness, and other platitudinous qualities. News of the attack on Fort Sumter washed much of the ground out from under the Unionists. And when Lincoln issued his call for troops, there was no ground left to stand on at all. Overnight, newspapers in the western towns picked up the gauntlet of war, as evidenced by the words that appeared in *The Carolina Watchman* on April 23:

> Old lifelong conservative men, who throughout had labored and prayed for a peaceful solution to the national troubles and have never once given up all hope, yielded with anguish of the heart when they could hold out no longer. The miserable duplicity of Abraham Lincoln stung them to the quick, one and all are freely bringing their

sons and their treasures to offer on the altar of liberty...Who would
measure the deep damnation due to those, North and South, who have
through years of ceaseless agitation, brought this terrible calamity
upon us. As there is a just God in heaven, they will get their reward.[7]

William W. MacDowell formed the first volunteer outfit from
the western counties: the Buncombe Riflemen, who departed
Asheville on April 18 and became part of the First North Carolina
Regiment. They would take part in the first land battle, Big Bethel,
on June 10. Zebulon Vance's company, the Rough and Ready
Guards, left for service on May 4. The Henderson Guards left
Hendersonville two weeks later; on their flag was emblazoned the
motto "Follow your banner to victory or death!". Up in Madison
County, a then-obscure local bigshot named Lawrence M. Allen
formed Allen's Rangers, which eventually became part of the
notorious 64th North Carolina, a unit whose banner would be
soaked in both shame and blood. During this first and most intense
wave of Confederate patriotism, some counties hastily passed new
taxes to equip locally raised companies, and one county, Transylvania, actually took out a commercial loan from the Cape Fear Bank
in order to pay its volunteers their enlistment bounties.

The total white population in western North Carolina, from the
Virginia border in Ashe County to the Georgia state line in Cherokee County, was 68,000. By October 1861, 4,000 volunteers had
entered Confederate service from the mountain counties — one-
sixteenth of the eligible male population, and actually a higher
percentage of eligibles than was obtained from most of the Piedmont counties. By December, the total number of mountain volunteers had risen to more than 8,000. Before the war's end, an
aggregate total of 20,000 men would serve the Confederacy — one-
third of the entire white population. However, Unionist sentiment
showed up early by virtue of the low enlistment rates in Yadkin,
Surry, Madison, Henderson, Polk, and Wilkes counties. Wilkes, in
fact, although it had the largest white population of any western
county, had the lowest rate of volunteers: 2.7 percent.

During those same months when 8,000 mountain men were
joining the Rebel cause, another 2,000 or so were quietly making
their way to Kentucky and enlisting in the Union Army. Thousands

more, who sympathized with the Union cause, simply kept their mouths shut and tried to sit out the war in peace. The only alternative was a long and hazardous trek over rough terrain, and the trauma of abandoning one's wife and children to a very uncertain and lonely fate. Only the most dedicated Unionists, therefore, embarked on such an odyssey during the war's first years. But after the Union army under General Ambrose Burnside had established itself in Knoxville in September 1863, the steady trickle of mountaineer recruits for the Union turned into a flood. Before the war's end, about 5,000 western North Carolinians would bear arms for the Union.

For every man who joined the Confederate Army out of political conviction, probably three or four more enlisted because it gave them a chance to get beyond the hills, see the world, and experience the great adventure of war. The naive quality of their enthusiasm is reflected in everything from the songs they sang to the advertisements in their hometown newspapers. For sheer drum-whacking jingoism, it would be hard to beat this advertisement from an Asheville paper:

HURRAH FOR BUNCOMBE! Some weeks since we noticed the fact that Drums of an excellent quality were being manufactured here; and now we are gratified at being able to state that we have examined, and heard tested a lot of Fifes, manufactured by our ingenious townsman, Mr. John Hildebrand, Jr., for the 25th Regiment. They are pronounced...equal to the best. We repeat, hurrah for Buncombe! We are cutting, one by one, and in rapid succession, the fetters which bound us down in galling dependence upon the North. It is eminently right and proper that as our gallant soldiers march to meet the enemy to the tune of Dixie, the music should be extracted from Southern made instruments. Buncombe can supply orders for any number of Drums and Fifes, warranted equal to any in the world.[8]

All the local companies which departed the mountains that first spring and summer were given romantic, emotional farewells. The whole village would turn out, speeches would be made, sermons delivered, and handmade flags presented by young women whose eyes devoured the gilt and glitter of brass, braid, leather, and steel. A gangly youth who weeks before had been nothing more than another local plow-puller, now stood proudly before his peers, drawn up in ranks, belted, buckled, and capped, standing ramrod straight behind a musket as tall as he was.

Government contracts poured into the region's forges and mines. A musket factory was set up in Asheville and was soon turning out some of the finest firearms ever made in the South. Up at Cranberry, on the Tennessee line in Mitchell County, a moribund complex of iron mines was reinvigorated with state funds and soon was turning out high-grade ore.

After the first wave of six-month volunteers were called up in April 1861, the state called for 50,000 more in May. By the beginning of 1862, however, it was painfully clear to the Confederate government in Richmond that a lot of that naive enthusiasm for combat had lasted about as long as it took for the volunteers to see their first grapeshot casualty. Most of the volunteers did stick out their term, at least, but when their six months or year was up, they came home. And that's where they intended to stay, figuring they had done their share. How quickly a man became disillusioned depended on a number of things: what happened to him in combat, his experiences when dealing with officers or Confederate officials, and how secure he felt his wife and children to be during his absence.

A new tide of popular emotion swept through the western counties between the spring of 1862 and the summer of 1863. The realities of the war turned what had been mere political disagreements into deadly animosities. Gradually, the hills themselves became a sort of battlefield. The deepening hatred and polarization can be traced by some very specific benchmarks. The first and most devastating in its effects was the passage of the hated Conscription Act in April 1862.

If any factor can be identified as the single greatest cause of unrest in the mountains, it was the Confederate government's imposition of the draft. Under the Conscription Act, all able-bodied males between 18 and 35 were subject to being drafted. There were a lot of loopholes in the law, though, which made it less odious to the very class of people who had always been in favor of secession. For men of property there were exemptions, such as the so-called "20-nigger law" which let the big plantation managers off the hook. For men of wealth, there was the offensive practice of hiring, for a fee, some poor neighbor to go fight in his place. The exceptions and substitutions brought considerable relief to citizens in other parts of the state, but for the rural poor in the western counties, there was very little relief. None of them held exemptible jobs, owned twenty or more slaves, or could dream of hiring a substitute. Conscription struck this class of people with staggering force.

The first waves of volunteer enlistments had already taken away all but the minimum number of men needed to keep the western farms going. The pro-Confederate farmers who were left, or who had returned after the expiration of their six-month enlistment terms, felt, with plenty of justification, that they and their class had already done its share. For them, the new law was a disaster, and it was resented accordingly. Loyalty began to waver, even among people who had hitherto been enthusiastic about the Southern cause. And for a large part of the population that had been trying to sit out the war in a posture of neutrality, the draft law served to push many over the borderline into active Unionism. Almost overnight, the future of thousands of families became clouded. What day would the recruiting party come for the man who ran the farm? What should he do, when confronted with their legal forms, their authority, and their bayonets?

The Richmond government professed to be fighting for the God-given right to be left alone -- something, by God, all the mountain people believed in! But this conflicted with the naked coercion the Confederacy was now using to obtain its cannon fodder, and it struck many mountain folks as just plain wrong.

Desertions increased as the conscription agents filled their quotas of warm bodies. It was one thing to round up a man and march him, an gunpoint, into a training camp; but once he was at the front lines, nobody could watch him around the clock. The opportunities for desertion were numerous and the path back home not hard to find: just head west until you hit the mountains, then turn left and follow the valleys south. For men who had grown up in wilderness terrain, it was not a particularly arduous journey in season, and the Confederate patrols couldn't guard every route. The same manpower shortage which had forced conscription also made sure of that.

There were only two North Carolinian votes against the Conscription Act when the matter was before the Confederate Congress; both came from the mountain counties. In December 1862, four state senators and 12 congressmen from North Carolina petitioned President Jefferson Davis to suspend conscription in the mountain district. In many counties, nearly the entire voting population was already in service. To take the remaining men, from areas where there were no slaves to replace them, would entail dreadful hardship on the civilians.

Letters from the period are full of references to the effects of the conscription policy. One typical example is this excerpt from a letter written by Ella Harper of Lenoir to a relative, dated November 8, 1862: "If there is not something done for the support of the soldiers' families, they *will not* stay away when their wives write to them that they are suffering for the necessaries of life, and many of them are doing that now, as they cannot foresee how they [the families] are going to be provisions for the winter."[9]

By the middle of 1862, the first Unionist guerrilla raids had started from Tennessee. Crops were poor that year, too, with many areas suffering from drought. Wool, cotton, hogs, corn, and especially salt were all becoming scarce. Prices inflated as a result of shortages and rampant speculation. By the end of 1862, land prices were up 60 percent, wheat and oats were beyond the economic means of the rural masses, and the price of an ordinary farm horse — if you could find one for sale — was nearly $500.

Two other Confederate policies also contributed to the gradual decline of conditions in western North Carolina: the tax-in-kind, and the policy of impressment.

The tax-in-kind was really a "tithe-tax." Farmers were required to contribute one-tenth of everything they produced to the Richmond government. For the gentlemen farmers of the coast and Piedmont, this was not necessarily a problem, or even more than a minor inconvenience. For the subsistence farmers of the mountains, it was an agonizing turn of the screws. Already stricken by a shortage of manpower, horses, and usable farming implements, not to mention the drought, most rural families were barely able to feed themselves. Whatever minuscule surpluses they might have set aside before the war had vanished. By the end of 1862, a ten percent bite out of their crops amounted to Richmond literally snatching food from the mouths of children.

This was also the first time the lower and lower-middle classes of North Carolina had ever been subject to any kind of tax. The tax-in-kind stirred generational memories of why so many mountaineers had fought the British back in Revolutionary days — was it not something about taxation? What rankled almost as much as the taxes themselves was the method of their collection. The taxation agents sent out by Richmond did not till the soil, or cope with the vicissitudes of the weather, or suffer visits from Rebel foragers and Unionist raiders. In fact, the tax collectors were exempt from both taxation and the draft. The whole system didn't seem fair, and it wasn't. The burdens fell heaviest upon those least able to cope with them.

Equally, if not more, odious was the Richmond government's policy of impressment, of arrogating the right to take provisions, animals, slaves, wagons, or whatever else was needed for the cause, and then to set the price which would be paid (if the owner were lucky) in compensation. The compensation was invariably pegged much lower than the inflated market value of the commodities taken. The policy was enforced, in some districts, with a very heavy hand. The property and livestock of suspected Union sympathizers was often impressed without so much as a promissory receipt, leaving many small farmers virtually helpless. How could you raise enough to feed your family, much less pay the tithe-tax, if you were forced to plow by hand, like some kind of primitive savage, after your own government had taken your horse?

In the realm of military strategy, the mountainous district of North Carolina was irrelevant to events that transpired on the coast and in the Piedmont, not to mention the main front in northern Virginia. To the west, it was a very different story. Military events in eastern Tennessee had direct, intimate, and profound consequences for the mountain counties of North Carolina. Those counties were, most of the time, a peripheral part of the eastern Tennessee theater of war, and the stakes in that part of the Confederacy were high indeed.

The region watered by the lower third of the French Broad River was of great strategic importance. It stood between the strong

Federal presence in Kentucky and the vital Confederate heartland
that stretched from central Tennessee to the Mississippi River. It
was also one of the most fertile regions in the Confederacy, produc-
ing not only wheat and corn, but also hay for fodder, and bacon and
beef for the army.

But it was a politically volatile region, and every commander on
either side who ever pulled a tour of duty in eastern Tennessee had
ample reason to curse his luck. The passions that war had unleashed in that region seemed to corrode the morale, and sometimes
the reputation, of every man who held command there. For a while,
on the Confederate side at least, it prompted a game of military
musical chairs.

There was a cruel irony here. Geographically, this was the very
center of the Confederacy; yet it was here, in western North Carolina and eastern Tennessee, that a large percentage of the population -- in some places a majority -- utterly rejected the Confederate
cause. Indeed, some 9,000 North Carolinians rejected it so utterly
that they crossed the mountains and donned blue uniforms, along
with three or four times that many men from eastern Tennessee.
(Tennessee, as a matter of fact, ended up contributing more men to
the Union Army than Delaware, Rhode Island, or Minnesota.)

The very existence of such intense regional disloyalty had a
corrosive effect on Confederate morale. Mountain Unionism was
regarded as a dangerous contagion. It was common for the politicians in Raleigh to thunder about the danger of "infection" from
eastern Tennessee, as though skepticism about the rebel cause
could be spread by the very wind that blew through the mountain
passes.

There were tangible military effects, too, from this state of
affairs. Until the Confederacy lost eastern Tennessee (most of it,
anyway) for good in the autumn of 1863, Richmond was forced to
commit 5,000 to 10,000 troops in that region just to keep the
Unionist disaffection at a tolerable level, to keep the railroads from
being sabotaged and bridges from being burned, to keep snipers
from ambushing conscription officers up in the hills, and to keep
supplies coming up the eastern Tennessee railroad into Virginia,
where they were always badly needed.

As a rule, there was considerable tolerance toward mountain

Unionists on the part of the state government in Raleigh. How could it be otherwise, with Governor Zebulon Vance at the helm? Vance was himself a mountain man. He knew how people thought up in those hills. He knew how much pushing those people would stand for before they began to push back. For that reason he was constantly petitioning Richmond to suspend, at least during planting season, its conscription drives in the western counties. Even during the period of grimmest strife in Madison County, the bastion of rifle-toting, hard-core Unionism, Vance was careful not to speak of the Unionist bushwhackers as "bandits" or "traitors," but rather as wayward souls. "Do not let our excited people deal too harshly with these misguided men" he telegraphed to General Heth in Tennessee.[10] Heth was another of those Confederate commanders who wanted nothing more than to get as far away from eastern Tennessee as he could. He didn't heed Vance's telegram, and instead sent Colonel William Allen into the Shelton Laurel valley with a set of open-ended orders that were virtually guaranteed to provoke the kind of atrocity that did, in fact, take place.

Conditions in the Carolina mountains deteriorated rapidly after General Burnside took Knoxville, and when General James Longstreet's halfhearted attempt to dislodge Burnside failed bloodily on November 29, 1863 — the same day the news broke of General Braxton Bragg's humiliating and catastrophic defeat at Chattanooga. Desperate for supplies, Longstreet's men foraged across a wide swath of mountain country, including the upper edge of North Carolina, sending wagon trains deep into the hills to strip the local farms like locusts. Thirty miles south of Longstreet's winter encampment, Burnside's army was doing the same thing in the counties closer to Knoxville. Hard times grew harder.

General Ulysses S. Grant arrived in eastern Tennessee in December of that year to inspect the Union armies. For a time, Grant seriously contemplated launching a full-scale army-sized offensive straight through the mountains of North Carolina, following the course of the French Broad River to Asheville and beyond. This would have divided North Carolina lengthwise, cutting off General Robert E. Lee's supply lines into Virginia, and it would have linked up the Union army in the West with the Federal enclaves on the Carolina coast — sort of a Sherman's March in reverse. It was a bold, all-or-nothing operation, but Grant was talked out of it by General Sherman. Sherman hated eastern Tennessee, and he used to advocate stripping everything of value from the entire region, then simply abandoning it to let the locals fight it out among themselves. Sherman pointed out to Grant the logistical and physical problems of trying to move a large army through such rough terrain. At one point, Grant himself rode into the mountains to take a firsthand look, and he readily admitted that the terrain was a great deal rougher, and more easily defensible, than the maps made it appear to be.

It is interesting to speculate on what might have happened if Grant had decided to begin 1864 with such an offensive. It's true that the difficulties were real enough -- but at the time, the Confederate commander of western North Carolina had a grand total of 500 regular troops with which to oppose him.

The
Enforcement
Of
Conscription
Suffers A Setback
In Yadkin County

Captain John West woke up on the morning of February 11, 1863, feeling good about the day that stretched before him. A light snow had fallen during the night, but the morning sky was clear and the sharp winter sunlight was evaporating the last streaks of white. The ground would be damp, no more than that, and the air invigorating.

John West was commander of the Yadkinville Home Guard, and so far his duties had been routine, if occasionally strenuous. He had arrested some deserters, turned out a few times when there had been rumors of Unionist bushwhackers, and had patrolled some mighty long stretches of bad road, but so far there had been no real action. As a man of middle age, though still vigorous, Captain West had ambivalent feelings about that. He supposed, as he dressed that morning, that this day would be as routine as most of his other days in Confederate service. But at least, on this occasion, he would be performing a valuable service for the Southern cause.

Reports had reached Captain West the night before that a party of deserters and draft dodgers -- 15 or 16 men who had been hiding out in the forest near the Quaker schoolhouse at Deep Creek — had taken shelter from the cold inside the schoolhouse. For several days, local Quaker women had been providing food to the rascals, but it was not until the previous night that West had learned of their whereabouts. An informer had come in the night, bearing word that the outlier band was planning to flee the county as soon as the weather cleared, then head for Kentucky and the Union lines.

Well, Captain West told his wife over breakfast, those were 15 recruits the Union would never get. "I'll get those deserters or roast in Hell," he vowed. Mrs. West cautioned him to be careful; there was no longer any such thing as an unarmed deserter, and if those men were on the verge of lighting out for Federal lines, they were apt to be edgy.

"They won't shoot," West assured her. "They won't fight for their state or their country, why should they fight us? They won't shoot me."

West was accompanied on that bright winter morning by most of the Home Guard company from Yadkinville, plus a few Confederate loyalists who came along just to see what was going to happen -- maybe 50 men altogether. West felt like a soldier that morning, something that didn't often happen in Home Guard duty, not for real. He was an officer with a mission, and it had more significance than his usual duties. His step was resolute as he led his men to the Quaker schoolhouse.

Inside, the 15 men West was coming to arrest had spent much of the night laying plans for their flight to Union territory. Most, if not all, were conscription dodgers, not deserters. At first they had just wanted to be left alone, but a few months of living in the woods had turned that mild emotion into an active detestation of the Confederacy. Now most of them were gathered around the hearth inside the schoolhouse, eating breakfast and listening to one of their number who had just arrived with a fresh newspaper, one which might contain information about the military situation that could prove useful to them on the journey to come.

Outside, Captain West deployed his men around the little

building. Through its windows, the gathering of men around the fireplace was visible, and one of West's men could not restrain himself. He raised his rifle and fired into the room. One of the men standing at the hearth fell dead, a ball through his heart. The rest of the Home Guard then fired a ragtag volley at the log building, tearing up splinters and breaking glass, but otherwise hitting nothing else.

Unaware that his ill-disciplined force had already killed someone inside the schoolhouse, Captain West strode bravely up to the front door, armed with a shotgun. He pounded on the door and threw it open, crying out, "Men, surrender!"

He found himself staring at the muzzles of several weapons. West reached out with his shotgun and parried the muzzle closest to his breast, just as the draft dodger holding it pulled the trigger. The shot missed Captain West, blowing the door-joist over his head in two. Simultaneously, however, another draft dodger fired his weapon, and this time the ball struck John West above his left eye, blowing off a six-inch slab of his skull.

Seeing their captain falling lifeless to the ground, the Home Guard opened fire at will as the conscripts came boiling through the door, guns in hand. The first man out the door fell with six balls in his body. One of the fleeing conscripts took time to kneel by the front steps and return fire, killing a militiaman. Soon the front yard of the schoolhouse was obscured by powder smoke and the air was filled with screams, yells, and oaths.

When it was all over, four men lay dead: Captain West, two conscripts, and the unlucky Home Guardsman. Three or four others were wounded on each side. At least four of the men in the schoolhouse got away during the confusion and succeeded in making their way to Kentucky.

The schoolhouse battle polarized the political situation in Yadkin County. Only a day or two after the event, almost 500 eligible conscripts left their homes en masse and fled the county, assisted by a well-known guide. According to one (unfortunately very sketchy) account, the now-aroused Home Guard, together with some state troops, intercepted the mass of deserters near Rich Mountain and fired on them as they marched, killing several and capturing a few dozen.

The others, nearly 400 men, escaped to the west. It was a terrible journey, in weather that alternated between freezing rain and snow. Part of the time, the men marched with their clothing frozen to their bodies. Several died from exposure, and others were so injured by the ordeal that they were never the same afterward. After a journey of almost 500 miles, they reached Lexington, Kentucky and enlisted in the Union Army.

PART 2:
RAIDERS
AND REGULARS

Awake! and to horse, my brother! For the dawn is glimmering gray;

And hark! in the crackling brushwood there are feet that tread this way

Who cometh?" "A friend." "What tidings?" "O God, I sicken to tell,

For the earth seems earth no longer, And its sights are the sights of Hell!

-- S. Teackle Wallis, "The Guerrillas: A Southern War Song," 1864.

'LITTLE WILL' — WHITE CHIEF OF THE CHEROKEES

The history of how the Appalachians came to be settled has been told many times, and too often without a proper awareness of the one precondition for that settlement: the Indians had to be moved out first.

It would be difficult to find another Indian tribe in North America that suffered more from the policies and attitudes of the white man than the Cherokees who once inhabited a vast area of Georgia, Tennessee, and North Carolina. Each wave of white immigration into the mountain regions was accompanied by a treaty which resulted in the Cherokees being deprived of more land and more rights, starting with the Treaty of Hopewell in 1785. There was at times fierce Cherokee resistance, but each time they went to war, the white man's superior firepower and organization took a heavy toll. By the third decade of the 19th century, the 17,000 or so Cherokees remaining in eastern America were too weak to offer more than last-ditch resistance, which surely would have resulted in their complete annihilation.

What happened instead was sad enough. By 1835, the U.S. government had determined to remove, by force if necessary, all of the remaining eastern Cherokees. In the Treaty of New Echota, Georgia, signed on December 29, 1836, the Cherokees yielded all claim to whatever lands remained under their control. In exchange, they were to receive $5 million and a big piece of land out in

Oklahoma Territory, adjacent to land already occupied by the Western Band of Cherokees — those who had already journeyed along the aptly named "Trail of Tears."

General Winfield Scott assumed command of the removal operation in the spring of 1838. Most of the Georgia Cherokee submitted to their removal peacefully, but a large portion of the North Carolina Cherokees balked and fled deeper into the mountains. The majority of these settled in what would become Haywood County, establishing a central village which they named Quallatown, situated on the banks of Soco Creek near the junction of the Tuckaseegee and Oconoluftee rivers.

That they managed to remain in their beloved mountains, even to this day, was due in large part to the efforts of a single man: William Holland Thomas, the only white man ever known to be elected chief of a North American Indian tribe. And 23 years after the great Removal, when the Civil War started, Thomas led virtually every able-bodied Cherokee male into battle on the Confederate side. He created and commanded one of the most colorful and least-known Confederate units: Thomas's Highland Legion. In its ranks, the Cherokees served side by side with hundreds of white mountaineers descended from the very men who had decimated their tribe a few decades earlier. It was a remarkable achievement by a remarkable and somewhat elusive man.

Next to Zebulon Vance, William Holland Thomas was probably the best-known character to come from western North Carolina in the mid-19th century. He was born in 1805, on the banks of Raccoon Creek, near Waynesville. When he was 12, he went to work in a general store in Soco Valley. During the three years he held the job, he discovered within himself not only a talent for trade and speculation, but also a deep emotional affinity for the Cherokee Indians who dwelt close to, and often patronized, the store.

When Thomas was 14, his mother, Temperance Thomas, moved to a 50-acre plot on the west side of the Oconoluftee River. One of their neighbors happened to be the revered Chief of the Oconoluftee Cherokee, Yonagushka ("Drowning Bear"). For whatever reasons of temperament or impulse, the aging Indian chief and the young merchant became close friends, so close that Yonagushka "adopted" William Thomas as his son and gave him his official Cherokee name: "Wil-Usdi," which meant "Little Will."

It was not a particularly tactful name, but it was often the Cherokees' custom to designate a man according to his most striking physical characteristic. And Will Thomas was short: five feet, four inches. No photographs of him taken before his middle age have been found, but the one surviving formal portrait reveals a man with a lofty forehead, intelligent but rather mild blue eyes, a round face with full cheeks, and a thin, almost prim, mouth.

He more than compensated for his short stature and less-than-charismatic features by virtue of his keen, omnivorous mind and his remarkable physical stamina. He had a vast capacity for both intellectual work — he would often stay up all night working on his business ventures or writing legal papers on behalf of the Cherokees — and for physical labor. His business interests in the mountains were far-flung indeed, yet he kept in personal touch with all of them and thought nothing of spending 20 hours in the saddle, alone, in some of the wildest country east of the Mississippi. In one youthful diary entry, he casually mentioned killing a five-foot rattlesnake near Soco Creek.

Thomas was largely self-educated, but he was as diligent in those pursuits as he was in his business ventures. His correspondence sometimes reveals the awkward syntax and unsure spelling of a self-taught person, but it also reveals clarity, logic, and force. He taught himself mathematics, law, and such portions of literature as he could come across in his remote location. He seems to have been, by temperament, a great compromiser: tactful, judicious, and patient. Not surprisingly, he did well in politics.

Thomas's son once wrote that his father had "an almost romantic fondness for the Cherokee tribe." There was actually nothing "almost" about it; Thomas's identification with his adopted people was deep and lasting. And yet, there was a touch of ambiguity now and then to his relations with the Indians. That he sincerely loved them and successfully fought for their right to remain in their beloved mountains are matters of historical fact. Yet it is also demonstrably true that he was ready to use his Indian connections to turn a fast profit, particularly in the realm of real estate speculation — a business for which he had unbounded zest, unfortunately coupled with a lifetime of sloppy habits as a bookkeeper.

Thomas opened a general store of his own in 1821, when he was only 16. His chief source of income was fur and skins, which the Indians brought him in abundance. In those days, the Smokies were still well-populated with bears, panthers, and wildcats, as well as minks, otters, foxes, and raccoons. With the profits from his early bartering, Thomas became a real estate tycoon, eventually acquiring at least 100,000 acres of mountain land. He lent, he borrowed, he paid, he foreclosed, he wheeled, and he dealt. As it turned out later, a great deal of his wealth existed mostly on paper.

His activities included running a fleet of trade wagons to and from the market towns of Georgia and South Carolina, mining interests, milling operations, a tannery, beef cattle, and expanding his original store into the first "chain," consisting of seven establishments, ever created in that part of the state.

All along, while he was building his commercial empire, he was both reveling in and successfully exploiting his relationship with the Cherokees. In later years, when his chronic mismanagement of financial affairs embroiled him in endless legal actions, he freely speculated with land that, technically, belonged to the Indians and not to him. He also had no hesitation about using Indian money under his control for the purpose of staving off personal financial crises.

Nevertheless, the antebellum relationship between Thomas and the Indians was one of unbounded trust. They appointed him their legal representative in 1831, at a time when the remaining Cherokees in North Carolina were under intense pressure to pack up and leave the mountains altogether. Unlike the Georgia Cherokees, who had produced their own eloquent spokesmen, the North Carolina Cherokees had few members who spoke English very well, and without Thomas they would have been nearly helpless in their ongoing negotiations with Washington.

Thomas translated his personal identification with the Cherokees into a full-blown sense of mission. He would be their advocate in Washington, and if possible, their savior. He would secure for them every last dollar that was due them under the treaty of New Echota, and he would force the government to acknowledge the right of the North Carolina Cherokees to remain in their mountain homeland without molestation. If Thomas was not averse to making a quick buck from his Indian connections now and then, in this, the most important work of his life, he seems to have been motivated entirely by humanitarian impulses.

He was their lobbyist in Washington for a quarter-century, from 1836 to 1860, and he tirelessly pursued two main objectives: permission for the mountain Cherokees to remain in the East, and their fair share of the "removal and subsistence" fund that had been created, under the New Echota Treaty, to compensate the Cherokee nations for the barbarous uprooting inflicted on them by Washington.

Thomas seems, however, to have played a slightly ambiguous role in "The Removal." He set up stores near the camps where the soon-to-be-displaced Indians were under guard, and he peddled his wares to victims and oppressors alike. He also played fast and loose with real estate opportunities that arose as a result of the Indians' removal.

He played a key role in the capture of the rebellious renegade warrior Tsali, whose armed resistance to The Removal had generated a virtual guerrilla band of recalcitrant Cherokees hidden deep in the mountain wilderness. Thomas traveled to Tsali's camp and persuaded the rebel warrior to give himself up for the good of the tribe. Tsali and his closest associates were subsequently executed by a firing squad made up of other Indians — a tactic designed to impress upon the entire tribe the futility of resistance.

Thomas's solitary trek to Tsali's hideout was unquestionably a brave act, and it may well have averted a major outbreak of violence. But the rest of Will Thomas's role in the whole sorry episode of The Removal remains a bit cloudy. Certain documentation suggests, albeit indirectly, that he may have been acting as a double agent, receiving payments from a fund set up to help subvert Cherokee leaders in favor of government policy.

Whatever shady dealings Thomas may have had on the side, his basic loyalty to the Cherokees was never questioned by Chief Yonagushka. When that revered leader passed away in April 1838, he bestowed upon Thomas a signal honor. Realizing he was near death, Yonagushka summoned the other tribal leaders to his headquarters, the council-house at Quallatown. He admonished the tribe never to leave their mountains, and also to practice temperance (something Yonagushka himself was inclined not to do; Will Thomas, in fact, helped keep the old man supplied with liquor). Then Yonagushka did something astonishing: he named William Holland Thomas, a white man, to be his successor as chief of the Oconoluftee tribe. So great was the prestige of both Yonagushka and "Little Will" that this decision was accepted without question, and Thomas enjoyed the utter devotion of "his tribe" until the day he died.

Whether Thomas was accepted, officially, as chief of all the eastern Cherokees is not clear from the records. Certainly, however, he was treated as if this were the case. Whatever the truth may be, Thomas took his new responsibilities very seriously. When he was not in Washington, lobbying for the Indians' right to remain in their homeland, he took an active role in tribal affairs. He met in council with the sub-chiefs, he took part in ceremonies and rituals, and he organized the reservation's land and government in a manner so consistent with common sense that some aspects of his system remain in place to this day.

Maybe his financial wheeling and dealing, his dubious relations with the white soldiers who had supervised The Removal, his occasional appropriation of Indian funds for other than strictly tribal purposes -- maybe all of these acts were subsumed under the heading of "just business," for there can be no doubt that the man's heart really belonged to the tribe. Lesser men have had no trouble rationalizing much greater hypocrisies than any Thomas may have been guilty of. When starvation threatened, in 1864, Thomas spent thousands of dollars of his own money to import food from South Carolina. And when he spoke or wrote about the Cherokees, Thomas could approach Governor Zebulon Vance's level of eloquence:

> A larger portion of them can read and write than is found among the White population, in a majority of the States of the Union. Their lands are situated at the base of the Great Iron or Smoky Mountains, which furnishes rich pasturage for their cattle, both winter and summer, and where game is plenty. Their lands are productive, their orchards supply them with fruit; springs and brooks of the purest water from the sides and base of the mountain[s]; and the atmosphere

is one of the healthiest on the globe. No local causes for disease; no chills or fever which are so prevalent in the South, And that country is endeared to those Indians by the graves and sacred relics of their ancestors — the bones of their children, sisters, brothers, fathers and mothers lie there; they say we cannot leave them; let us alone in the land of our fathers.[1]

And when it was pointed out to Thomas, midway through his crusade on the Indians' behalf, that his activities were alienating many of his white acquaintances, he replied: "If my advocating their rights has offended any of my friends...I have one consolation[,] that I have faithfully discharged my duty to those people...I had much rather be blamed for doing my duty than neglecting it and when entrusted with defending the rights of white or red man I hope I shall always be found faithful to my trust...the Indians are as much entitled to their rights as I am to mine."[2]

Thomas was very active in state politics, serving in the Senate for seven consecutive terms, beginning in 1848. His most effective role seems to have been that of chairman of the Committee on Internal Improvements, in which capacity he supported the development of North Carolina's transportation network. He was a force behind the creation of the 130-mile-long Fayetteville and Western plank road, and, somewhat later, the laying of the Western North Carolina Railroad tracks as far as Morganton. For a while, there was even talk of Thomas running for governor. But the war, which set back economic development of the mountain region by more than half a century, also put an end to Will Thomas's political career — if not his politicking.

In 1861, the total population of North Carolina Cherokees was slightly under 2,000. On the face of it, there was nothing on earth the Cherokees stood to gain from joining the war in any capacity. It is surely doubtful if many of them had even the dimmest comprehension of the constitutional, economic, and philosophical issues that attended the secession debates. That they did participate, and on the Southern side, is due entirely to the persuasiveness of Will Thomas, their white chief. Even then, some of the Indians must have wondered at the strange ways of white politics. Here Thomas had been telling them for years to trust the government in Washington to make good on its obligations to them, and now here was

Little Will back among them, telling them that Washington was inhabited by demons in blue uniforms and that they should be prepared to defend their corner of the South against armies sent from Washington. Little wonder that, when Thomas held his first discussion with tribal authorities on the matter of secession, their initial reaction was one of utter confusion.

That the Cherokees did eventually go to war, more or less just because William Thomas asked them to, speaks volumes about his personal influence over the tribe. Their active cooperation probably dates from May 1861, just after Thomas had returned from performing his duty as a delegate to the secession convention in Raleigh. It was apparently on this visit that Thomas organized the first Indian unit, a 200-man outfit picturesquely dubbed the "Junaluska Zouaves." For the time being, however, the unit existed mainly on paper and in Thomas's imagination, for Thomas had to return to Raleigh and attend to his duties as a state senator.

Some Cherokees did apply to join a unit being raised in Buncombe County, but were turned down because there was no clear Confederate policy regarding their status. Two or three Cherokees did get into a cavalry company organized by one George Hayes, a political foe of William Thomas, but it is doubtful if they stayed long. Hayes made no secret of his prejudices, saying that he would "just as soon be caught in a voting booth with a free Negro" as to be seen socializing with an Indian.

Thomas stood for reelection in November 1861, and most of the early autumn found him campaigning in Raleigh. He continued to agitate on behalf of an Indian volunteer force, however, and he succeeded in persuading the state senate to pass a bill authorizing North Carolina to raise a battalion of Cherokee regulars. When this measure was passed, Thomas ebulliently wrote to President Jefferson Davis, telling him that such a force, in embryo at any rate, was already available.

Splendid, Davis wrote back; then, in a paragraph which reflected his usual level of military expertise, he suggested that the Cherokee unit be sent to the coastal swamplands for duty -- hundreds of miles away from the terrain the Indians were familiar with, into the same pestilential environment that absolutely ravaged the Lumbee Indians who were impressed to serve in labor battalions near the coast.

Fortunately for the Cherokees, Davis never had a chance to carry out his idea. The bill authorizing a Cherokee battalion, though passed by the state senate, was torpedoed in the state house of representatives by politicians who felt it was too radical. They felt it would bestow de facto citizenship on the tribe — something, one would think, they were already entitled to. Thomas found this reasoning specious as well as morally abhorrent. In his opinion, the three existing treaties the Cherokees had signed with the government already recognized them as citizens of North Carolina.

So Thomas decided to organize a Cherokee battalion anyway. He had written authorization from Jefferson Davis to form an Indian unit, and that is what he intended to do.

At age 59, Thomas surely did not contemplate an active field command, and in the autumn of 1861, his ambitions were clearly more political than military. He chose not to run for the senate again, but for the house, and he was defeated by the incumbent, Colonel Allen Davidson, largely because Davidson had the support of the more influential newspapers.

Thomas was, however, still a member of the Third Session of the North Carolina Convention, and he was still an ardent Confederate. Through the winter of 1861-62, until the dissolution of the Convention in February, Thomas busied himself drawing up plans never to be fully realized — plans for making North Carolina's western boundary militarily impregnable. Thomas had lots of firsthand knowledge about the extent of Unionist sentiment in East Tennessee, and he was concerned about the possibility of an invasion from that direction.

He returned to Quallatown in March 1862, and under his direction, the Indians and some local whites began the construction of defensive earthworks to block the critical pass at Oconoluftee Gap. This was the main route between the Cherokee capital at Quallatown and nearby Sevier County, Tennessee, known as a cauldron of divided loyalties. As for the troops to man these defenses, Thomas now envisioned a composite force that would combine an existing white regiment with his own "Zouaves," as well as whatever additional companies of recruits, red or white, could be scoured from the hills. The whole thing was to be called *Thomas's*

North Carolina Highland Legion.

Even counting all the possible raw material in that part of the mountains, Thomas did not yet have the ingredients of a "legion." One suspects he just loved the sound of the word, as well as its classical associations with ancient Rome. In the military parlance of Civil War times, a "legion" was a single command which contained all three component elements: infantry, cavalry, and artillery. Legions formed in the war's first months usually carried the names of their founders or commanders: Wade Hampton's Legion from South Carolina, for instance, or Phillips's Georgia Legion. As the war dragged on and units were reshuffled, most of the legions ended up being "brigaded" — in other words, attached to regular line units, at which time they were given less romantic numerical designations, usually as regiments. Of all the units designated as legions, only the one formed by William Thomas remained a legion throughout the war. It would, in fact, be the last Confederate unit in North Carolina to lay down its arms.

Throughout his military career, despite the trouble he often got into with superior officers, William Thomas managed to retain an amazing degree of independence. This resulted from a byzantine, and thoroughly Southern, arrangement of bloodlines. Thomas's mother was Temperance Calvert, of the Maryland Calverts (and, according to some sources, the grand-niece of Lord Baltimore himself). And Thomas was blood-related to ex-President Zachary Taylor, whose daughter happened to be married to Jefferson Davis. To cinch the matter, Thomas was a first cousin of John Strother, a prominent member of the Virginia aristocracy who enjoyed plenty of clout within the Richmond administration.

Thus it came about that, while Thomas's men were digging trenches in the Oconoluftee Gap, word came that his Cherokee battalion had been accepted into Confederate service. Moreover, it had been accepted by, and was reportable only to, the central government in Richmond -- completely bypassing the chain of command in North Carolina. The unit would not, however, be used simply to guard the mountain passes near the Cherokee homeland. Instead, it would be attached to the Department of East Tennessee, where General Edmund Kirby-Smith was serving as the first of nine Confederate generals who would be saddled with that odious and thankless command.

To muster-in the Indian companies, Kirby-Smith sent Major Washington Morgan to Quallatown. Morgan, as it happened, was himself part Cherokee. He was the half-breed son of Gideon Morgan, a chieftain who had led Cherokees at the Battle of Horseshoe Bend, and he bore the tribal name "Aganstata." Major Morgan succeeded in whipping up the enthusiasm of his Cherokee braves, but Will Thomas was unhappy about Morgan's appearance on the scene. Thomas feared that if the Indians marched away under Morgan's command, they would be sacrificed on some distant battlefield, whereas Thomas wanted to employ them as close to home as possible. Unfortunately, Thomas had little choice. Because the Cherokees had been accepted in the Confederate Army, they would have to go where ordered, with or without him. So Will Thomas made a momentous decision. Despite his age and lack of military experience, he took a commission as a captain, and elected to ride into Tennessee at the head of his legion. So great was Thomas's prestige that Major Morgan folded up his recruiting operation as soon as Thomas took a commission.

Not many Confederate units could have gone to war in a more colorful fashion than Thomas's Indians. Few of the Cherokees could possibly have had more than a casual understanding of Confederate ideology, such as it was, but they could certainly understand the desire to fight back against men who were invading one's homeland. For many braves, the existence of the Legion seemed to offer a chance to do something they would never have dared to do otherwise: go forth and confirm their manhood by killing white men.

Before the Cherokees went to war, however, they held a great feast, complete with elaborate rituals of oracle-consultation and war dances in full ceremonial regalia. Will Thomas even donned war feathers on top of his gray officer's uniform and participated in the rituals.

The whole show was witnessed by hundreds of fascinated and slightly bewildered white Confederate recruits, who must have felt as though they were caught in a momentary time warp. Observing the spirited dances and the ferocious appearance of the warriors, they also must have been glad the Indians were on their side.

THE LEGION IN EAST TENNESSEE

With William Thomas as its elected captain, the first Indian company of what would become Thomas's Highland Legion was officially mustered into Confederate service on April 9, 1862. Second-in-command was Lieutenant James W. Terrell, a longtime friend and business associate of Thomas. The unit's two second lieutenants were both Cherokee: Peter Graybeard and John Astoogatogeh. The latter was one of the most highly regarded men in the tribe. Astoogatogeh was respected as the grandson of the great chief Junaluska, and was well liked for his own qualities. A born leader, blessed with keen intelligence and a magnificent physique, he had earlier become a devout Christian and had been instrumental in getting the New Testament translated into Cherokee. In addition to these officers, several other Cherokees who would later become prominent in tribal affairs were also enrolled in the company as junior officers (what would today be considered noncoms).

Numbering just over 130 men, the company began its march to Knoxville several days after its official mustering-in. One Confederate regular officer who observed the first Legion troops on the march thought them to be "as fine a body of men as ever went into the service."[1] Indeed, they must have been. The Cherokees had not actually been to war, as a tribe, since the Creek campaigns of 1814, but they had a strong tradition of battlefield bravery. In the images of chiefs such as Oconostota and Junaluska, these young soldiers had powerful role models. And they were in better physical shape, by far, than most Confederate recruits. The endless hours of lacrosse-like ball games that were part of the routine upbringing of every Cherokee male, plus the conditioning of long hunts through rough, mountainous terrain, built them into muscular yet graceful men. As trackers and navigators, they had no peer in Confederate service, as the Unionists of eastern Tennessee would soon learn.

At every mountain village along the way, Thomas paused to recruit more soldiers, red and white alike. They were delayed a few days when the Hiawasee River flooded, but a day's march after the waters receded brought them to Sweetwater, on the Tennessee and Georgia Railroad. Thomas went ahead to Knoxville by train to make arrangements for billeting the unit, leaving Terrell in charge. The Indians got their first-ever train ride a day or two later and arrived in Knoxville to find themselves already famous.

The citizens of Knoxville reacted to Thomas's men as though an expeditionary force of Martians had come to town in Confederate uniforms. Their first parade through the city was followed by a large, excited crowd. Thomas led them to an unimpressive hill north of the city, which the Indians promptly named Camp Agan-stata, in honor of Major Morgan, and there they settled in. Now their training began in earnest, and they were drilled in the rudiments of tactics. Other units comprised of mountain-born men were marching through Knoxville all the time, and several contemporary observers remarked on how much better disciplined, and how much smarter on the drill field, the Indians appeared to be than the average company of white men.

During the weeks they were bivouacked at Camp Aganstata, the Indians were the subject of intense local scrutiny. Crowds gathered at the edge of camp every day to gawk at what one newspaper called "the wonder of the city." The highlight of the Indians' stay in Knoxville came on April 27, when they held a well-publicized worship service at the local Baptist church. A colorful account of this incident was published in the *Knoxville Daily Register* on May 2, 1862:

> ...At the appointed time the battalion formed in double file, and marched under an elegant Confederate flag, under command of Major G.W. Morgan. Entering the city at the east end of Main Street...the troops attired in their new dress, continued the march, and entered the Church in an orderly and quiet manner. It was at once seen that public expectation was so high as to have drawn out a larger

crowd than the building could accommodate. An offer was made of the First Presbyterian Church, and the meeting was adjourned to that large and commodious building. The pews on the south side of the aisle...were assigned to and at once occupied by the Cherokee braves. The Rev. W.A. Harrison, pastor of the Church, introduced to the audiences 'our brother Unaguskie, Chaplain of the Cherokee battalion,' and the services commenced by reading and singing (in the standing posture) a hymn in their own dialect. The types resemble a little the Hebrew, but are read from the left side, as our common language. Prayer followed, the chaplain and his braves all kneeling. Another hymn was sung, and the text announced, as found in Luke, 6 chap.: 43 verse. The sermon was, like the entire service, delivered in the original Cherokee language, but was addressed alike to all his auditors, wherever seated or of whatever complexion...[the services] were probably two hours long, and in every part of them secured the fixed attention of a very large auditory. Every part of the church was filled, and yet not a word was understood by any one...

Unagushkie is the grandson of a Cherokee chieftain...he has many of the attributes of a natural orator. In person he is about six feet high — tall, slender, and erect; has an excellent voice, graceful and rather emphatic gesticulation with little of the mannerism of the modern pulpit. His sermon seemed to be persuasive rather than denunciatory, advisory and parental rather than condemnatory and authoritative...Of his theology, of course nothing can be known certainly....[2]

About two weeks later, the Indians were ordered to the village of Strawberry Plains, northeast of Knoxville. Strawberry Plains would be their headquarters for quite some time. The Indians settled agreeably into camp routine, naming the place Camp Junaluska. There were now enough recruits for Thomas to form two companies — the first of many shifts of organization and command which would vastly confuse historians — and designate the unit a "battalion."

One bit of confusion should perhaps be cleared up at the outset: It is common to read, in nearly every account of the mountain war published before the 1970s, that Thomas's Legion and the 69th North Carolina were one and the same unit. Indeed, the outfit is even designated as the "Sixty-Ninth" in Walter Clark's *Histories of the Several Regiments and Battalions from North Carolina in the Great War, 1861-65.* In fact, however, it was not so designated during the war years. Instead, it was known always by either its formal appellation -- Thomas's Legion of Indians and Highlanders -- or more often, simply as Thomas's Legion. How the confusion with the 69th North Carolina came about is itself highly confusing and probably of interest only to specialists; readers wishing to pursue the matter are directed to pages 145-147 of Vernon Crow's book about the Legion, *Storm in the Mountains*, where he makes a nearly superhuman effort to untangle the intricacies of the nomenclature.

By the time they went into bivouac at Strawberry Plains, Thomas's men were handsomely clad in new uniforms and had acquired a soldierly appearance in their drill. But they were, as yet, poorly armed. There were few modern rifles in the unit, although in the preceding weeks a large number of small-caliber "squirrel rifles" had been rebored to accept balls of man-stopping caliber. A significant portion of the command, however, was still armed with steel-tipped spears or traditional bows and arrows (which one officer suggested were probably more lethal than the regrooved and under-powered squirrel guns). All this equipage, of course, merely made the unit more picturesque to the locals. But by the end of the year, the unit seems to have traded these colorful artifacts for more modern rifles and carbines, some obtained from fallen Federal troopers or from Unionists who were disarmed by Legion scouts.

Now trained and ready for battle, the Indians and their white mountaineer comrades drew a vital but dull assignment. There was an important railroad bridge at Strawberry Plains which spanned the Holston River, a major tributary of the French Broad River. From there, the Tennessee and Virginia Railroad ran northeast to Bristol on the Virginia border, and thence to Lynchburg, passing the vital salt mines at Saltville on the way. Along this rail line came a significant amount of the supplies consumed by the Confederate forces in Virginia. And the region through which the tracks ran was swarming with Unionists — many of them defiantly militant — and was conceivably within striking distance of a quick cavalry raid from Kentucky. Thomas's job was to make sure nothing happened to the bridge or to the tracks for some distance in either direction north or south of his encampment.

Not long after settling in, the Indians suffered their first casualties — from measles, a disease which they had never encountered in the mountains, and which proved fatal to several of them. Another trooper was accidentally run over and killed by a train.

While his men were guarding the railroad and becoming acclimated to the customary fevers, fluctions, and discomforts of 19th-century field service, William Thomas was doing one of the things he did best: politicking. He traded subtly on his connections in Richmond, and mobilized his own remarkable fund of diplomacy and charm, to ingratiate himself with General Kirby-Smith and his entourage. Thomas wanted to expand the forces under his command, convinced that it was his personal mission in the war to forge a shield for his beloved mountains.

In some ways, he was remarkably successful. He obtained authorization to send out agents to recruit more men from the border region, and he was allocated three other companies. Two of the companies were from Virginia, and one was from Haywood County, North Carolina — led by a prominent mountain citizen, Doctor Elisha Johnson. The first of these new companies, Johnson's, was added to Thomas's command in late summer; the others trickled in during early autumn.

Thomas also crossed paths, in mid-summer, with a handsome, blue-eyed, 24-year-old native of Strawberry Plains who was destined, through a series of adventurous circumstances that would do credit to a Victor Hugo novel, to become one of the Legion's last and best battlefield commanders. William W. Stringfield had already seen considerable action, but at the time he met Thomas and Terrell, he was chafing under a truly obnoxious assignment. As deputy provost marshal of Upper East Tennessee, it was his thankless job to round up deserters and to enforce the hated conscription law that had been enacted in April 1862. So intense was Unionist sentiment in this part of the state that Stringfield escaped bushwhacking only because his family was well-liked and he himself was an exceptionally tactful and sensitive young man.

When Thomas, along with second-in-command Terrell, became lodgers at the Stringfield family home, Stringfield quickly befriended the two officers and soon found himself attached to Thomas's command as his enrollment officer. Stringfield's first assignment was to go back to the Legion's home territory in North

Carolina -- Cherokee, Macon, and Haywood counties -- and muster-in all the new recruits that Thomas's agents had been drumming up in the region.

At about the time he was befriending Captain Stringfield, Thomas himself received his first taste of action — or glimpse of it, anyway. In June 1862, when a Federal move on Chattanooga seemed to threaten the stability of the eastern Tennessee theater, General Kirby-Smith sent Thomas and half a company of his Indians into that sector to act as scouts. The Indians did their job well, although by the time they got to the front, there was not much going on besides the usual skirmishing between pickets. Thomas himself had the good fortune to capture a Federal straggler, although by Thomas's own admission, the Yankee didn't require much capturing:

> ...When on the enemies [sic] side of the river alone except [for] a fisherman I had hired to aid me, I met up with a lost Yankee belonging to the Lincoln army. He had lost his regiment which I ascertained from him was from Michigan, and surrendered to me no doubt to avoid being shot by the pickets[.] I took him across the river and turned him over to the commander of the Regt. He seemed to be an intilligent [sic] and gentlemaney [sic] man. The mob came near shooting him after he surrendered and it was all I could do to prevent it. The Indians say as I took the first prisoner each of them must take one to be even with me. While at Chattanooga news came that a battle was going on, 20 miles below...and I with a few of my Indians was immediately ordered there. Upon our arrival we found the two armies separated by the River and the army of the enemy slowly retreating from the field. I sent ten of my men across the river to watch the movements of the enemy and to report to me at Chattanooga. I came back to Chattanooga and received their report which was, that the enemy was moving toward the Cumberland Gap. I then returned to Knoxville and from that to this place....[3]

Thomas's force was considerably augmented when Captain Stringfield returned from North Carolina at the end of July. All told, Stringfield had mustered-in about 500 new recruits. Thomas divided them into five companies, adding three to his own regiment and allocating two companies as the nucleus of a new battalion commanded by his old friend, William C. Walker. Walker had met Stringfield at Valleytown with about 300 recruits, and had accompanied him back to Strawberry Plains.

So far, Thomas's plan to enlarge his force was working splendidly. As befitted the leader of such a growing contingent, he was promoted to major on July 19, 1862. For a while, Thomas had been calling his force the Highland Rangers, but in a letter to President Jefferson Davis, written in late August, he plainly stated: "I have increased the battalion of Indians and Mountaineers to a regiment and am progressing with a legion."[4]

Thomas's troops were formally organized as a regiment, in Knoxville, on September 27. Thomas, it goes without saying, was elected colonel. As his second-in-command, however, the troops chose a man who was not even present: James R. Love. Love was at that time still commanding a company in Virginia, one of the two which earlier had been transferred to Thomas on paper, but which had not yet arrived.

James Robert Love, one of the finest soldiers the Legion ever produced, was the scion of a great mountain clan. The Loves, at one time, had owned most of the land in Haywood County. His grandfather, Colonel Robert Love, was a Revolutionary War hero who had moved into the western country after his service and had founded the town of Waynesville, in 1809. Another one of the Colonel's grandchildren, Sarah Love, had married William Holland Thomas, in 1858. James Love had been a member of the North Carolina legislature when the war broke out; he had immediately resigned and taken a commission in the 16th North Carolina Regiment. He had seen intense action at Seven Pines, the Seven Days Battles, and Second Manassas, and he had survived the butchery of Sharpsburg-Antietam. After Antietam, his company was at last permitted to entrain for Tennessee to join Thomas, five months after the transfer had been authorized on paper.

Another Love boy, Matthew, was promoted in September to command one of the Indian companies, and Lieutenant Terrell was elevated to the rank of captain and assigned the duties of quartermaster for the regiment.

Both of Thomas's Virginia companies arrived in October. Meanwhile, Thomas had ingratiated himself with the new Confederate commander in eastern Tennessee, General McCown, just as he had done with the recently transferred Kirby-Smith. Thomas obtained permission to beef up another part of his force, Walker's battalion. Two new companies were enrolled in that unit, one comprised of Tennesseans, the other of men from Clay and Cherokee counties back in North Carolina. General McCown also authorized the transfer of three cavalry companies to Thomas. Walker now had seven companies in his battalion and was promoted to lieutenant colonel on October 1, 1862. All Thomas lacked now was integral artillery before he could realize his dream of commanding a legion.

It was during this period of intense recruiting and organization that the Legion saw combat for the first time, in a small but rather spectacular engagement up in the Cumberland Gap. The Confederates had spotted a Federal advance, presumably a thrust aimed a cutting Knoxville's communications with Confederate forces in Kentucky. General McCown ordered all the secondary passes through the mountains guarded, and Thomas's two Indian companies duly marched out to reconnoiter a place called Baptist Gap.

A reconnaissance detachment of enemy soldiers — probably not much larger than a company — had already reached the gap. It was from an Indiana regiment, part of General George Morgan's command. Its scouts had spotted the Confederate companies entering the gap and had hurriedly set up what must have seemed like a perfect ambush. Several Yankee sharpshooters drew beads on a man who appeared to be in command of the leading company: He was a tall, swarthy individual wearing a curious headdress which looked, from a distance, not unlike a turban. It occurred to more than one Indiana rifleman that they seemed to be getting ready to shoot at a Hindu.

But the man killed instantly by that first volley from the sharpshooters was the beloved Lieutenant John Astoogatogeh. And instead of recoiling from the surprise attack, the two Indian companies spontaneously charged straight into the ambush. It was a wild and terrifying moment for the Indiana troops, resembling an action scene in a dime novel. Fierce, ululating war cries echoed from the rocky mountainsides, and some of the dark-skinned Confederates dropped their rifles in favor of cold steel, brandishing Bowie-style blades about the size of Roman short swords. These barbaric-appearing apparitions charged fearlessly into the trees and were among the ambushers before another volley could be fired at them. The engagement was brief, savage, and bloody. In their rage over the death of Astoogatogeh, the Indians attacked with rifle butts, bayonets, knives, and even the steel-tipped spears some of them still carried.

Then, before their horrified officers could stop them, the Cherokees began to scalp their victims — the wounded as well as the dead. The air was torn by screams, pleas for mercy, shots, and curses. Every man in the Indiana detachment who had survived the Indians' first onslaught took off running, and they didn't stop until they stumbled, lathered and still pop-eyed with fear, into their base camp near the Cumberland Gap. By nightfall, the story of the "savage redskins" had spread through the entire Union force, magnified in the retelling until it reached Little Big Horn proportions. If Will Thomas had been seeking to give his men a reputation for battlefield savagery, he could not have engineered a better incident.

But Thomas was actually rather upset by the affair. He had, after all, spent most of his adult life pleading with the white authorities that the Cherokees were decent, civilized, responsible citizens...and now, in the heat of battle, they had reverted to savage tribal atavism.

If it had ever been Thomas's intention to use the Indians as a partisan strike force, the Baptist Gap incident would surely have multiplied their effectiveness far beyond their numbers. For the rest of the time the Indians were stationed in eastern Tennessee, they were feared and respected by regional Unionists. When tracked to their lairs by Cherokee patrols, deserters tended to come along peacefully rather than resist. Indeed, when the unit was finally compelled to abandon Strawberry Plains, one prominent local Union man actually came up to Lieutenant Terrell and said: "...I am truly sorry you are going to leave, for since you have been here there has been no stealing or raiding."[5]

The Indians' reputation for savagery followed them throughout the war. Although any mention of such things is conspicuously absent from the *Official Records*, there can be little doubt that the practice of scalping continued. Whether it happened often in eastern Tennessee seems doubtful, if only because the Indians' very presence helped to keep the lid on that region. But outlier bandits in North Carolina, stragglers from guerrilla forces such as Colonel George W. Kirk's command, and men known to have committed atrocities against mountain-folk the Indians considered friendly, must surely have felt the knife from time to time.

William Stringfield, as close to an official chronicler as the Legion ever had, denied that scalping ever happened after Baptist Gap. Another source states that a letter of apology was sent by courier to the Indiana regiment after that engagement, along with a grisly sackful of scalps, so that the "trophies" could be given Christian burial along with the rest of their former owners. Stringfield was unquestionably a sterling gentleman, but he was writing many years after these events had grown cold in his memory, and he often got important things wrong or left out crucial information. Moreover, by the time he wrote his account for Clark's *Histories of the Several Regiments*, he had lived among the Indians so intimately for so many years, that he sometimes claimed a condition of virtual sainthood for them which rings false.

James Terrell, on the other hand, had been an Indian agent for ten years before the war. During the conflict, he saw the Cherokees in action on any number of occasions, particularly in the small, unrecorded skirmishes that took place in the mountains of North Carolina. Terrell flatly stated: "Throughout the war they did scalp every man they killed, if they could get to him, which they generally managed to do...and while they operated where they were but scantily reported, at the end of the war, they had at least as many scalps as there were survivors among them."[6] This indicates that the Indians killed many more men than either the official or unofficial records give them credit for. If Terrell was not exaggerating — and in most instances, he seems a credible guide — the number of scalps taken could have been anywhere from 300 to 400, an impressively grim total if the Baptist Gap scalps, probably the largest number ever taken in one battle, were indeed returned to their previous wearers.

There seems no reason to doubt the credibility of what Terrell says. In the last winter and spring of the Appalachian war, there were dozens of bloody encounters, on nameless mountain paths and in secretive forest coves, that no one ever wrote about in any official reports. Too insignificant in the overall scheme of the war to be labeled even as "skirmishes," these encounters were just as lethal as Gettysburg to the men who were involved in them.

Discord Along the Tennessee-North Carolina Border

About six weeks after the Baptist Gap fight, eastern Tennessee boiled over in a brief, convulsive spasm of fratricidal violence. It had been building up for a long time, and it would continue, in spasms, long after the Legion had departed for other fronts. Indeed, in some places, it would continue long after the war itself was over.

In some ways, eastern Tennessee and western North Carolina were mirror images of each other. Both regions were quite distinct — economically, politically, and socially — from the Southern culture in which they were geographically embedded. If anything, eastern Tennesseans felt themselves even more isolated from what was happening in the rest of Tennessee than western North Carolinians ever felt from the rest of their state. Yet, eastern Tennessee had more connections with the outside world, thanks to the railroad which flanked the mountains and ran, for part of its length, through the foothills. Something else which set the two regions apart was the fact that eastern Tennessee was in the path of several major campaigns during the war, which was not true of western North Carolina until Stoneman's raid in 1865.

There was always a direct relationship between the situation in eastern Tennessee and what was happening in the mountainous part of North Carolina. When guerrilla activity heated up on one side of the border, it tended to heat up on the other side as well. And when eastern Tennessee came under Federal control in the autumn of 1863, Unionist activity in North Carolina increased dramatically, as did the danger of raids into the state from the west.

Like western North Carolina, eastern Tennessee had developed an economy that was not greatly dependent on slavery. Small numbers of slaves were held in the region, and they were used, as they were in North Carolina, for mining and milling as well as agriculture, but their economic importance was marginal. In western Tennessee, by contrast, the population was one-third slave; in central Tennessee, it was 29 percent slave. But in eastern Tennessee, the slave population was less than ten percent. There were 31 counties in eastern Tennessee in 1860, and in only two of those counties did slave-owners make up as much as four percent of the population.

The idea of turning eastern Tennessee into a separate state had not expired with the failure of the state of Franklin in the 1780s. The idea was still being pushed, well into the 1850s, by Knoxville's crusading Whig publisher, the Reverend William G. Brownlow.

When the lines were drawn between pro- and anti-Confederates at the start of hostilities, there was an economic pattern discernible that matched the one found in North Carolina. Generally speaking, it was the wealthier and more aristocratic families who supported the Confederacy, while the more numerous, and much poorer, yeoman farmers remained steadfastly in favor of the Union.

In the editorial pages of the *Knoxville Whig*, Reverend Brownlow spoke with feisty eloquence for this class of citizens:

> We belong to the "low flung" party of Unionists, and don't aspire to any higher class of associates. We have always despised, in our heart of hearts, a hateful aristocracy in this country, based on the ownership of a few ashy negroes, and arrogating to themselves all the decency, all the talents, and all the respectability of the social circle.
>
> The "low-flung," aye, the "mudsills" of society, the hard-fisted yeomanry of this country are going to govern it, and the respectability of the land may prepare to meet their humiliation. Educated labor will take the place of your slave-ocracy, and it will not be long until it will be looked upon as no disgrace for a man to eat his bread by the sweat of his brow.[7]

When Tennessee voted on the issue of its own statewide secession convention in February 1861, eastern Tennesseans voted against the idea by a total of 33,000 to 8,000. As in North Carolina and other Southern states, Abraham Lincoln's call for troops did push many previously neutral people into the rebel camp, but the region as a whole was still Unionist by a ratio of about two-to-one when the war broke out. Eastern Tennessee's Unionists even held their own convention, in June 1861, and resolved that the Unionist counties were, in fact, the "legal" part of the state. Resolutions were passed calling for armed resistance to any Confederate attempt to coerce the region. The delegates backed down from their more inflammatory propositions, however, when it became possible to look out the windows of their meeting places and observe companies of Confederate troops marching past. In secret meetings, however, ardent Union men made plans to arm and train their own paramilitary companies.

The Confederates were aware that they had a major security problem in this region: one of their most vital railroad lines went through the heart of this disputed land. Lacking the manpower to come down hard on the Unionists, the Confederacy at first adopted a policy of benevolence, hoping that Unionist sentiments would fade as the inhabitants lost their fear of mistreatment. It was too idealistic a policy to last long

Almost from the start of the war, eastern Tennessee acquired a reputation as a rotten place to pull duty. As early as the summer of 1861, Confederate soldiers stationed in the region were growing paranoid. When one unit experienced a rash of food poisoning (common enough in those days before refrigeration), wildfire rumors spread of mass poisonings plotted by the Lincolnites around Knoxville.

Something much more serious than food poisoning was afoot by November 1861: a plan for a concerted guerrilla strike against the critical railroad line. The plot was hatched by a dedicated Unionist named William B. Carter and had been approved by no less a personage than President Abraham Lincoln, who also saw to it that Carter received Federal funds to finance the undertaking.

It was supposed to be one of the most ambitious guerrilla strikes of the entire war. On a single night, Carter and other Unionists planned to attack, seize, and burn all nine major bridges on the railroad, knocking out a stretch of line 225 miles long. Simultaneously, the Federals would launch a strong thrust down from Kentucky, which the Confederate defenders would be unable to parry because all reinforcements would be cut off by the destruction along the railroad line.

Carter's plan was upset, however, when the Confederates made a preemptive attack of their own into Kentucky, resulting in a hot little battle at a place appropriately named Wildcat. This sudden action on the part of the previously docile Confederates prompted the Federal theater commander at the time, General William Tecumseh Sherman, to cancel the planned thrust into Tennessee. But by then it was too late to abort Carter's attacks on the bridges.

Nevertheless, Carter's men achieved total surprise and partial success. On the night of November 8, 1861, five of the nine targeted bridges were damaged or destroyed, and the attacks sent a shock wave of apprehension throughout the Confederate command in eastern Tennessee.

One of the bridges that was not destroyed, however, was the one at Strawberry Plains. William Stringfield rode across the bridge that night at about ten o'clock and stopped to chat a moment with one of the two sentries posted at either end, a Legion mountaineer named James Keelan. Then he rode on to the Stringfield family house, just on the other side of the bridge.

Approaching the bridge on that dark night was a raiding party of ten men — all natives of Sevier County, Tennessee — led by a militant Unionist named William Pickens. The approach to the bridge, on Keelan's end, was steep and narrow, so the party had to scramble, single file, up a considerable embankment in pitch darkness. They were unable to do this very stealthily, and Keelan was alerted to their approach. Keelan had a rifle, but it was propped against the bridge some distance away — too far for him to reach before the men he heard would be on the bridge. He therefore stood his ground armed only with a single-shot pistol and a Bowie knife.

Pickens was the first guerrilla to reach the top of the embankment. Rather stupidly, he struck a match. Keelan blasted him with the pistol at point-blank range. The raiding party responded by firing a wild volley of shots at Keelan, wounding the sentry in the hip and right arm. Another attacker, feeling Pickens suddenly go limp ahead of him, clawed his way up the slope, growling, "Let me up there, boys, I'll fix the damned rebel!" Keelan slashed him to death with his "Arkansas toothpick."

A frantic knife-fight then broke out at the top of the embankment. Exactly how many of the attackers Keelan killed or wounded, no one seems to know with any certainty. Some of the more lurid accounts of the incident say he killed four and wounded four or five more; others reduce the raiders' fatalities to just

Pickens and one other man, while admitting that several other attackers were severely gashed by Keelan's blade.

Keelan himself suffered numerous serious wounds. In addition to the two pistol balls that struck him, he suffered gashes in the head, neck, and right hand from the attackers' knives. Worst of all — although Keelan didn't realize it until he tried to pick up his rifle — a vicious blow from one of the raider's blades had almost severed his left hand.

What happened next is a matter of some confusion. The shots and commotion from the bridge had alerted the occupants of the Stringfield house, and lights were coming on — indicating that Confederate reinforcements were likely to arrive in a matter of minutes. (The sentry at the opposite end of the bridge apparently ran away in terror at the first sounds of Keelan's struggle.) According to Confederate accounts, Keelan stood his ground, rivered with his own and the attackers' gore, until help arrived. According to accounts from Unionist sources, Keelan finally jumped, or fell, over the embankment, and the raiders proceeded to try and burn the bridge anyway. They had brought containers of flammable liquid, but then discovered that they had only one box of matches, and it was wet. The raid was then aborted and the attackers withdrew, taking their injured with them.

James Keelan's Horatius-like stand was heroism of the Medal-of-Honor class, but there were numerous attempts both during and after the war on the part of local Unionists to denigrate it. Whether Keelan killed two, three, or four men that night is irrelevant; he single-handedly thwarted the raid and clearly put up an astonishing fight. The severity of his wounds attested to that, and his wounds were authenticated by several inhabitants of the Stringfield house who helped administer first aid to the blood-drenched man. Keelan survived his wounds, although it took him a year to recover. He even rejoined the Confederate Army after his convalescence.

News of the bridge attacks sparked several Unionist uprisings in other parts of eastern Tennessee — not everyone had received word that there would be no supporting Yankee attack from Kentucky. Groups of as many as a thousand "Tories" appeared in the open, and there was some skirmishing of a desultory nature before the Unionists realized that a general uprising was both premature and suicidal, and they eventually went back home to wait for better days. These Unionist movements were never much of a threat to anyone — they were poorly armed, undisciplined, and lacked strategic direction — but they added fuel to the backlash that now came down from the Confederate authorities. A number of suspected bridge-burners were rounded up and hung. In one place, the bodies were left dangling alongside the railroad tracks, and Confederate passengers on the railroad amused themselves by swiping at the bodies with their canes and taking potshots at them with their sidearms.

For the men of Thomas's command, the rest of the autumn and winter were relatively uneventful. The unit was dispersed in small packets along the railroad, guarding bridges and supply depots, and the Indians were sent out on an endless series of patrols, looking for draft dodgers and deserters, of whom there were plenty. It was not very glamorous work, but it was necessary, and the Indians did it well. Their very appearance was usually enough to trigger terror, although apparently they did not engage in much unnecessary brutality.

Some of the stories about what they did were fairly harsh, and perhaps not all of them should be dismissed — there are simply too few records about what happened when the Legion went out looking for conscripts. Only one thing can be said with certainty: the "bloodthirsty savage" stereotype clung to them like flypaper, and every rumor of a scalping that drifted out of the hills was seized upon and luridly embellished by the regional press. "England, in her wars with America, received and deserved the execration of the world for her barbarity in employing the Savages," wrote one Unionist demagogue in eastern Tennessee, "and the Southern Confederacy will become equally odious."[8]

Colonel Thomas occupied his considerable leisure time by drafting strategic plans for developing the foothills of eastern Tennessee into a kind of forward defensive zone for the mountainous border country — plans that were fully in keeping with his maturing concept of the Appalachians themselves as a kind of impregnable Confederate bastion. During his long political career, Thomas had passionately argued the benefits of new roads and rail lines into and across the mountains; this experience had given him a genuine expertise with regard to the strategic possibilities of good roads. With an impressive grasp of the essentials, and with a sense of vision he unfortunately never displayed as a tactician, Thomas outlined his plans in several letters to President Jefferson Davis. These plans were not only feasible, but also, if brought to fruition, would have significantly improved the Confederacy's overall posture west of the Blue Ridge — and fairly economically, too, in terms of manpower and resources. Here is one of them:

Headquarters
Strawberry Plains, November 8, 1862

President Jefferson Davis

DEAR SIR:

Summer is gone; fall has come. During the latter we came near losing East Tennessee. At present, we have to look out for the future.

I beg leave to submit a plan for the defenses of East Tennessee, which has been submitted to General Jones and others, and received their approval:

1st. Let a depot be established at the west end of the bridge at Strawberry Plains.

2nd. Let the road be completed from that point into the road leading to Blain's Cross-Roads.

3rd. This would complete the opening of the wagon communication between East Tennessee and the Virginia Railroad and Kentucky.

To secure this communication to be kept open, I would respectfully recommend the establishment of a line of posts, from 15 to 20 miles apart, on the road leading from the Mississippi Valley [into Kentucky]. The wagons, by stopping at a post each night, could be protected, which would secure us permanently.

To complete this communication with Kentucky, a guard of Indians or other soldiers would be necessary to pass from post to post, and an old-fashioned blockhouse should be built at such post to protect our troops against sudden emergencies.

The present prices of salt produce the necessity of putting into operation the Goose Creek salt works, where coal is in convenient distance to the salt works, and carting a few hundred yards completes the connection between the salt works and fuel. But there is another advantage to be anticipated. It will secure the control of

the article of salt in the hands of Government agents. That is worth
more than 5,000 troops. Besides, it will secure a communication
with Southern Kentucky, to be kept open, which will facilitate trade
in beef, bacon & c., of much advantage to us. We need their
breadstuffs, beef, bacon &c.

Yours, truly,

Wm. H. Thomas Colonel, Commanding Legion of Indians and
Highlanders[9]

It was a sensible, workable, comprehensive scheme, well
thought-out by an officer who was intimately acquainted with the
terrain and the situation. Had the "Thomas Plan" been put into
effect, the Confederates' hold on this strategic region would have
been strengthened and, as Thomas pointed out, some 5,000 men --
at that time tied down as little more than traffic cops and security
guards -- would have been freed for service on more active fronts.

But President Davis never even bothered to reply to this letter,
or to other, similar, communications from Thomas. This seems
odd, in view of his lenient and protective attitude toward Thomas
in other matters. But then, Davis's mind had a way of glazing over
whenever he was confronted with a military proposal based on
common sense. In this case, he simply passed the plan on to his
secretary of war, without comment. The secretary of war glanced at
it, initialed it, and filed it away without taking further action.

Thomas also worked out a rational and effective way of mini-
mizing anti-Confederate sentiment in his area of responsibility.
There was little he could do about gun-toting guerrillas except keep
them at arms-length by means of constant patrols, but there were
many other pro-Union men in that part of Tennessee who were not
quite militant enough to go underground, or not able, for personal
reasons, to flee to Federal territory. These men, naturally, were
most unwilling to bear arms for the Confederacy. Conscripting
them into combat units was a waste of time, Thomas believed —
time and time again, the process only resulted in their being
moved, at Confederate expense, close enough to Yankee lines for
them to desert in large numbers at the first opportunity.

Thomas devised a plan for enrolling several hundred of these men into an "engineer battalion." The unit was to include blacksmiths, masons, coopers, miners, gunsmiths, and carpenters. They would build, repair, and perform maintenance for the Legion, thus technically serving in the Confederate Army, but without being asked to fight, or even to carry weapons except in self-defense. It was a rather Solomonic scheme, in that it would have given Thomas a very valuable support unit while permitting many reluctant east Tennesseans to avoid either having to flee their homes or face imprisonment as draft-dodgers. It would also have gone a long way toward reconciling the balky inhabitants to Confederate authority. Unfortunately, this plan, too, never came to full fruition.

The Legion Sees More Action

Thus closed the year 1862, with William Thomas devising plans to help keep the lid on eastern Tennessee, while his Legion devised ways to stave off terminal boredom.

In January 1863, however, Thomas and his Indian companies got a firsthand look at how badly western North Carolina had become divided during the year they had been stationed elsewhere. Ordered to take part in a sweep against a band of outliers who had raided the town of Marshall, North Carolina, early in the month, Thomas marched his Indians from the rail depot at Greeneville into rugged Madison County and spent a fruitless week marching around the French Broad Valley, looking for bushwhackers. They found plenty of signs of both disaffection and increasing destitution but, fortunately for the Legion's honor, they had no part in the massacre at Shelton Laurel — the climax of this grim operation and the act which marked the start of intensified and bitterly cruel conflict in the mountains.

Back at Strawberry Plains, at the end of January, Thomas found further unpleasant developments. The Department of East Tennessee, rapidly acquiring a reputation as one of the least desirable postings in the Confederacy, had acquired yet another new commander, General Daniel Donalson. Donalson soon attached Thomas's hitherto independent command to the brigade of General

Alfred C. Jackson. This change was not popular with Thomas or his troops. Some idea of Jackson's reputation can be read from the nickname his men had given him — "Old Mudwall" — to distinguish him from Confederate hero General Thomas "Stonewall" Jackson.

Old Mudwall lost no time undoing whatever good Thomas had done in the Knoxville area. He ordered all but one of Thomas's noncombatant "engineers" into combat units and shipped them off to General Braxton Bragg's army at Chattanooga, where nearly all of them deserted within a week or two, just as Thomas had predicted.

Thomas could, however, take pleasure from one development. In March 1863, with the arrival of a four-gun battery of artillery, Thomas could finally and legitimately think of his force as a true "legion." The unit was organized into two main sub-units: Love's regiment, with ten companies, and Walker's battalion, with five. The artillery was under the command of a Virginian named John T. Levi. The total strength of Thomas's Highland Legion, as of the spring of 1863, was about 1,400 men.

All through the spring, the Legion's companies were shuttled back and forth, criss-crossing the upper part of eastern Tennessee in response to one rumored Federal thrust after another. Finally, in June, one of those threats materialized in the form of a 1,500-man cavalry raid led by Union Colonel William Sanders. About half of this Federal force was comprised of "Home Yankees" — that is, native eastern Tennesseans who had fled to Kentucky and donned the blue uniform.

Taking full advantage of his scouts' knowledge of the terrain, Sanders maneuvered skillfully around rebel defenses and actually reached Knoxville on June 20. After scouting the city's defenses, however, he realized he could not take it with his lightly armed column. Going after the consolation prize, Sanders swung northwest and fell upon the defenders of the Strawberry Plains bridge — after Knoxville itself, the most vital objective in the area.

There were about 400 Confederate troops guarding the bridge, including two Legion companies, both from Walker's battalion, plus Levi's artillery. At first, Levi's guns held the Federals at bay, but Sanders had the advantage of numbers as well as mobility.

After an hour's fighting, with light casualties on both sides, the defenders were routed and the bridge taken. All four of Levi's precious guns were captured, along with a great quantity of supplies. Sanders destroyed everything, including the bridge, before making his escape.

Some 130 Legion soldiers were captured and "paroled" by Sanders. Nearly all of them — honor-bound not to bear arms again until the terms of their paroles expired — promptly returned to their homes in North Carolina. Once there, they were appalled to learn that conditions in the mountains were deteriorating rapidly. "Tory" bushwhackers were marauding in every county, stealing food and horses, terrorizing the defenseless families of absent Confederate soldiers. In Cherokee County, they had recently murdered a Confederate lieutenant home on leave. Reports of these outrages soon got back to Thomas's men in Tennessee. Since the Richmond government had not seen fit to give any of them leave in more than a year, scores of men elected to slip away on their own and pay a visit to their families across the state line.

Partly to make up for the desertions -- and partly, one suspects, to teach the stubborn mountaineers who was boss -- Mudwall Jackson ordered all of the paroled men to return to active duty, contrary to custom, honor, and common sense. The men refused. They wanted to remain at home and protect their families at least as long as their paroles lasted. Colonel Thomas sided with them. There were some extremely heated exchanges between Thomas and Jackson, and the older man, Thomas, did little to hide his contempt for his putative commanding officer. The result was that Jackson actually had Thomas arrested on charges of insubordination on August 15, 1863.

But Thomas was not brought to trial -- not this time, anyway. Two weeks after he had Thomas brought up on charges, Mudwall suddenly had more serious things to worry about than the willfulness of a few hundred hillbilly soldiers.

Flanking the Cumberland Gap defenses just as Sanders had done earlier, Union General Ambrose Burnside struck eastern Tennessee like thunder with a force of 20,000 men. By September 3, without having to fight a single battle, he was enjoying a parade down the main street of Knoxville, wildly cheered by the town's Unionist population. The fall of Knoxville effectively terminated the already shaky Confederate hold over the central part of eastern Tennessee, although the rebels would hang on grimly to the northeast corner of the state for months to come.

Burnside then scored another triumph by boldly marching one of his brigades — 60 miles in 52 hours! — back toward Kentucky and investing Cumberland Gap from the southern side, while strong Federal forces menaced the vital mountain pass from the Kentucky side. John Frazer, commanding the Confederate garrison at Cumberland Gap, was unnerved and totally unaware of the military situation elsewhere in eastern Tennessee. Should he dig in and fight, in hopes of being relieved, or should he attempt a breakout before the ring around him grew too solid to penetrate? And if he broke out, with whom should he link up, and where? He urgently needed orders...from somebody. But thanks to a series of snafus, remarkable even for the Davis administration, Frazer heard nothing. Assuming the worst, Frazer abjectly surrendered on September 9. The loss of the Cumberland Gap was a staggering blow to the Confederacy.

Colonel Thomas, meanwhile, had been lucky enough to be elsewhere when Sanders attacked Strawberry Plains. He was back there again, however, trying to sort out the damage from that raid, when Burnside captured Knoxville. Thomas thereupon received orders to take his two original Indian companies, fall back on the Smokies, and block the mountain passes.

The rest of the Legion, under the active command of Love and Walker and still attached to Mudwall Jackson's brigade, found itself for the first time, on September 8, engaged in a large-scale battle. On September 5, the 100th Ohio Infantry had moved into Jonesborough, the last stop on the Tennessee and Virginia Railroad before the strategic bridge at Carter's Depot. Mudwall Jackson was gathering troops at Bristol, on the Virginia line, and he had screened his southern flank by stationing Love's regiment at Carter's Depot. When Jackson heard about the Ohioans' advance, he signaled Lieutenant Colonel Love: "Urge the holding of Carter's Depot at all hazard...reinforcements are coming." Love and his men were sick and tired of guarding railroad bridges; his reply to Jackson read: "Push forward the cavalry and let us have some fighting...."[10]

On September 8, Love got his wish. The Ohio regiment, doubtless feeling themselves too far out on a limb at Jonesborough, had
pulled back a few miles to a whistle-stop called Telford and had
dug in. During the same 48 hours, Mudwall had gathered his
forces: Walker's battalion of the Legion, plus some Georgia
infantry and Kentucky cavalry.

Taking the Legion's desire to fight seriously, Jackson ordered
Love's regiment to lead the attack. So fired up were the mountaineers that their first charge broke the Federal line and sent the
Ohioans reeling back down the railroad tracks. The Yankees rallied
about six miles below Telford, anchoring their defense around a big
limestone blockhouse. Walker's battalion took over the advance
now — at a crawl, for the enemy's fire was too heavy for a charge —
and drove the supporting Yankee infantry away from the flanks of
the blockhouse, which was then smothered by concentrated artillery
fire. Jackson, who proved himself on this day to be a much better
tactician than he was a diplomat, worked his other units around the
Federals' flanks and surrounded everyone who was still holding
out. A white flag went up not too long after the Ohioans realized
their predicament.

Thanks to the Legion's spirited performance, Jackson had won a
splendid little victory. At a cost of only 20 casualties, he had killed
or wounded 50 of the enemy and taken 350 prisoner. An especially
welcome windfall from the engagement was the capture of 400
modern rifles, which were immediately issued as replacements for
the motley collection of firearms the Legion had been using up to
this time.

There was more fighting in that corner of Tennessee through
October 1863. Love's regiment fought with conspicuous gallantry
during a hotly contested engagement at Bull's Gap, below
Greeneville, on October 10. In November, Confederate General
James Longstreet was detached from the Chattanooga front and
ordered to recapture Knoxville. Longstreet was not in his usual
form in this campaign, however. He moved sluggishly, and some
of his decisions were pig-headed; one suspects he was more
obsessed with getting rid of Braxton Bragg than he was with
beating Burnside. Burnside repulsed him bloodily at the end of

November.

With the onset of winter, both sides went into camp, Burnside's army in and around Knoxville, and the Confederates about 30 miles away in the Greeneville area. Love's and Walker's units encamped at Carter's Depot and spent a wretched winter.

In the spring, both units were transferred to Virginia to meet a growing emergency in the Shenandoah Valley. They remained in Virginia for the next year, fighting first in the valley campaign and then joining General Jubal Early for his breathtaking raid on Washington. Despite Will Thomas's desperate entreaties to Richmond, and despite the intense desire of Love and his men to return to North Carolina, that part of the Legion would not be able to leave Virginia until December 1864.

More than 400 men marched into Virginia with Colonel Love in the spring of 1864; less than 100 would return with him to the mountains of North Carolina in December.

THE CHEROKEES ON GUARD

William Thomas was tending to routine duties at his Strawberry Plains headquarters on September 1, 1863, when the electrifying news reached him that General Ambrose Burnside's advance guard had been seen just outside of Knoxville. Not long after that, he received orders to take his two Indian companies, a total of about 300 men, and race for the passes of the Smoky Mountains. At the time Knoxville fell to Burnside, the mountain gaps were virtually undefended and there seemed a strong possibility that Unionist partisans might block them, effectively cutting off the lower half of western North Carolina.

Thomas left Strawberry Plains on September 2 and moved with what must have been an exhausting pace for a man approaching 60. A detachment of the Fifth Indiana Cavalry pursued him vigorously and at one point got close enough to exchange shots with Thomas's rear guard. But once "Little Will" and his Cherokees reached the Smokies, there was no catching them. Upon his return to Sevierville, the Federal cavalry commander reported, "I pursued the Indians as far as their encampment. The [Unionist] citizens failing to blockade the road in their rear, I was able to capture but one. They won't fight and the country is so mountainous it is almost impossible to catch them."[1]

Once the Indiana horsemen had turned back, Thomas set his tiny army to work fortifying all the gaps between Ducktown, Tennessee, down near the Georgia state line, to Paint Rock Gap, in Madison County. A permanent observation post was constructed atop Clingman's Dome. Thomas also established a small fortified camp near modern-day Chimneys Campground, on the Tennessee side of the mountains. This camp was known, for reasons now lost to historians, as Fort Harry. As Thomas knew from his prewar experience, there had been considerable small-scale mining in this region, and there are indications that he put some of his remaining engineers and miners to work extracting quantities of alum, magnesium, saltpeter, and low-grade copper, all of which were valuable strategic commodities in great demand by the state.

Once again, as soon as he had time to catch his breath, Thomas scanned the local terrain with a road-builder's eye and soon had his entire force at work hacking out a new road that would connect his home territory with his deepest outpost in Tennessee, about 15 to 20 miles east of Sevierville. The road began somewhere in or near Quallatown, followed the twisting Oconoluftee River for a ways, then wound up the steepening ridges of the Smokies and crested at Indian Gap, near the top of Clingman's Dome. Traces of the road can be seen today, both at Indian Gap and near the Oconoluftee, north of the village of Cherokee, at a point close to the Pioneer Museum. The term "road," however, must be understood in its contemporary context: Long stretches of it would have been impassable even for a modern-day Land Rover, and not all of it was navigable even by ox-cart in Thomas's day. But wagons could navigate some of it, and men on horseback could make relatively good time. It was a remarkable feat of engineering, considering how few men and tools Thomas had to work with, and once again it demonstrated Little Will's strongest points as a military commander.

With the coming of autumn, Thomas was able to return to his home for the first time in nearly a year and a half. Even there, however, he found little rest. The mountains themselves had become a battleground by the winter of 1863. The local Unionists had grown bolder, and marauders from eastern Tennessee began making regular raids into North Carolina, coming in to steal horses and food, and to recruit local Unionists for their partisan bands.

Almost from the day they returned, the Cherokee troopers found themselves engaged in deadly games of hide-and-seek with these troublemakers. One of their earliest encounters, in fact, gave them a chance to settle an old score — and there would be a lot of score-settling in western North Carolina during the last two years of the war.

Back in 1856, on a cool August night, a prominent Cherokee named John Timson had been murdered in cold blood. Timson had been the first Christian convert among the Valleytown Cherokees and a trusted go-between in numerous dealings with agents of the U.S. government. But on the night of August 31, 1856, a band of marauders had set fire to his house, then gunned him down as he ran from the flames. A local rowdy named Goldman Bryson was fingered, by a mixed-blood witness, as the perpetrator of this senseless deed. The all-white jury, however, threw out the witness's testimony and permitted Bryson's brother and sister to swear that he had been elsewhere on that night. Bryson went free, but many area residents, red and white alike, continued to view him as a vicious killer.

He was also viewed as a renegade in the eyes of local Confederates, for he had gone "over the mountains" as soon as there were Federal troops within riding distance in eastern Tennessee, taking a commission as captain of a Unionist partisan outfit called the First Tennessee National Guard. The outfit probably numbered no more than 150 men, and was of dubious conventional military value. Most of Bryson's men were mountaineer Unionists, and he was under a legitimate Federal commission, with written orders to go inside North Carolina and recruit new volunteers. But a portion of his band was little more than armed riffraff, and his actions were less those of a recruiting agent than of a highwayman. On a dozen or more occasions, Bryson led his men into the state to not only recruit, but also to rob and terrorize numerous families, both Confederate and neutralist alike.

Word of these depredations finally reached the Confederate theater commander, Braxton Bragg, who labeled Bryson's band "nothing more than mounted robbers" and dispatched part of a brigade of regular cavalry to deal with the matter.

Bryson's band was brought to bay inside Cherokee County and nearly bagged entire. There was a desperate horseback gun battle as Bryson's men tried to break out of their encirclement. Many succeeded, thanks to their knowledge of the terrain, but two were killed, five or six wounded, and 17 captured. Bryson also lost so many weapons and horses that his unit was forced to disband. The survivors made their way back to Tennessee as best they could, some on foot.

Bryson himself seemed to have vanished into thin air. Learning what was going on, Will Thomas dispatched a part of Company B of the Legion, some 25 or 30 men led by a half-breed lieutenant named James Taylor, from Murphy. These men had known Bryson, and had hated him, for a long time. And unlike the detachment Bragg had sent in, they knew the terrain in microscopic detail. It didn't take long for them to pick up Bryson's trail. The guerrilla leader was evidently in a panic, for he was doing something very stupid: heading for home.

Taylor and his men clung to Bryson's tracks like avenging furies. They tracked him, on foot, for two days without even pausing to eat. Then, not far from Murphy, they spotted him. Taylor called out for Bryson to halt. Bryson, exhausted but terrified, put on a fresh burst of speed. Taylor took careful aim and winged him with the first shot. Bryson, bleeding and clutching his wound, kept running, zigzagging desperately through the trees...with half a company of angry Indians in hot pursuit. They shot him to pieces while he was still trying to run.

A few hours later, a party of Cherokee braves came galloping down the main street of Murphy, whooping lustily and waving above their heads the blood-soaked, bullet-ripped uniform of the bushwhacker chieftain.

The mountains were also starting to fill up with deserters. By the autumn of 1863, members of Thomas's Legion on active duty in southwestern North Carolina were probably outnumbered by Confederates who had deserted other units and returned to their mountain homes, either sick of the war, disillusioned with the Confederacy, or just plain worried about their wives and kids.

From the larger portion of Thomas's Legion that was still serving in the upper part of eastern Tennessee, Lieutenant Colonel William Walker, who had been in poor health for some time, was given leave to return to Cherokee County. Walker was allowed to bring along several other officers, in hopes that they could persuade some of the deserters to return to duty. Not long after he arrived back home, Walker was formally relieved of front-line duties and reassigned to help Thomas with the regional defense. But as the winter of 1863-64 deepened, Walker's health deteriorated. By Christmas, he was home in bed; so was his son, Columbus, who had been furloughed home from the battalion with typhoid fever. On the bone-freezing night of January 3, 1864, a small band of men rode up to Walker's home, dismounted, and hammered on the door.

Mrs. Walker answered -- the hour was late, but because of Colonel Walker's rank and station, it was not unknown for messengers to arrive an inconvenient hours. She did not, however, recognize these men, and a feeling of unease came over her as she summoned her husband from his bed.

Colonel Walker came slowly and painfully to the door. Not a word was said. The strange man standing on the other side of the door frame waited until Walker was close, then pointed a large-caliber revolver at him and fired point-blank. William Walker fell back, mortally wounded, into the arms of his wife.

Walker's killing was an augury of the anarchy and violence that the new year would bring to the mountains. The men who slew him were never precisely identified — one set of rumors said they had ridden over from Tennessee for the assassination, and yet another set of rumors said they were native bushwhackers from Jackson or Haywood County. But no one ever learned for sure. The obsidian mountain night engulfed them like wraiths.

Conventional Operations, September 1863–June 1864

On September 16, 1863, in a somewhat belated knee-jerk reaction to the fall of Knoxville, the Confederate government designated western North Carolina a separate military district. To command the district, the government selected Brigadier General Robert B. Vance, younger brother of Governor Zebulon Vance. Robert Vance had a good war record as commander of the 29th North Carolina Regiment, and, later, as a brigade commander at the Battle of Stone's River, where he was cited in dispatches for conspicuous gallantry. His tenure as commander-in-chief of western North Carolina, however, would be brief and bitter.

Little is known about the operations mounted from North Carolina during September and October 1863. It would seem that Vance wanted to employ Thomas's Indians in a fairly forward, aggressive manner, rather than simply leaving them standing around, guarding the mountain passes. In early November, General Vance reported to his brother that forces under his command had raided two Tennessee counties "pretty thoroughly, and brought out

95

safely 800 hogs and some horses and cattle...[I am] threatening the enemy on his lines, and keeping him uneasy, and drawing some of his force away to watch me."[1]

There were certainly targets aplenty within easy striking distance, not the least of which was the East Tennessee Railroad, which was now just as vital to the Union as it had previously been to the Confederacy -- and it remained as vulnerable as ever to guerrilla sabotage.

Even a small force of 300 men, properly employed and aggressively led, could have inflicted considerable damage on the Federals west of the Smokies. And there seems no question that the Indians had the "right stuff" to be turned into a crack guerrilla force. Their morale was still high at this time, and their soldierly qualities were remarked on favorably by several contemporary observers. One Confederate officer recorded seeing a Cherokee sentry standing guard, without shelter, in one of the mountain passes during a snowstorm for 14 straight hours. Man to man, guerrilla style, the Indians were fearless. On patrols, they were dogged, strong, and utterly without peer as trackers. About the only thing that frightened them — as indeed it frightened almost everyone on the receiving end — was artillery (or, as the Cherokees called it, "big-guns-on-wheels"). A force of such men, large enough to take on any routine patrols, yet compact enough to move swiftly, and operating on familiar ground, could have been a formidable asset to the Confederacy.

But Will Thomas was no Lawrence of Arabia. If the number of Federal regulars actually in the field south of Knoxville was not very large on any given day, the aggregate total of forces available to General Ambrose Burnside astronomically outnumbered Thomas's Legion (and every other Confederate unit in the mountains). Thomas had not chosen to lead his beloved Indians into the field in order to risk their lives recklessly. He couldn't replace his Indian casualties — virtually every able-bodied male in the tribe was already under arms — and his Legion was the only coherent rebel force of any significance south of Asheville. It was probably all Thomas could do to keep some kind of control over the activities of local Tories and outlier bands. And, finally, it had never been the Cherokees' style of combat to go looking for stand-up battles with formations of enemy regulars; like most North American Indians, they quite sensibly preferred to fight when the odds were favorable, and melt into the landscape when they were not.

But the Legion companies must have been fairly active west of the state line during that autumn of 1863. Even though the Confederate records contain only a few oblique references to their activities, the enemy seems to have taken them quite seriously for a time. Granted that the Indians were a Godsend for Unionist propaganda, they must have been both effective and aggressive in their border operations in order for one Yankee general to complain that they had "become a terror" and were "daily perpetrating atrocities."

Andrew Johnson, the newly appointed Unionist governor of eastern Tennessee, claimed that the Cherokees had begun slicing the ears off their victims and were wearing the leathery objects as trophies on thongs around their necks — a grisly detail that is not mentioned by any other source, and almost surely has to be an exaggeration. One thing emerges from the Federal records: Ear-collectors or not, the Indians scared the living hell out of all the Unionists living within a day's ride of the Smokies. How else to explain the tone of this description from a Unionist commentator: "Wretched, ignorant, half-civilized offscourings of humanity...long-haired greasy-looking savages who could not even speak a word of English or understand a plea for mercy...."[2]

Perhaps the best assessment of the Indians' performance in the field came from the pen of Daniel Ellis, a Unionist from east Tennessee who had a long, action-packed, and spectacularly successful career as a guide for refugees seeking to reach Federal lines. Outliers and deserters, Ellis said, had "the greatest dread" of the Cherokees; "there was not a day passed but some of the poor Union men were either killed or captured by these infernal Indians." Rather curiously, in view of their supposed "savagery," Ellis then went on to state that the Indians were not, as a rule, nearly as cruel to their prey as the white Confederate patrols — which may be damning with faint praise, considering the prevailing standards of brutality in the mountain war.

Ellis's final word on the subject was his verdict that any and all captured Indians should have been killed on the spot, and he admitted that he himself had greatly desired "to kill some of them

97

for the mischief they had done...when they were engaged in catching conscripts, murdering white men, plundering houses, and frightening women and children to death."[3]

Whatever Thomas's command was doing in September and October, besides building roads and frightening Unionist women and children "to death," the enemy was not idle. In late October 1863 (the exact dates are not clear), the largest Federal penetration to date took place. Colonel George W. Kirk, who would soon become notorious as the deadliest and boldest Union partisan commander, brazenly led a force estimated at 600-800 men into Warm Springs, North Carolina. Digging in there, he seemingly dared anyone to eject him.

The nearest Confederate force was in Marshall, about 16 miles away. It consisted of a battalion of mounted troops, about 150 in number, commanded by Major John Woodfin — a life-loving and immensely popular Asheville lawyer who had once been Governor Zebulon Vance's teacher. Woodfin's response to Kirk's incursion was amateurishly impetuous, but certainly brave. Mounting his fine black charger, Prince Hal, Woodfin led his men straight toward Kirk's position.

Kirk's men not only had the high ground, screened by trees, but also were stationed in the tourist hotel and its outbuildings. Confronted by an acute angle in the road, around which he could not clearly see, Major Woodfin signaled his cavalry troop to halt. He then rode ahead, with several of his staff, to the bridge that led across the French Broad River to the hotel. From an outbuilding only a few yards away, a party of Kirk's men fired a murderous volley. Woodfin was blown from his horse, killed instantly. Two of the men closest to him were wounded, one mortally. Stunned by the loss of their leader, and clearly up against a superior and well-entrenched foe, the little Confederate battalion quickly retreated to Marshall.

A delegation of citizens from Asheville went out the next day, under flag of truce, to recover Woodfin's body. They found that Kirk had gone, and that Woodfin's corpse had been stripped of all its valuables and left where it had fallen.

When news of Kirk's probe reached Raleigh, 250 miles away, Governor Vance was so alarmed that within hours he boarded a train and swore to his staff that he intended to join the battle personally. But by the time he had ridden from Morganton, where the railroad ended, to Marshall, the whole incident was over. He arrived only in time to learn that his friend and mentor, John Woodfin, had just been buried. It was a stunning personal blow to the young governor, and the ease with which Kirk had penetrated the mountains made him apprehensive.

Colonel Thomas evidently planned to make Gatlinburg, Tennessee, then no more than a tiny hamlet of a few dozen cabins, his winter headquarters. He must have felt he would be secure there, for his men took the time and trouble to erect permanent log huts, and some of the Indian troopers even sent for their squaws and set up regular housekeeping.

In early December, however, a detachment of well-armed Unionist militia from Sevierville got the drop on one of the Legion's routine patrols. The Indians were marched back to town in triumph and locked up in the county jail. But Will Thomas was still, at this stage of the war, capable of aggressive action, especially when his beloved Indians were at risk. As soon as he learned about the capture, he stormed Sevierville at the head of 200 men, taking the town completely by surprise and quickly liberating his imprisoned troopers. He also captured — and apparently paroled, since he had no means of dealing with a large number of prisoners — 60 Home Guard and a half-dozen Federal regular officers acting as advisers. An added bonus were the dozens of brand-new rifles he captured, enough to equip half a company.

The Sevierville affair stirred up a hornet's nest of reaction. From Knoxville came the bold Colonel William Palmer and a battalion of the hard-riding, battle-wise 15th Pennsylvania Cavalry. Palmer had no trouble obtaining good intelligence: "The people everywhere evinced the greatest delight to meet our cavalry, and attested the sincerity of their loyalty by feeding our men and horses and guiding the command through the difficult and unknown mountain paths."[4]

Thanks to the help of local scouts, and Thomas's complacency, Palmer was able to reconnoiter the Gatlinburg position before laying his tactical plans. Thomas's position was a strong one, at the head of a long, narrow defile. If Thomas had been on his toes,

Palmer would have had a tough time mounting his attack. One of Palmer's officers, writing about the engagement 50 years later, thought it would have been impossible to carry Thomas's position with a frontal assault, so strongly did the terrain favor defense.

But Palmer wasn't planning anything so unimaginative as a frontal assault. He decided to wait an extra day — obviously, if the Indians had taken the time to build log huts, they weren't planning on going anywhere soon. He used the time to set up a simultaneous attack to be launched from two sides. Leaving about 40 percent of his force in front of Thomas's position, Palmer took the remaining men on a long and strenuous march around Gatlinburg, using several intervening ridges to screen his movements from any observation posts Thomas might have above his camp.

The 15th Pennsylvania had been through some hard campaigning in its time, but one veteran of that December expedition remembered the flanking march at Gatlinburg:

> [It was] one of the most toilsome journeys that was ever undertaken by any body of cavalrymen, as we were obliged to lead our horses, single file, up the terribly rocky and steep trail, horses falling, men stumbling and swearing the entire length of the line. We were dripping with perspiration...not daring to discard our overcoats for fear of delay or surprise. Such was the intense darkness of the forest that we were not able to see our hands before our faces. After marching about eight hours, having lost the trail twice, we indeed felt ourselves a forlorn hope. At last we arrived on a fair level about 1 a.m., gathered the stragglers and took a rest for a few minutes. We pressed onward along the crest for a number of miles, and long before the break of day began the descent.
>
> The mountaineer scouts lighted their long pine torches and led the column down the trail single file. The men bumped against the horses and the horses bumped against the men. As we moved down the wild mountain trail, I thought the column resembled an immense serpent, with every vertebra in its back in violent action, winding its way into the darkness of the forest.
>
> I was very thirsty, as my canteen had been emptied two hours before, and my horse kept licking my frosty saber hilt at every opportunity...after an unusually long, toilsome, and continuous march, we succeeded in getting to the base of the mountain. Immediately we noticed a very beautiful stream of spring water rushing from the mountain base. We hurriedly watered our famished and hungry horses, then mounted and assembled for combat.[5]

At the Indian encampment, it was breakfast time. Thomas did have pickets out — he wasn't that much of an amateur — but they were too close to the camp to give more than about two minutes' warning. By the time the Indians had snatched up their rifles, the Federal cavalry was upon them. The advancing Yankees soon overran the line of huts, some of them even pausing to gobble up the hot corn-cakes they found stacked by the cooking fires.

The Cherokees recovered from their surprise rather quickly. They retreated up the wooded sides of the draw, but were never actually routed. They reformed with the steadiness of veterans and traded volleys with the Pennsylvanians for about an hour before a flanking movement compelled them to retire into steeper terrain where the Yankees dared not follow. A corporal from Pittsburgh named James Over later described the engagement: "A brisk fight from behind trees, rocks and fallen timber, in regular Indian fashion...the enemy seemed to think it necessary to accompany every shot with a genuine war whoop, which must have interfered with their aim, as they only wounded two of our men...."[6]

It was a noisy and spirited fight, but after the first Yankee volley, most of the firing must have taken place at fairly long range, which would explain the light casualties on both sides. Colonel Thomas was mute about the engagement in any of the documents he left to posterity, but Colonel Palmer estimated that the Cherokees suffered only five or six wounded, all of whom they carried away with them when they retreated.

For all the dash and effort that went into the attack, Palmer came up more or less sucking wind. He captured only one Indian straggler, ten horses, some miscellaneous supplies of no great worth, and William Thomas's personal hat — a trophy of which he seems to have been inordinately proud, since he went out of his way to boast about it when writing his official report.

Still, in strategic terms, the skirmish at Gatlinburg was a solid Confederate defeat, in that it drove the Legion back into the mountains. Never again would Will Thomas, or any other Confederate officer, succeed in establishing a permanent encampment on the Tennessee side of the border.

Following this repulse, the Legion retired to its home base at Quallatown, for what Colonel Thomas must have hoped, in his

weary, middle-aged bones, would be a quiet winter. But it was not
to be. Scarcely after the Indian companies had thawed out from
their march back from Tennessee, orders came through that would
send them back. They were about to become part of what turned
out to be the biggest Confederate offensive ever launched from the
mountains of North Carolina.

Attack From The Mountains

During the period when he was besieging Knoxville, Confederate
General James Longstreet had been nagging General Vance to push
over the Smokies with "all available forces" and give him assistance. Given the weakness, disarray, and geographically scattered
nature of his command, it was not possible for Vance to comply;
and given Longstreet's inexplicably bull-headed and obtuse handling of the campaign, it wouldn't have mattered very much if he
had. But now, as 1863 rolled into 1864, with Knoxville firmly in
Union hands and the main Confederate army encamped in winter
quarters around Greeneville, Vance thought he could comply with a
new set of orders. Longstreet wanted Vance to move virtually his
entire command to Newport, Tennessee, just across the Great
Smokies from Warm Springs, North Carolina, on the banks of the
French Broad River. From Newport, Longstreet reasoned, Vance
could continue to screen the main approaches to North Carolina
and also guard the left flank of the main Confederate force at
Greeneville.

Vance certainly gave it a game try. The Indian Gap road that
Thomas and his engineers had been hacking through the mountains
toward Sevierville was passable as far as the crest of the Smokies,
but beyond that the route was little more than a mule-path: steep,
rocky, and too narrow even for an ox cart. But what oxen could not
do, men could. At the crest, Vance's men dismantled their artillery.
Teams of men carried the wheels, axles, rigging, and ammunition.
The gun barrels themselves were harnessed to ropes and rolled,
pushed, or dragged down the far side, gun metal screeching on
naked rock. The march was characterized not only by Homeric
physical exertion, but also by vile weather; Vance and his men did
all this in the teeth of savagely cold winds that scoured the moun-

tain tops like a sand-blaster, from time to time lashing them with pellets of ice. In was Hannibal crossing the Alps in miniature.

"Miniature" indeed...Vance's little army barely amounted to a regiment in strength. He commanded one battery of artillery and about 700 soldiers, including Colonel Thomas and a force of 125 of the Legion's best men. Astonishingly, this pathetic little force represented the largest conventional military operation the Confederacy was ever able to mount in or from western North Carolina.

Robert Vance must have had considerable powers of leadership to accomplish as much as he did. But as events were to prove, he was nowhere near as good a tactician as his brother was a governor.

Once Vance's men reached the foot of the Smokies and reassembled their guns, Vance immediately divided his already small force. His reasons for doing this are unclear; perhaps he had intelligence that convinced him the area was free of Federal regulars. In any case, divide his force he did. He sent Colonel Thomas and his troops, along with 350 cavalry under Lieutenant Colonel James L. Henry, to Gatlinburg, on or about January 12, 1864. General Vance himself, with his remaining 200 or so men, mostly cavalry, rode on toward Sevierville.

At first, luck was with him. On January 13, his scouts spotted a Yankee wagon train. Vance immediately swept down on the caravan and captured it without losing a man. The problems faced by historians who research the war in the mountains can perhaps be illustrated by the difficulty of pinning down even so simple a fact as how many wagons Vance captured. One usually reliable source says 80; another says 77; two or three more say 17 — quite a range of discrepancy. There is one obscure account, though, by a Yankee soldier who was actually there and had a chance to count the wagons; he gives a total of 28, and that seems reasonable.[7]

In any case, it was a splendid little victory. The wagonloads of military supplies were a Godsend to the Confederates. This alone would have justified all the effort that had gone into the offensive, and the sudden disappearance of the wagon train would certainly have caused a ruckus in the Federal command at Knoxville. Vance should have quit while he was ahead. But the ease with which he had captured the wagon train appears to have made him cocky — a trait he shared with his illustrious brother in Raleigh — and he pushed his luck too far.

His original intent was to rendezvous with Colonel Henry and his cavalry at Schultze's Mill on Cosby Creek. Colonel Thomas, apparently, was supposed to stay close to Gatlinburg, where he could at least guard Vance's rear and protect the escape route back into the Smokies.

But Vance was outsmarted and outridden by the mountaineer's current nemesis, Colonel William Palmer, who led his detachment of the 15th Pennsylvania Cavalry out of camp at 3 a.m., as soon as he received word of Vance's presence from local Unionists. Palmer soon discovered that Unionist partisans had already been at work, felling trees and trying to box in the wagon train column. Palmer's advance guard spotted the ungainly formation, struggling to get back on the road to Asheville. Vance's first thought seems to have been to take the wagons north and give them to Longstreet, but common sense prevailed and he was now making for home. Even so, the weariness of the wagon teams was discernible even to Palmer, as he watched the wagons creak along the banks of Cosby Creek from a rocky bluff a mile or so away. Finally, the wagons halted and campfire smoke began to rise in the still, clear, winter air. Vance and his men were getting ready to eat breakfast. Amazingly, he didn't bother to post pickets.

Along with the rest of Palmer's column, Sergeant E.W. Anderson, from Phoenixville, Pennsylvania, observed these developments with growing excitement:

> All this time our command was standing on the rise of the descent to Cosby's Creek watching all these maneuvers. The Confederate vedette had gone down for...[his breakfast], leaving no one on lookout. We could plainly see the wagons coming up the stream, and those in front going into camp, when the order for the charge was given. With a yell such as the mountains have never heard before or since, our command fell upon the Confederates in the center, forcing them up and down the stream in direst confusion, with little or no resistance.
>
> The fight, to the best of my recollection, lasted but five minutes, several of the Confederates being killed or wounded. But a great surprise was in store for us. With a little squad of men we were moving among the wounded and dead, and I was taking a revolver

from the pocket of a Confederate officer, when one of the men called my attention to General Vance and a squad of men, consisting of two aid[es] and orderlies, advancing toward us. I was soon in the saddle and demanded their surrender.[8]

Vance and Sergeant Anderson met again after the war, and exchanged gentlemanly letters on several occasions. In one of them, dated September 3, 1887, Vance tried to reconstruct the events of that morning. He had been misled, he insisted, by treacherous local scouts (a very real possibility). "Believing that most of my command was down the creek, I turned there, but soon after found my mistake. Nearly the whole of the command was up the creek."[9]

Truer words were never penned by a general.

Vance was also let down by his subordinates. He had been expecting the momentary arrival of Colonel Henry and his command, and indeed, if Henry had followed his orders and joined Vance when he was supposed to, Palmer would have been, if not outnumbered, at least equally matched.

But Henry didn't and Palmer wasn't, and his men had swept down on the unsuspecting Confederate column like a blue avalanche. During the confusion, about two-thirds of Vance's men managed to get to their horses and ride out of the trap, but as a coherent force, they were, for the time being, finished. And they had lost all of those bountiful Yankee supply wagons. General Vance spent the rest of the war languishing in a Federal prison, and the rest of his life trying to explain how this calamity had occurred.

The lack of clarity in Vance's written orders made it look as though some of the fault belonged to Will Thomas. From a distance, it must have looked that way to General Joseph E. Johnston, now in command of the Army of Tennessee, because for a time, he wanted to convene a court martial in Asheville to bring charges against both Henry and Thomas. Exactly why that never happened is unclear, but there is indirect evidence that Jefferson Davis exerted some pressure on Johnston to have the matter dropped. Not for the last time, Will Thomas's connections in Richmond had helped to keep him out of trouble.

It was not until the exhausted remnants of the abortive expedi-

tion had straggled back to their base at Quallatown that Thomas
learned about the murder of William Walker. The compound effect
on him of, first, the disastrous operation in Tennessee, and, second,
the cold-blooded assassination of Walker at the man's own front
door, seems to have provoked a profound change in Thomas. He
became morose and cautious. He all but stopped planning aggressive moves against the enemy in Tennessee, and thought only in
terms of keeping peace and order within his beloved mountains. He
also became fearful for his own life — the night riders who had
gunned down Bill Walker might come for him, too, one moonless
midnight. From January 1864 until the end of the war, whenever he
went abroad in the mountains, Will Thomas was accompanied by a
personal bodyguard of 20 heavily armed Cherokees.

With the ignominious capture of General Vance, command of
the Western District of North Carolina shifted to the shoulders of
Colonel John B. Palmer. Palmer took a lot of verbal criticism from
his contemporaries — Governor Zebulon Vance accused him of
being a good bureaucrat but a lousy soldier — and he evidently was
one of those people who have a talent for rubbing subordinates' fur
the wrong way. A dispassionate examination of his record, however, reveals no dramatic symptoms of incompetence; on the
contrary, he seems to have been a man of character, sense, and no
small ability. But the psychology of the mountain theater demanded a leader with extraordinary charisma and imagination, and
these qualities John Palmer lacked to a conspicuous degree.

He also lacked an army. To say that Palmer's command was
"thinly spread" does not begin to suggest how desperate his
situation was. To maintain order within the entire western third of
North Carolina, and to protect a mostly hostile border 250 miles
long, Palmer's entire resources consisted of 475 "regular" infantry
(Thomas's Indians, together with the 62nd and 64th North Carolina
Regiments, neither of them anything to brag about) and some 250-
odd cavalry under the balky and undependable James Henry. Truly,
the only protection North Carolina had in the west at this time was
that provided by nature: the unconquerable ramparts of the mountains themselves.

To augment these puny forces there were, of course, the Home
Guard companies...such as they were. One contemporary observer,

disturbed enough by what she saw during a Home Guard parade to write Governor Vance, described a procession that more closely resembled something from Gilbert and Sullivan than it did a serious military force. The company had only a few modern weapons. Some men were armed with antique fowling pieces, some with heirloom flintlocks from Revolutionary days; others carried homemade pikes and spears, and some were armed with nothing but knives and clubs. Marching in the same column were men on foot, men on mules, men on horseback, and a few men riding in buggies — all of them, ostensibly, in the same unit.[10]

To make matters worse, an unknown but significant percentage of the militiamen were themselves Unionist, or at least were related to someone who was. In some counties, the Home Guard was zealous and bloodthirsty and actively feared, however inadequately armed; in other counties, or in other regions of the same county, it was cowed by or actively in league with the very people it was supposed to be arresting.

Palmer barely had time to adjust to his new responsibilities before he had to cope with the first Federal incursion of the new year. It was mounted for the express purpose of eliminating Thomas's Legion from the war — yet another indication that the enemy took the Indians more seriously than the Confederate records might lead one to believe.

There was a sizable Federal cavalry command stationed at Maryville, Tennessee, south of Knoxville. On the first day of February 1864, Major Francis M. Davidson moved out at the head of a 600-man column with orders to "pursue and destroy" Colonel Thomas's entire force. Once he had moved into the hill country, Davidson picked up an advance guard of 40 to 50 local Tories who acted as guides. They had no trouble penetrating the mountains. Thomas had grown so passive by this time that he had neglected to maintain rigorous security even in the passes leading to his own headquarters — even though, in his reports to Raleigh and Richmond, he was still claiming that his men were constantly on duty and continually "fortifying" the gaps.

Davidson's force followed the Tennessee River until they picked up the Tuckaseegee branch, then emerged from the forest near Deep Creek, a few miles below Quallatown. Thomas was caught flat-footed. The terrain made a cavalry charge out of the question, so Davidson's troopers had to fight dismounted. Although surprised by the attack, the Cherokees again rallied with remarkable discipline and in the words of one eyewitness "fought nobly until their ammunition gave out."[11]

Davidson crowed excessively about his victory, and his account was picked up by the Northern press, which gave him credit for one of the most daring and effective cross-border strikes of the war. The "bloodthirsty savages" were eliminated, he claimed: 200 of them had been killed, 54 captured, and only 50 or so escaped. Those figures seem not just inflated, but ludicrous, as Thomas's entire command on that day probably did not much exceed 200 men, and Davidson's body count, if true, would have made this paltry little skirmish the biggest and bloodiest encounter ever fought in the mountain region. In his own report, written three weeks later, Thomas admitted that he had heard about Davidson's claims, and he quietly denied them. His own force, he said, had suffered only five casualties, and he estimated they had inflicted at least twice that many on the enemy. Simple logic, the matter-of-fact tone of Thomas's documentation, and the fact that the Indians could still field a 300-man force would all seem to indicate that Thomas's figures are reliable, and that Davidson's were either the product of inflamed imagination or rampant ambition.

Davidson did, however, capture some two dozen Indians and take them back to Knoxville, along with a slightly larger number of white soldiers. According to an oft-quoted report that later appeared in the *Raleigh Daily News*, once the Indians reached Knoxville they "were flattered and feasted [and] promised their liberty and five thousand dollars in gold, if they would bring in the scalp of their chief, Colonel William H. Thomas! The Indians...agreed to the proposition. They were released, returned to their native mountains, sought the camp of their chief, told him all, and ever since have been on the warpath — after Yankee scalps!"[12]

February 1864 proved a busy month for Thomas's command. Only three weeks after Davidson's force had returned to Tennessee, another Federal raid — 250 men of the First Wisconsin Cavalry under Major Nathan Paine — rode all the way through Cherokee County and got to within 20 miles of Franklin, in Macon County, before having to turn back. The exact purpose of Paine's raid, other than to generally stir things up, seems unclear. Nor, frustratingly, are there any details about what appears to have been a solid defensive victory for the local Confederates. Paine's route of march took him through country patrolled by the same Indians who had tracked down Goldman Bryson, aggressively led by their mixed-blood lieutenant, Campbell Taylor. Finding little food on his route of march, Paine was forced to send out foraging parties daily, and some of these were effectively ambushed by Taylor's Indians. His losses are unknown, but clearly things were so hot that he exited the state much more rapidly than he entered it.

He did take a small number of Cherokee deserters with him — maybe 15 men. These were new, young recruits into the Legion and their fighting spirit had been sapped by the appalling conditions under which their families were now compelled to live. These Cherokees became renegades, donning the blue uniform back in Tennessee and serving as scouts for Kirk and other raiders. According to local tribal stories, they were never reconciled with their people following the war's end, and several who did attempt to resettle in Quallatown appear to have been murdered.

Paine's raiders weren't the only ones suffering from a lack of sustenance during that bitter winter. Conscription had reduced the number of men available for farming. Repeated hard frosts, some of them quite unseasonable, stunted the already sparse crops that had been planted. The Cherokees shared in the general misery. By the end of 1863, flour, salt, and even cornmeal had become scarce or had vanished altogether from Quallatown. By February 1864, Thomas reported that his men were in "starving condition" and appealed for extra provisions from his nominal superior, Colonel Palmer. But by this time, the rift between the two men had grown so great that Palmer passed the buck to Richmond — the equivalent of telling the Cherokees that they could either starve or leave Thomas's command and join a "regular" Confederate unit, where they would be able to draw rations through "regular" channels. Thomas turned to the governor of South Carolina, on the grounds that the Indians were protecting part of his state, too. The argument proved persuasive, and Thomas, using his own money, was able to purchase 100 bushels of corn and have them delivered to Walhalla,

South Carolina, from where his own wagons and mules were able to bring the food into the mountains.

The strain between Palmer and Thomas had been evident almost from the beginning of Palmer's tour as commander-in-chief of the Western District. Thomas insisted that, because of the peculiar circumstances of his original charter from Richmond, his command was independent of any authority less than General Joseph E. Johnston. Palmer -- who, on paper, was in command of the territory where Thomas and his men operated -- not unreasonably expected them to do as they were told. After all, Thomas had showed no reluctance to obey the orders of General Vance. But then, General Vance, in some ways, had seemed a kindred spirit and had never tried to bring Thomas to heel, as Palmer wanted to do. Thus, the already parlous state of Confederate defenses in the west was further jeopardized by a growing paralysis of command.

Thomas was also under orders to retain command only of his Indians — now organized into a slightly enlarged force of three companies (a total of 350-400 men). But since the autumn of 1863, he had also been enrolling white troopers who had deserted from Love's part of the Legion, still encamped at Carter's Depot in upper east Tennessee. Despite Love's affection for Will Thomas, and his intense personal desire to see the command reunited and returned to its home district, Love found it necessary to remind Thomas that he had absolutely no authority to tell the deserters that it was fine for them to stay home in the mountains and serve near home, when those same men were still officially carried on Love's rolls. "Men who had deserted from here," Love chided Thomas in a letter dated December 28, 1863, "are sending back letters to their friends, saying that they have reported to you — that you have furloughed them home, and that it is all right. You can readily see that this causes disaffection in [my] command...."

This time, in fact, Will Thomas had put himself on a collision course with the Confederate hierarchy, and not even his free-and-easy relationship with Jefferson Davis was going to keep him out of serious trouble.

Not that command problems did not exist in Love's part of the Legion, too. In Love's view, the obvious solution was to permit the Legion's sundered parts to reunite immediately — it would solve the desertion problem, greatly strengthen the defenses of western North Carolina, and relieve the impossible situation that had arisen with Love's immediate commanding officer, Mudwall Jackson.

On February 25, 1864, in what amounted to a gentlemanly form of mutiny, Love and every other officer in his regiment signed a petition to Governor Vance. The petition asked to be freed from Jackson's command and allowed to reunite with Thomas in the mountains. The petition was strongly worded, accusing Jackson of having "diseased nerves" and of being "morally and physically unfit" for command. Vance had heard enough about Old Mudwall to know these feelings were not confined to the Legion companies, but he was starting to have some doubts about William Thomas's effectiveness as a leader, and he surely had some doubts about whether Love's men would fight as hard under Thomas, close to their homes, as they had done while brigaded to General Jackson. After mulling over the petition for a while, he agreed only to forward Love's arguments to Jefferson Davis — the equivalent of putting Love "on hold."

It was the Legion's fate not to be reunited for quite some time to come. Love's men would win their share of battlefield glory, but the battlefields would not be in North Carolina. In the spring of 1864, General James Longstreet began pulling his Confederate forces out of their remaining enclaves in east Tennessee in response to enemy activity in a more sensitive area -- Virginia.

The worsening military situation in Virginia unfortunately coincided with the breakup of the bureaucratic logjam that had been keeping the Legion divided. Governor Vance had a change of mind, for one thing; as letter after letter reached him detailing the worsening economic and political situation in the western counties, he began to think that it might, after all, be a good idea to bring Love's men back to the state. Vance simply had no other troops in North Carolina who could be sent to the mountains.

In April, he wrote to President Davis: "The condition of [the mountain counties] is truly deplorable, and if the militia could be depended upon, starvation must ensue...wholesale if they are kept from their crops in a country where there are no slaves. Times will not suffice to tell you of the horrors to which [those counties] are exposed. I beg you to relief them, and quickly, by sending troops there."[13]

This time, Davis prodded the matter along. On April 25, General Braxton Bragg added his approval. On May 5, orders were released that would finally have allowed Colonel Love to take his troops — about 400 men, give or take whoever was missing from one roll call to another — back home to the mountains.

But before they could entrain for North Carolina, a major Federal offensive erupted in the Shenandoah Valley. Richmond was forced to rush every available man into that important region, including the Legion companies. It was a bitter disappointment, but duty was duty, and Love's men went where they were ordered to go. At least they wouldn't have to fight in Virginia under the detested Mudwall Jackson. Poor Mudwall was relieved of his Virginia command and packed off to the Army of Tennessee, where his career went into permanent eclipse. That was about the only consolation Love's mountaineers could take with them into the hotly contested Shenandoah Valley, where many of them would leave their bones.

LIGHTNING OUT OF TENNESSEE — KIRK'S RAID ON MORGANTON

Of all the violent men who launched raids into western North Carolina from east Tennessee, none was more feared, or more effective in causing trouble, than George W. Kirk. In 1864, he was 26 years old. Although wartime rumors sometimes identified him as a North Carolinian, he was in fact a native of Greene County, Tennessee. In Confederate records, he is invariably referred to as a "scoundrel," a "renegade," and a "traitor" — and it does seem as though he enlisted in the Confederate Army, early in the war, for the sole purpose of getting close enough to the enemy to desert at the first opportunity.

Kirk's first assignment for the Federals was to act as a "pilot" for escaped prisoners of war and Unionist mountaineers, on both sides of the state border, who wanted to get to Federal lines. He was exceptionally good at this work, and while making his forays into Confederate territory, he took pains to set up an informal kind of "fifth column" network in North Carolina, establishing safe houses for refugees, learning who could be trusted, and recruiting other men to act as guides and part-time guerrillas.

His usefulness to the Federal cause, and his courage, were rewarded with steady promotions and increased responsibilities. By mid-1864, he was in command of two small regiments of mounted partisans, comprised largely of "Home Yankees" — pro-Union mountaineers from the border counties — designated the Second and Third North Carolina Mounted Volunteers. Not all of them served full-time in uniform, and the units were informally organized. If Kirk needed a large force, he sent out word and the men came in; and if he needed a small, stealthy reconnaissance force, he knew just who to pick for that kind of mission, too. Included in his ranks were some of the turncoat Cherokees who had accompanied Major Nathan Paine back to Tennessee in February, plus a fluctuating number of outliers, deserters, and men who were little more than bandits. At least 60 men in Kirk's command were from Madison County, a further indication of the depth of disaffection in that rugged corner of North Carolina.

Since most of the surviving accounts of Kirk's activities are from Confederate sources, it is possible that his reputation for bloody-mindedness has been exaggerated. He was a passionate Unionist, bold to the point of recklessness, and he certainly had no hesitation about killing people who tried to get in his way. But for the most part, he seems to have confined his personal violence to property rather than people whenever possible, and what looks like murderous behavior to the enemy may appear simply to be ruthless efficiency to one's own side. Of Kirk's efficiency as a partisan raider, there can be no doubt.

During 1863, he led or ordered dozens of small raids into North Carolina. Aside from intelligence gathering, the only purpose of some of these incursions seems to have been horse-stealing, and invariably, some poor rebel farmer's barn got burned in the bargain. How many raids Kirk initiated is anyone's guess. Few of them were ever described in any kind of official reports. And to judge from the man's reputation, even making allowances for wartime propaganda, many of the raids must have been accompanied by gratuitous violence on the part of his troops, if not of Kirk himself. An example was a raid that was launched sometime in 1863 against, of all things, the annual meeting of the French Broad

Baptist Association, at Middle Fork Baptist Church, about four
miles from Mars Hill. Two men were killed and another wounded
(presumably because they were Confederates, not Baptists).

But, contrary to much that has been written about him by
historians of the western counties, George Kirk was a legitimate
soldier with a regular commission. His activities were sanctioned
by General John M. Schofield at Headquarters, Department of the
Ohio, as provided for in Special Order No. 44, dated February 13,
1864:

> ...Authority is hereby granted to Maj. G.W. Kirk, of the Second
> North Carolina Mounted Infantry, to raise a regiment of troops in
> the eastern front of Tennessee and western part of North Carolina.
> The regiment will be organized as infantry and will be mustered
> into the service of the United States to serve for three years, unless
> sooner discharged. The regiment will rendezvous as soon as
> practicable at headquarters Department of the Ohio, or other place
> to be hereinafter designated, to be mustered into service. The
> commanding officer is authorized to mount his regiment, or such
> portion of it as may from time to time be necessary, upon private
> or captured horses. This regiment will be known as the Third
> Regiment of North Carolina Mounted Infantry.
> By command of Major-General Schofield....[1]

If nothing else, this explains why Kirk was such a horse thief.
He also took care that his men not only had good mounts, but were
well-armed, too. Using, no doubt, the proceeds from some of the
valuables taken during his raids, he purchased several hundred
Spencer repeating rifles for his two regiments, thus giving them an
even greater edge of firepower over the obsolete, slow-firing
muskets and squirrel rifles of the Home Guard companies they
were likely to meet in battle. The Spencers were ideal weapons for
Kirk's kind of operations. Only 42 inches long (even shorter in the
carbine configuration), they were lever-action repeaters that could
carry eight rounds (one in the chamber and seven in the tubular
magazine inside the stock), and they could fire their .52-caliber
slugs at the rate of 20 per minute — about ten times the rate of fire
of a percussion-cap musket. The Spencer was also a state-of-the-art
weapon in terms of its manufacturing technology. During its
acceptance tests, the weapon was immersed in salt water and buried

under dirt for long periods of time, and it always came up firing. In a theater of operations in which wet weather was common and "keeping your powder dry" could be a matter of life or death, the waterproof nature of the weapon was especially desirable.

Kirk counted on that firepower to help him pull off one of the boldest and most devastatingly effective raids ever staged on either side of the Tennessee-North Carolina line.

On June 13, 1864, under orders from General Schofield, Kirk left Morristown, Tennessee at the head of a compact force of experienced partisans. As usual, different sources give different figures, but according to several who either witnessed the column's departure or actually rode with it, the total force amounted to only 130 men, including about a dozen turncoat Indians and about a company's worth of Madison County Unionists. Kirk's objective was the Confederate training camp at Morganton, Camp Vance, and the nearby railroad depot, along with any supplies that happened to be there when he struck.

There were secondary objectives, too, which Kirk could tackle at his discretion. Burning down the bridge over the Yadkin River was at the head of the list, and Schofield would have been mighty happy with that alone. Kirk, true to his nature, wanted to do something even more daring: he brought with him from Tennessee a railroad engineer. At the railhead in Morganton, he hoped to capture a working locomotive, load several cars with troops, dash down the rail line into Salisbury, overwhelm the local guards, liberate the hundreds of Federal inmates languishing in the infamous Salisbury prison camp, and somehow get them all safely back to Tennessee. Morganton alone was 75 miles behind Confederate lines; the audacity of the plan was breathtaking. One cannot help but speculate on what might have happened if Thomas's Legion had been commanded by someone like George Kirk.

Not far from the state line, Kirk was joined by Joseph Franklin, a local Unionist who was reputed to be a member of the secret "Heroes of America" underground. Franklin guided them over the mountains at a place near the Toe River, about six miles south of the Cranberry iron works. There, Kirk encamped on the property of another local Unionist named David Ellis (possibly a relative of a legendary Unionist guide, Daniel Ellis). Kirk's march was swift and stealthy. He crossed all of Mitchell County undetected, and pushed fearlessly into Burke County, driving his men hard. The raiders reached the vicinity of Camp Vance in time to hear reveille on the morning of June 28.

Camp Vance was one of the many training facilities established by the state government in the fall of 1861. When it was first opened for business, its occupants were volunteers — Burke County contributed 400 men out of a voting population of just over 1,000. But by mid-1864, all it held were conscripts who would have preferred to be just about anywhere else.

The camp covered about five acres of ground and was primitive in the extreme. The men lived in log huts in a forest clearing, with inadequate food and no water except what could be carried, by hand, from a pair of small springs. Sanitation facilities were but one step removed from the barnyard. Life there must have been dismal almost beyond endurance. Of the few surviving letters known to have been written from Camp Vance, every single one mentions the wretchedness of living conditions there. As one soldier named J.B. Gaither stated it bluntly, "Paw, I want you to hire me a substitute if you can, for I would not stay here fore [sic] all that I ever expect to be worth in this world."[2]

For reasons that have never been discovered, the camp's commandant, a major named McClean, was absent on that morning. The senior officer present was a mere lieutenant named Bullock. Present for roll-call that morning were a total of 277 conscripts and officers, few if any of them armed. Kirk simply marched out of the woods under a flag of truce and demanded the camp's immediate surrender. Bullock appears to have stalled for time and tried to get some of his men armed from the camp's magazine. For nearly a hundred years, every account of the incident has stated flatly that there was "no resistance," but archaeological digs carried out on the site of the camp in the early 1970s turned up a fair number of fired Minie balls, indicating that some of the garrison did put up a fight (Kirk's Spencers fired a copper-jacketed cartridge and so would not have left such evidence). There was some firing, at any rate, because ten conscripts and one officer were killed before a surrender went into effect. Maybe Kirk just wanted to impress on them the fact that he was serious.

Kirk's men torched the camp utterly, except for the hospital, and destroyed all of its records in the process. Then he proceeded into town and struck the railroad depot. A locomotive and four cars were burned, as well as 250 bushels of corn and about two tons' worth of assorted military supplies. An arms depot was also uncovered, and 1,200 weapons destroyed.

Kirk regretfully abandoned his more ambitious schemes for knocking out the Yadkin bridge and raiding Salisbury — the alarm was out now, and he began to receive from his scouts reports of Confederate detachments converging on Morganton from all directions. By the end of June 28, he had decided not to press his luck and had begun his withdrawal to Tennessee. Marching with him were 40 of the conscripts who had surrendered at Camp Vance; they had elected to join Kirk's regiment rather than return to Confederate service. This, in itself, is a striking illustration of the state of Confederate morale in the mountain counties at this stage of the war.

About 14 miles from Morganton, at Brown's Mountain, Kirk made contact with a pursuing detachment of about 65 Confederates, mostly old men and boys under the command of Colonel George Love, whose home was only a mile away from the battlefield. When Kirk dug in, he took the ruthless precaution of placing about 20 of his prisoners from Morganton in front of his position for use as a human shield. When the Confederates began firing, Kirk hollered: "Look at the damned fools, shooting their own men!" And indeed, one of the prisoners, a 30-year-old man named Bowles (carried on the rolls, oddly enough, under the designation of "drummer boy"), was killed by the Confederate volleys. At least one other prisoner was wounded.

The militia unit made a game try, but the terrific fire from Kirk's Spencers, the confusion over whom to shoot at, and their obvious numerical inferiority all kept the Confederates from inflicting any serious damage. Kirk was wounded in the arm during the encounter, but it didn't prevent him from disengaging when he felt like it, more or less.

Kirk turned to fight again when the Morganton Home Guard, accompanied by a detachment of prison guards hurried up from Salisbury, caught his column at Winding Stairs Road, near Piedmont Springs. Kirk held the high ground, and could be approached only along the accurately named road that wound steeply up toward the crest. With the Spencer firepower at his disposal and a splendid defensive position, Kirk easily repulsed the halfhearted assault thrown against him.

In both engagements, Kirk's total casualties were two killed and five wounded. Confederate losses in the Winding Stairs fight are not known exactly — a half-dozen dead would be a good estimate, including the commander of the Morganton troops, a colonel named Avery.

After this skirmish, Kirk was able to retreat unmolested all the way to Knoxville, Tennessee, taking with him 40 new recruits, 132 prisoners, and 48 horses and mules.

The effect of this raid was electrifying. Kirk had penetrated the mountain "defenses" effortlessly, struck a stunning blow at Morganton, and escaped virtually unharmed. Colonel John B. Palmer, Confederate commander of the Western District of North Carolina, expressed emotions of helpless fury in his report about the incident. If he had received only a few hours' notice of Kirk's presence, Palmer remonstrated, he could have bagged the whole raiding force -- a not unreasonable proposition, since Kirk's men had moved on foot in order to be stealthy, and since there were only a handful of exits open to them for their withdrawal. Confederate loyalists in the western counties felt despair, anger, and embarrassment over Kirk's success. Unionists, however, interpreted the incident (correctly) as a sign that Confederate control over the western counties was feeble at best, and they were accordingly much emboldened.

While the Confederates were beating their breasts with post-mortem discussions over what went wrong, Kirk was being feted in Knoxville as a hero. This wasn't unreasonable, in view of the daring nature of the enterprise and its remarkable success. General William Tecumseh Sherman even sent his congratulations — this was the kind of soldiering he liked to see! But he also admonished Kirk not to take such a chance again, cautioning him that, next time, he might not be so lucky.

Next time, he wasn't. But he still got away with it.

THE
LEGION IN DECLINE

The first officer of Thomas's Legion to return to North Carolina
from Virginia, other than men on furlough, was Major William
Stringfield. On the evening of October 31, 1864, Major Stringfield
(soon to be a colonel) sat down in a cabin in Quallatown, propped
his weary legs up in front of a log fire, and jotted in his pocket
diary: "After a long and tiresome journey of one month I arrived at
this haven of rest — this long heard of place of security where
Yankees never come and conscripts find shelter. I will now rest
awhile before I undertake to straighten out this end of the Legion."[1]

In his later years, Bill Stringfield had ample time to chuckle
sadly over that diary entry: rarely had so many naive assumptions
been packed into such a short paragraph. The mountains outside the
cabin, still rusty and sharp-scented with the last glories of autumn,
might have looked eternally peaceful, but every other assumption
Stringfield made was dead wrong. The Yankees would be coming.
He would have reasons to curse the deserters, and on more than one
occasion would find himself staring down the muzzles of their
guns. He would get precious little rest until the war was finally
over. And, last on his list but first in real-life priorities, the Legion
would require a great deal of "straightening out."

Bill Stringfield was in Quallatown, in fact, to assume command
of all of Thomas's men in the vast wilderness region between
Asheville and Murphy. Colonel William Holland Thomas was not
on hand to greet his old comrade and housemate from the Strawberry Plains days; "Little Will," it turns out, had been placed
under arrest in late September and sent to Goldsboro, where he was
to be court martialed.

This dramatic turn of events represented the climax of the crisis that had been building ever since Colonel John B. Palmer had assumed command of the Western District of North Carolina. The central issue was that recurring pestilence of the Confederacy, desertion.

By mid-1864, there were more deserters in the mountain counties than there were troops on duty. There was no longer the slightest social stigma attached to desertion. Many of the latest arrivals now lived openly on their family farms, their loaded rifles always within arm's reach. Few were the counties where Confederate ardor was still sufficiently strong to permit the local Home Guard to perform its duties in strict compliance with the law. Too many people now sympathized with the deserters. A Home Guard officer who acted too aggressively toward the "outliers" in his district was likely to find himself caught in a very personal ambush.

Trying to make the best of this chaotic situation, Colonel Thomas had gradually stopped tracking and arresting deserters. Instead, he began trying to woo them into his ranks, where they would at least serve some useful function in defending their home ground. The outliers were, after all, the only source of fresh manpower in the whole region. At first, Thomas went through the proper motions and wrote several memoranda to the War Department in Richmond, asking for permission to do this. Permission was, of course, angrily denied. So Thomas just ignored all subsequent directives from the War Department, as well as a series of direct orders from his putative superior officer, Colonel Palmer, and went right on enlisting whomever he pleased.

For Palmer, the situation became intolerable. Ever since he had taken command, he had sought to exert proper control over the disposition of Thomas's troops; and Thomas had fought him, or ignored him, every step of the way. Thomas continued to maintain that, because the original sanction to form the Legion had come directly from President Jefferson Davis, his was still an independent command, answerable only to the President -- who, presumably, had more important things on his mind than the deployment of 300 or 400 Indians and mountaineers. Thomas's contention was arrogant nonsense, of course, as well as the most flagrant kind of insubordination. Thomas obeyed Palmer's directives only when their contents coincided with his own wishes; otherwise, he continued to do exactly as he pleased.

Unfortunately for the Confederate war effort, what Will Thomas now wanted, more than anything else, was for his men and his home region to be left alone. All summer long, he had virtually hunkered down in that corner of the state, assuming a military posture that had become, by summer's end, entirely passive, even timid.

His personal behavior, too, had become puzzling and erratic. Long spells of silent brooding would suddenly yield to spasms of manic emotion. Thomas was, in fact, experiencing the first symptoms of the progressive mental deterioration that would lead him to spend many of his declining years inside a madhouse.

Sadly for the historian, next to nothing is known about the court martial of William Thomas. No transcripts of any part of the proceedings have ever been uncovered. The charges drawn up against him, however, are known:

* That he did "knowingly entertain and receive deserters into his command";

* That he was guilty of "conduct unbecoming an officer and a gentleman...in that he...did publish and make known that he was authorized to receive into his command to wit the said Thomas Legion and place on duty all dismounted cavalry soldiers";

* That he had been guilty of conduct "prejudicial to good order and discipline";

* That he had repeatedly disobeyed the direct orders of his superior officer;

* That he was incompetent.

All in all, it was quite a list. Confronted with charges like those, many an army officer would have resigned his commission and taken up a career in life insurance. Not Thomas. He pleaded not guilty. Lacking any transcript of the court martial, one can only speculate on how the proceeding went. Thomas probably defended his actions by arguing that they were based on the realities of the situation in the mountains, and on the need to reconcile, rather than further antagonize, the deserters and Union sympathizers in the region. Major Stringfield, for one, thought that "Colonel Thomas, in his excess of kindness, goes too far," but did not for one moment doubt that Thomas was "a true Southerner."

Neither, apparently, did Jefferson Davis. Although the Goldsboro tribunal found Thomas guilty, Thomas appealed in person to the President in Richmond. In November 1864, his conviction was reversed by Presidential order. Stringfield had never doubted that Thomas, through guile and political connections, would somehow come out of the mess with his commission intact. In his diary entry for November 1, Stringfield had scrawled: "As he [Colonel Thomas] is a very shifty and polite man he is likely to come out OK in the end."[2]

With the exoneration of William Thomas, there were no longer any reasons why the long-sundered parts of the Legion should not be reunited. James R. Love's Virginia detachment staged a final parade before their brigade commander in Virginia, Colonel Thomas Smith, on November 17. Smith bade them farewell with ringing words of praise. Aside from the complications of command, the main reason Love's men had been kept in Virginia was for their fighting qualities. In fierce engagements at Piedmont, Winchester, and Cedar Creek, the mountaineers had held crucial parts of the rebel line and had fought with exceptional steadfastness and bravery. General Jubal Early had taken them on his stunning, whirlwind invasion of Maryland, and in that great cavalier's vanguard, they had glimpsed the very gates of Washington. A few Legion Cherokees -- who had through unusual circumstances not only remained with Love's companies, but also had become attached to other units during the complicated maneuvers of the Shenandoah Valley campaign -- actually remained in Virginia and are said to have been present at Appomattox when Lee surrendered.

After Thomas was cleared of all charges, he remained for a while in Richmond, mending his political fences, renewing old friendships, and making sure all his connections were still in place. Operational command of the Indians and the newly raised white troopers (legitimate volunteers and reenlisted deserters alike) became the responsibility of Stringfield. It was to prove a hard-riding command. By the time Stringfield got to Quallatown at the end of October 1864, the Confederacy's hold over the western counties of North Carolina was so tenuous, and its defenses on the

Tennessee border so porous, that nothing less than two full brigades of regulars, at least one of them comprised of first-rate
cavalry, would have sufficed to contain the situation.

By the end of the year, all Stringfield had were four Indian
companies — although whites must have comprised part of two of
them — to patrol Cherokee, Clay, Macon, and Jackson counties.
Thomas, when he was in the region, continued to make his headquarters at home, in Quallatown. Stringfield, for his part, could
most often be found in Franklin, Macon County, which was more
centrally located.

Lacking any telegraphic communications, Stringfield had to
spend a lot of time in the saddle, just riding from one outpost to
another. He described the terrain as "a wild section...almost a
pathless wilderness...lonely, perilous and desolate."[3] He was
usually alone and had to cover 20, 30, sometimes 50 miles between
his far-flung detachments. And all of this was through country that
harbored armed deserters, Unionist bushwhackers, Federal raiders
from Tennessee, and, not infrequently, cut-throat robbers who
preyed indiscriminately on anyone who came under their hand.

"These counties were much infested by the Union element,
some very good men among them," wrote Stringfield, many years
later. "There were some very indiscreet and unwise men...on our
side in this section. Much bad feeling existed...I gave protection to
such as deserved it and ordered the others to leave the State.
Several bands of 'scouts' [Confederate partisans] caused much of
this trouble. I ordered these to their commands, took horses, cattle
and other property from them, several times at the muzzles of their
pistols."[4]

On one of these rides, Stringfield came upon some men from
Love's Virginia detachment. These men had recently arrived back
in the mountains and no doubt were affected by the conditions they
found there — so different from what they must have longed to find.
They had captured two Federals from Tennessee, probably recruiting agents, and when Stringfield happened along, they were in the
process of hustling the two Yankees into a laurel thicket, prepara-
tory to shooting them. Stringfield reined to a halt, assessed the
situation with one glance, and ordered the prisoners untied. No one
moved. Stringfield turned to the lieutenant in charge of the patrol

and gave the order a second time. Again, there was no response except angry glares of disbelief. Stringfield calmly got down from his horse and cut the prisoners' bonds himself. At this point, the Confederate lieutenant angrily drew his revolver and advanced on Stringfield. Standing his ground, Stringfield drew his sword and raised it above his head. Fortunately, a couple of privates intervened, placing themselves between the two officers. This gave their choleric lieutenant a moment to recall that shooting a superior officer was a hanging offense. Upon further reflection, the lieutenant admitted that it was probably better for all concerned to march the two Yankees to the jail in Asheville than to kill them by the roadside. Stringfield remounted and rode on, and two lucky men survived the war because of his intervention.

Governor Zebulon Vance had by now become so concerned about the defenseless condition of the mountain passes, and about the anarchy that prevailed in the growing number of counties where the outlier bands outnumbered and outgunned the local militia, that he begged Richmond to send regular troops to the region. Preferably, the troops would come from General Breckinridge's command in southwestern Virginia. Breckinridge was sympathetic, but could not spare a man or a gun. In the end, Richmond did what governments have always done when they lacked the resources to deal with the causes of such situations: they switched commanders. Colonel Palmer was sacked in mid-August of 1864 (too late to stop the machinery of Thomas's court martial, which had already creaked into motion), and command of the Western District was given to one of the ablest men in North Carolina: General James Green Martin.

General Martin was then 45 years old. A stern disciplinarian and a man of the highest personal integrity, he had lost his right arm during the Mexican War and was known by his men as "Old One-Wing." Martin was a weary man by the autumn of 1864; in addition to several battlefield commands, he had worked himself to exhaustion during the early months of the war in his post as adjutant general of North Carolina. He had achieved miracles of organization, raising and equipping more than 40 regiments between April 1861 and January 1862. He had also been one of the main inspirations for Governor Vance's program of state-sponsored blockade running, an adventurous expedient which had turned out to be remarkably successful in augmenting both the state's, and the Confederacy's, supply of strategic imports.

Martin probably wanted the mountain command about as much as he wanted to loose his other arm, but he dutifully took the job. He set up his regional headquarters at Morganton on August 16. The man whom he replaced, the long-suffering Colonel Palmer, seems to have taken his medicine with remarkably good grace. He remained loyally on duty as a subordinate commander, operating out of Asheville. Palmer's conflicts with Thomas aside, he had learned a lot about leadership during his thankless tenure as commander of the Western District. More comfortable in a subordinate, tactical role than he ever was as commander-in-chief, Palmer's subsequent performance (to deduce from the admittedly sketchy documentation) was marked by a fair degree of energy and competence.

General Martin's overall effort was hampered not only by local squabbles, but also by enemy action in a distant, though very much related, part of the Appalachians. In October 1864, in order to relieve Federal pressure on the vital salt works near Saltville, Virginia, Colonel Palmer was ordered, by no less a personage than Robert E. Lee himself, to create the strongest possible diversion in east Tennessee.

Palmer collected 800 men — the fact that Martin could spare that many troops proves that his efforts were indeed having a positive impact on the overall situation in the mountains — and departed Asheville on October 17. Martin ordered him to leave the Indians behind in North Carolina — possibly for political reasons, but more likely because the Cherokees, still nominally under Thomas's personal command, would have been a very dubious asset without Thomas to lead them. They might even have refused to budge, and then Palmer would have had yet another problem to deal with. Instead, a company of white soldiers from Thomas's Legion accompanied the expedition. These men were drawn from the predominately Indian companies and were led by Matthew Love, Will Thomas's brother-in-law, and Palmer was shocked by their condition. As he watched them cross the gap at Paint Mountain, he observed that half of them were without shoes and some of the more pathetic individuals actually left bloody footprints on the rocks as they passed.

The only result of this expedition was a brisk skirmish at Russellville on October 28. Love's detachment of white Legionnaires was assigned to an outfit of mostly cavalry led by John C. Vaughn, a mediocre officer on his better days. Against them came one of Union General Stoneman's most aggressive cavalry tacticians, General Alvan C. Gillem, an east Tennessean with a burning hatred of rebel mountaineers. Vaughn's horsemen were ill- positioned to receive Gillem's powerful charge, and they were routed within minutes. Only a determined stand by the Confederate infantry, which interposed its line between Vaughn's fleeing troopers and Gillem's attack, staved off a crushing rebel defeat. Matthew Love's Legionnaires held their part of the line with rock-solid steadiness, and their fire emptied several Yankee saddles. After disengaging, Palmer's dispirited force straggled back over the mountains, arriving in Asheville on November 3.

In his after-action report to General Martin, Palmer acknowledged the Legion company's bravery, but deplored the condition of the Legion as a whole. Scattered all over the southern half of western North Carolina, most of the Legion's companies were fragmented, raggedly dressed, and short of ammunition; the Indians were listless and balky without "Little Will" to energize them; and the chain of command had grown Byzantine, almost beyond comprehension. "Thomas's Legion," Palmer concluded, "as at present organized, is of but little, if any use, either for local defense or for aggressive movements."[5]

It is easy to sympathize with Palmer's vexation by glancing at the way the Legion was set up by the last weeks of 1864. Ostensibly a single, coherent tactical unit, Thomas's Legion was by then fragmented into four main groups, operating under a chain of command that was incredibly complicated and ill-defined:

* Five companies of what used to be Walker's battalion, now commanded by William Stringfield;

* A separate detachment of white troopers, drawn from the expanded and formerly all-Cherokee companies, commanded by Matthew Love;

* The original Indian companies and Colonel James R. Love's

regiment (now reduced in strength, by its Virginia losses, to a company's worth of manpower), which had finally arrived back in North Carolina, at Palmer's forward headquarters at Warm Springs, on December 2, 1864.

Technically, all of these men were still commanded by William Thomas. But Thomas was still in Richmond, politicking after his conviction at the court-martial was overturned. To confuse matters still more, Colonel James Love had to relinquish command, due to ill health, and retire to his Jackson County home for a period of rest. While he was gone, the day-to-day job of running that segment of the Legion fell to a lieutenant colonel named McDowell from the 62nd North Carolina Regiment.

No wonder Palmer was constantly complaining. There was no rational excuse for a unit that was not large to begin with to be scattered into such disorganized fragments and subjected to such a baroque chain of command.

Even though Thomas had managed to bob and weave his way out from under the court martial verdict, Palmer's complaints were finally being taken seriously by some authorities in Richmond -- especially after Governor Vance added his two cents worth in a letter to the War Department. Vance bluntly stated: "Colonel Thomas is worse than useless; he is a positive injury to the country. His command is a favorite resort for deserters, numbers of them, I learn are on his rolls, who do no service. He is disobedient of orders, and invariably avoids the enemy...."[6]

Perhaps some of the bitterness in the tone of this letter stems from the fact that Vance, at this time, still believed Thomas shared some of the blame for the capture of his brother, Robert Vance. In any event, it looked for a time as though Thomas's Legion would be broken up and its component parts brigaded to other, conventional, units — as indeed had already happened with every other "legion" in the Confederate Army.

Despite all this bureaucratic flak, however, William Thomas's connections, and his political skills, remained strong. On November 9, as a result of his intense political lobbying in Richmond, Confederate Secretary of War James A. Seddon issued a directive that gave Thomas everything he wanted: permission to raise new recruits on both sides of the state line; authorization to expand the

Legion by another three companies, if he could find the men; and, most gratifying of all, authority to keep the Legion intact and under his overall command. Neither Palmer nor anyone else could now break up the existing formations and attach them to other units.

As 1864 drew to a close, circumstances were leading to the final act of the mountain war -- Stoneman's Raid. As a kind of overture to that campaign, Union General Stoneman renewed his assault on Saltville on December 10, brilliantly capturing and sacking the place only ten days later. Once again, Colonel Palmer was ordered to use his little mountaineer army as a fire brigade. He was told to leave Asheville, cross the spine of the Smokies into Tennessee, and do whatever he could to siphon off enemy forces from the Saltville operation.

Palmer started off toward Paint Mountain Gap again, but this time his scouts reported that the much-hated George Kirk had encamped in the pass with a strong force of men. Kirk withdrew, however, without offering battle, and seemed to vanish into the haze. Palmer guessed that Kirk would be heading toward Greeneville. With admirable boldness of intent, Palmer laid plans to cut him off and bring him to bay.

First, Palmer ordered Bill Stringfield to link up with him at Warm Springs, which Stringfield did on December 26. As he reported to Palmer, Stringfield complained about the pokiness of his Legion companies in getting underway.

The following day, Stringfield and his 300-man battalion started on a terrible winter march, following the twisting course of the Nolichucky River, hoping to cut off Kirk's line of retreat. They got as far as Horse Creek, stumbling miserably through 18 inches of snow, when the weather conditions changed from wretched to appalling. A blizzard raked over the column, dumping ten inches of fresh snow and obliterating the trails Stringfield had been trying to follow. Kirk could have been lurking anywhere in the vicinity — their last good intelligence was 48 hours old — and instead of catching him, Stringfield's men were much more likely to be caught by him, and probably annihilated. At a council of war after the snowstorm, every single officer in the column agreed with Stringfield that it would be insane to press ahead under such conditions. The column about-faced and withdrew to their huts at

Warm Springs.

Palmer's report on this abortive operation does him little credit, for he accused Stringfield of disobeying orders. Given the impossible weather conditions and the weakness of his force relative to Kirk's (when last observed, Kirk had been leading at least 400 men), Stringfield's decision to retreat was entirely proper. He and his men had given it a game try, and had suffered great hardship in the process; by the time they elected to turn around, their original objective had become quite impossible to achieve. Palmer surely realized this. He probably wrote his report as one more maneuver in his campaign to force the authorities to give him full operational control over all of Thomas's units.

Palmer had to content himself with spreading out his little inventory of companies to cover the most critical areas, according to dispositions worked out in conferences with General Martin. Meanwhile, Stringfield and his battalion limped back to the Quallatown area and thawed out. The rest of the mountain front remained static for a while, as all movement was paralyzed by arctic cold, lashing snow, and winds that could reach hurricane velocities on the higher ridges.

Thus ended the year 1864 in the Western District of North Carolina. It had been a wretched year for Confederate arms, such as they were in that part of the state. The year had begun with the bagging of General Robert Vance and had ended with the failure to encircle George Kirk, probably the one man in the whole Union Army whom the mountaineers most wanted to whip in a stand-up fight. Not so far into the new year, they would have another chance.

William Stringfield as a young Confederate private in 1861. He ended up as a colonel in command of both Cherokee Indians and white mountaineers in Thomas's Legion in the counties west of Asheville.

Colonel William H. Thomas, "Little Will," commander of Thomas's Highland Legion and the only white man ever elected chief of a North American Indian tribe. This photo was taken in 1858.

Union General George Stoneman redeemed his military reputation by leading a wide-ranging cavalry raid into southern Virginia and North Carolina in 1865. But he never realized his ambition of liberating a POW camp.

Thrilling Adventures of Daniel Ellis

Daniel Ellis, the legendary Unionist guide who led thousands of Unionist refugees and would-be recruits to safety across the Cumberland and Appalachian Mountains. This engraving is from an 1867 autobiographical account of his adventures.

As a teenager, Malinda Pritchard Blalock cut her hair, donned trousers and a loose-fitting shirt, and joined the Confederate Army as "Sam" Blalock. Her husband enlisted with her, and the newlyweds shared a tent in the 26th North Carolina Regiment.

General Robert Vance, older brother of Governor Zebulon Vance, was the first commander of the Western District of North Carolina. In 1864 he captured a Yankee wagon train, but then pushed his luck and was captured himself in a surprise attack by Union cavalry.

Colonel James G. Martin, nicknamed "Old One-Wing" after losing an arm in the Mexican War. In 1864, he succeeded John B. Palmer as Confederate commander of the Western District of North Carolina. Martin was an able leader but was weary of the war by late 1864.

Thomas's Legion spent more than a year guarding this 1,600-foot bridge across the Holston River at Strawberry Plains, Tennessee. By the time the war ended, it had been destroyed and rebuilt four times. This 1864 photo was taken while the bridge was in Union hands.

Colonel John B. Palmer, Confederate commander of the Western District of North Carolina. Palmer felt helpless and outraged after Union raider George Kirk rode unmolested into North Carolina, captured Camp Vance, destroyed a supply train, and outgunned two local militia units.

Thrilling Adventures of Daniel Ellis

In the mountain war, hundreds of men on both sides were gunned down in their own doorways, and often their families never found out who killed them or why.

Thomas's Legion was feared by Union soldiers after some of the Cherokees scalped a few Yankees. Scalpings took place, but usually not when white officers were around. And unlike this 1867 engraving from Daniel Ellis's book, the Indians usually wore regulation Confederate uniforms.

Thrilling Adventures of Daniel Ellis

In the fall of 1863, Unionist refugees from Wilkes County were massacred in Tennessee by Confederate partisans. The incident was described in gruesome detail by Daniel Ellis.

Members of the 15th Pennsylvania Cavalry pose on top of a mountain. The 15th was one of the most disciplined and effective regiments in General Stoneman's entire command.

Enemies were dealt with harshly by both Unionist and Confederate guerrillas. Victims were sometimes hung to strangle slowly, rather than to die quickly from a broken neck. And sometimes they were beaten, stabbed, or burned as they died.

Thrilling Adventures of Daniel Ellis

Storm in the Mountains/Vernon H. Crow

Cherokee veterans of Thomas's Legion at a 1903 Confederate reunion in New Orleans. Colonel William Stringfield is in the back row, third from the left.

Unionist scout Daniel Ellis encounters three rotting skeletons hung from a tree —
victims of the partisan violence that raged in the mountains of North Carolina
during the war.

PART 3:
DESERTERS
AND DESPERADOES

On the banks of the battle-stained river I stood, as the moonlight shone,

And it glared from the face of my brother As the sad wave swept him on!

Where my home was glad, are ashes; And horrors and shame had been there —

For I found, on the fallen lintel, This tress of my wife's torn hair.

-- S. Teackle Wallis, "The Guerrillas: A Southern War Song," 1864.

THE
SONS OF
GRANNY FRANKLIN

In the late summer and autumn of 1864, Colonel George W. Kirk's men were coming over the Tennessee-North Carolina border at will, roaming the wilds of the Carolina border counties, stealing from and terrorizing anyone they suspected of Confederate sympathies. In Madison County, pro-Confederate citizens were, by this time anyway, a minority, but once you got beyond the hard-core Unionist areas such as Shelton Laurel, there still were a goodly number of them.

One Madison County inhabitant reputed to be a Confederate was Nance "Granny" Franklin, a widow with four sons, the youngest of whom, Josiah, was 15 in 1864. None of Granny Franklin's sons had actually joined the Confederate Army, but they had been known to join pro-Confederate bands that had gone out, sometimes into neighboring Haywood County, to bushwhack Unionists -- including, on occasion, some of Colonel Kirk's men. Now, Kirk's men decided it was time to make a pay-back call on Granny Franklin and her boys.

It was typical of the confused and tangled loyalties of the region that, although Granny Franklin had four sons who sniped for the rebel side, she herself was inclined toward the Union...at least, until the day Kirk's Unionists paid her a visit.

Three of the four Franklin boys were home that day: Josiah, Balus, and James. When they saw blue-bellies dismounting in the trees around their cabin, they knew instantly what was about to happen. All three grabbed their rifles, ran outside, took up positions near the cabin, and opened fire, wounding a couple of Yankee guerrillas. The boys were hopelessly outgunned, however, and return fire from the guerrillas' Spencer repeaters blasted up clouds of wood chips all around them and fatally wounded both James and Balus.

Young Josiah, seeing himself about to be outflanked, dove under the cabin and reloaded. He could see the booted feet of Kirk's men as they cautiously approached the house. They were coming for him, and he knew it. He fought them like a cornered mink. Two of the guerrillas crawled under the cabin to get the boy, and he shot them both dead.

Now it looked like a stand-off. Nance Franklin was screaming wildly as Kirk's men pinioned her arms and forced her to watch her two eldest boys bleed to death in their own front yard. Now she also had to watch as several of the men ran up with pine-knot torches and set fire to the cabin. Granny Franklin twisted like a madwoman in her captors' arms, and for an instant she almost broke loose. One of Kirk's men fired a pistol at her head, but only succeeded in clipping off a lock of her hair. Death would not release her, on that day, from one last horror.

Young Josiah stood the flames and smoke as long as he could, then bolted, his clothes smoking, from beneath the flaming cabin. He flew right into a knot of waiting Yankees, some of whom were guffawing obscenely at his plight. The boy fell. One of Kirk's men stepped up, swung his rifle like a club, and crushed the boy's skull. His mother watched while his brains spilled out onto the ground like the contents of a cracked egg.

There was no need to hold Mrs. Franklin now. She stood like a statue, three dead sons at her feet and her home burning to ashes, while the raiders remounted and rode away, congratulating themselves on having administered a salutary lesson to all Confederate bushwhackers in the area.

'THE COUNTY HAS GONE UP .....'

If early enthusiasm for the Confederate cause had been remarkably widespread in the western counties of North Carolina, it proved to be thin indeed after a few months of real fighting. There were individual desertions early on, of course; some young men endured one week of training camp and decided that was enough. But desertions in significant numbers really started when the mass of volunteers realized it was not going to be a short, victorious war, and that the primary cause for their early enthusiasm — the desire to defend their homes against a Yankee invasion — was not necessarily, or even primarily, what the war was really about.

President Jefferson Davis constantly railed against "disaffection" in North Carolina. Throughout the war, in a hundred instances both subtle and blatant, Davis revealed a deep prejudice against the state. But the percentage of deserters from North Carolina was about average for the Confederacy as a whole, and North Carolina was making the heaviest contribution of any state to the Confederate cause, in terms of taxes, supplies, and per capita manpower.

During the war, some 23,000 North Carolinians deserted the Confederate Army. Only a small percentage were disloyal Unionists, and fewer still were cowards. Indeed, the vast majority were men who had several heated battles on their service records. They drifted down from Virginia through the mountain valleys and along the deep cover of the ridges, or down through the sparsely inhabited swamps along the coast. And they drifted away for many reasons other than simple war-weariness: anxiety caused by letters from home; resentment over their conscription treatment; and furloughs and wages that were long overdue, thanks to the incompetence of Richmond bureaucrats. Whatever the reasons, the men who deserted found a civilian population in poor shape to support them, but unwilling to report them to the authorities. Often, bands of deserters just stuck together, guns in hand, staying out of sight, fighting if cornered, and were sometimes forced to turn to banditry just to survive. In a countryside which held little to support them, they became both a scourge and a pity.

The facade of romantic rebel patriotism began to crack, in the mountain region, as early as December 1862. At that time, a party of 2,000 Federal troops raided the appropriately named town of Union, Tennessee. Union was defended — if that's the right word — by two companies of the mountain-raised 62nd North Carolina Regiment. The Federal commander, General Samuel Carter, expected to have to fight hard for his objective, which was another one of those strategic bridges over the Holston River. But, as it happened, he only had to fire a few shots, and the defenders surrendered in a body. The North Carolinians, Carter reported, were happy to take parole and eager to get back to their homes in the mountains: "Their joy at being captured, seemed to be boundless."

Even before then, the state elections of November 1862 had shown that party lines were deepening in the mountains. Governor Zebulon Vance's famous remark that the conflict was "a rich man's war and a poor man's fight" seemed especially apt to the mountaineers — absolutely nothing in their experience so far contradicted it.

Certainly, the imposition of the Conscription Act in April 1862 seemed to underscore the truth of Vance's observation. You didn't have to be a rural socialist to see the injustice of the system. Slaveowners, wealthy farmers and merchants, speculators and government officials, all could wheedle or buy their way out of combat duty; the subsistence farmer, however, could not -- even if he had already served his six-month stint as an early volunteer, and even if he were the only thing standing between his family and hunger. To the burden of conscription were added the aggravation and hardship of the tax-in-kind and impressment laws. The basic reason for going to war in the first place — to defend the sacred right to be left alone — had, for the mountain citizens, been shunted aside and forgotten as Richmond found itself embroiled in a conflict it did not have the resources to sustain. Furthermore, Richmond pursued its goals by means of tactics that had not changed since the days of Napoleon, and found its armies chewed to shreds by firepower technology that had.

Conditions in the mountain counties had polarized by the start of 1863. The year was only a few weeks old before a party of Confederate conscript agents came into Cherokee County from upper Georgia, arrested three men, marched them off to jail in chains, and gave them the choice of rotting there or enlisting in the Confederate Army. Governor Vance, always sensitive to the touchiness of the mountaineers and keenly aware of how fragile the political balances were in that region, forced their release and threatened to use his militia units to shoot anyone who came into the state like that again.

By summer, the whole region was simmering. A gang of 100 outliers roamed Cherokee County, disarming Confederate soldiers who were trying to return to their regiments after a furlough at home. The same gang even had the audacity to stage a shooting spree in Murphy in broad daylight. The next week, from Henderson County, came news that a guerrilla band had attacked the house of a prominent citizen where several deserters were being held, and had freed them at gunpoint. From Wilkes County came a report that well-armed deserters numbering as many as 500 men had established a regular paramilitary force, holding drill in the open, living in guarded, fortified camps, and defying the local Confederates to do anything about it. In Salisbury, a mob of angry women armed with axes stormed the food warehouse of a speculator and took from him a great quantity of scarce and expensive flour.

Several mountain counties, by early 1863, virtually belonged to the deserters, at least by night. A Confederate officer in charge of rounding up deserters in Caldwell County frankly admitted that he and his men fraternized with these men at night, even while they were ostensibly chasing them during the day: "...at night I am generally out with the boys. Of course, they know enough to peek out of my sight during the day, which makes it exceedingly difficult for me to catch them."[1] In areas where Confederate support was spotty, it was common for local Home Guard commanders to make some kind of informal truce. Since most deserters brought their newly issued rifles home, along with all the ammunition they could carry, they were, in most places, better-armed than the ragtag militia outfits that were supposed to drag them from their hideouts. As the desertion problem escalated, and Richmond's efforts to deal with it became more heavy handed, armed clashes became common. More often than not, the deserters got the best of the exchanges. As another Confederate officer reported from North Carolina: "They [the deserters] are not only determined to kill in avoiding apprehension (having just put to death yet another of our enrolling officers), but their esprit de corps extends to killing in revenge...so far they have had no trouble for subsistence. While the disaffected feed them out of sympathy, the loyal do so from fear."[2]

Early in 1863, Jefferson Davis received a petition from community leaders in the counties west of the Blue Ridge Mountains, asking him to suspend conscription in that area, at least until local authorities had time to come up with a solution to the deserter problem. Davis refused, but did agree to send in men from outside the area, so as not to promote "inextinguishable feuds and mutual reprisals." This policy, of course, was guaranteed to produce just such results.

Another petition, this one from the loyal Confederates of Watauga County, spelled things out to Davis in blunt language: "We have very little slave labor in this mountain country, and if all the white labor is pressed into the army how are the troops in the field and the women and children to be fed next year? Unless a wiser policy prevails, our people will have to choose between starvation and emigration. We respectfully and earnestly call the attention of the authorities to this subject."[3]

Other expressions of disaffection were couched in bitter, more ironic terms, as reflected in this letter to a newspaper:

> Will you be so kind, Mr. Editor, as to inform Jeff Davis and his Destructives, that after they make the next draw of men from this mountain region, if they please, as an act of great and special mercy, be so gracious as to call out a few, just a few, of their exempted pets from Mississippi, Georgia and South Carolina, to knock the women

and children of the mountains in the head, to put them out of their misery.[4]

To many of the citizens of the mountain counties, it looked as if their region were being asked to bear an impossibly harsh and disproportionate share of the war's burdens. It also looked as if their entreaties for realistic, even-handed treatment were being snubbed by Richmond because a stereotype had already taken hold of the mountaineer-as-Tory. The fact that the mountain region was considered the heartland of Toryism in North Carolina -- a state which was already suspect because of its slowness in leaving the Union -- meant that the needs of the mountain people, even of those demonstrably loyal to the Confederacy, enjoyed a very low priority on the Davis administration's agenda.

Men not only hid to avoid conscription, but also feigned ill-nesses to avoid military service. In some extreme cases, they performed acts of self-mutilation. One Watauga County man named John Walker figured out a way to desert without marking himself as a target for vigilante retribution. As a member of the Home Guard, Walker was subject to a biweekly rotation of duties — for example, one local company pulled duty at Camp Mast, the regional Confederate stronghold, while the other local company tended their farms. One week, while it was his turn to be at home, Walker staged a mock "capture" of himself. Enlisting the aid of some trusted Unionist neighbors, he borrowed a genuine Yankee uniform and made up some wooden cutout rifles that might look like the real thing on a dark night. Then he had himself "arrested" at home by what, to a casual observer, would surely have appeared to be a Federal raiding party out of Tennessee, commanded by a well-dressed Yankee officer. The Yankee officer was actually Walker's neighbor, Levi Coffey, and his partisans consisted of several other local farmers and even their wives, dressed in guer-rilla-drag.

After being pulled from his home, to the accompaniment of realistic and well-rehearsed tears on the part of his family, Walker hid out for a week in the mountains, then returned quite openly, bearing a forged but authentic-looking parole document. He duly reported to the local Home Guard commander, who inspected the parole, did not question its legitimacy, and informed Walker that, as a gentleman, he was honor-bound to observe the full term of the parole before bearing arms again for the South. The war ended before Walker's "parole" did, and when local folks later found out about the scam, they gave him high marks for originality.

News from the outside world sometimes took a while to spread through the western counties — most of the telegraph lines stopped east of the Blue Ridge, and in the whole lower half of the region, the only town that had a telegraph station was Morganton. But that did not lessen the effect of the news when it was bad. The catastrophic rebel defeats of mid-1863 at Gettysburg and Vicksburg, coming on top of their deepening regional problems, had a staggering impact on the mountain inhabitants. That impact was quickly reflected in private correspondence, which in turn created an even worse desertion problem in the army. What was a soldier supposed to feel when he got a letter such as this one, written in Madison County from Martha Revis to her husband, on the last day of July 1863?

> ...The people is all turning to the Union since the Yankees has got Vicksburg. I want you to come home as soon as you can after you git this letter...I want you to come home the worst that I ever did. The conscripts is all home yet, and I don't know what they will do with them. Folks is leaving here, and going North as fast as they can, so I will close.

There followed a postscript, in a different hand, from one of the young men working on the Revis farm:

> I pen a line, Sir. I am well, and is right strait out for the Union, and I am never going into the service any more, for I am for the Union for ever and ever, amen...There was 800 left to go to the North, so will tell you all about it in the next letter...Your brother till death. Hurrah for the Union! Hurrah for the Union, Union!
> [signed] Thomas Hunter

As if it had not already done enough to alienate the mountain people, Richmond unleashed upon them, in January 1863, a veritable plague. A horde of cavalry horses -- described, even in the *Official Records*, as "broken down" -- were moved from

Virginia to North Carolina and put out to forage in parts of Ashe, Surry, McDowell, Yadkin, Wilkes, and Watauga counties. These counties had already been hit very hard by three successive years of drought and poor crops, compounded by a manpower shortage and punctuated by outbreaks of violence. The horses' foraging was bad enough — they are frequently compared to "locusts" in contemporary letters — but the behavior of the Confederate troops detailed to escort them was abominable. More than one mountaineer complained that they were worse than Yankee raiders. Without a by-your-leave, they broke into granaries, stole fodder, importuned meals (at gunpoint if need be) from poor isolated farmers, insulted the men, laid rough hands (at least) on any maidens they could catch, stole chickens, and appeared, more often than not, to be in a state of permanent drunkenness.

Governor Vance thundered away in fulminating letters to Richmond, calling these acts "a grievance, intolerable, damnable, and not to be borne!" At one point, Vance threatened to mobilize the entire state militia and "wage actual war" upon the vandals. The latter threat was a bluff, of course, and Richmond called him on it; the horses, and their rampaging escorts, stayed in North Carolina until recalled for duty in Virginia.

Another plague of horsemen was visited upon the mountains in the winter of 1863-64, when foraging parties from Confederate General James Longstreet's army (then in winter camp over in northeastern Tennessee) tore through Ashe, Wilkes, and Catawba counties. Longstreet's men impressed horses and mules, and appropriated, at much less than market value, wagonloads of grain from people who had been saving up every kernel of corn to survive the winter. The inhabitants made it clear that Longstreet's men were unwelcome, and Longstreet's men made it clear that, in their opinion, all mountaineers were traitors and ignorant "white trash." They bullied, insulted, robbed, molested, and in some cases, beat up anyone who got in their way or who manifested an "unpatriotic attitude."

Having stripped a wide swath of countryside bare of whatever the earlier wave of cavalrymen had overlooked, Longstreet's men finally departed. If the civilian population in these areas had been neutral before the foragers arrived, they were Unionists afterward...a reaction which American soldiers would encounter again, a century later, in Southeast Asia.

By the time the Battle of Gettysburg was raging in Pennsylvania in July 1863, there were no longer any clear distinctions in the mountain counties between armed deserters, Unionist guerrillas, and freelance outlaws. Some men were one thing one week, another the next. Governor Vance estimated that by mid-1863, there were at least 1,200 armed deserters in the western counties -- more than twice as many as the total of regular Confederate troops. Add to that a roughly equal number of full- or part-time Unionist bushwhackers, and the magnitude of the problem becomes more clear. Moveover, many deserters — even those who simply wanted to forget the whole dirty business — were forced to band together with the local Unionists to present a common front against a common enemy.

A Mitchell County resident, who was ten years old when the war broke out, remembered the times this way: "Hit was awful for the folks in the mountains, whichever army came through. They stripped the beds, cleaned anything they wanted out of the houses, robbed the bee gums and the hen roosts, lugged off the corn out of the cribs, and drove off the cattle, and hogs, and of course they took the horses. Anything that could travel."[5]

There were active bands of Confederate bushwhackers, too, on both sides of the state line. As these men gradually came to be outnumbered by their Unionist counterparts, their tactics became even more desperate. They even resorted to the frequent use of live Unionist prisoners as "human shields" when moving through unfriendly areas. Over in Tennessee, rebel snipers took cover in the steep hillsides near the railroad tracks and fired at Federal troops on the passing trains. So great a nuisance did this become that eventually the occupation troops had to clear all the timber from both sides of the rail line -- in certain troublesome sectors, to a distance of half a mile.

If Colonel George W. Kirk's attack on Morganton was the most spectacular raid of 1864, the runner-up for that distinction was an affair that took place on April 10, under the leadership of one of Kirk's North Carolina associates, an outlier chieftain named Montrevail Ray. With a band of 75 men, Ray marched boldly into

Burnsville and got the drop on the small Home Guard detachment there, wounding one officer in the process. He then looted the county magazine of 100 newly issued rifles and the local warehouse of 500 pounds of bacon. Just one day earlier, in the same area, 50 starving mountain women had descended on a Confederate depot and helped themselves to about 60 bushels of government-owned wheat.

In both of these incidents, the existing Home Guard units had proven utterly incapable of either preventing the attacks or of later apprehending those who committed them. And now, to add damage to insult, at least this one band of local marauders -- itself larger than many Home Guard companies -- was armed with brand-new state-issue rifles, while many of the militia detachments were still equipped only with old flintlocks, shotguns, and assorted civilian hunting pieces.

The situation became so bad that the Home Guard commander for western North Carolina, General J.W. McElroy, felt compelled to gather whoever he could at the site of Mars Hill College, fortify the position, and issue a call for help. His letter to Governor Vance, composed at Mars Hill on April 12, 1864, is worth quoting at length, for it gives a vivid picture of the chaos that was descending on the western part of North Carolina:

>...The county is gone up. It has got to be impossible to get any man out there [to do Home Guard duty] unless he is dragged out, with but very few exceptions. There was but a small guard there [at Burnsville], and the citizens all ran on the first approach of the tories. I have 100 men here [at Mars Hill] to guard against Kirk...and cannot reduce the force; and to call out any more home guards at this time is only certain destruction to the country eventually. In fact, it seems to me, that there is a determination of the people in the country generally to do no more service to the cause. Swarms of men liable to conscription are gone to the tories or to the Yankees — some men that you have no idea of — while many others are fleeing east of the Blue Ridge for refuge...that discourages those who are left behind, and on the back of that, conscription is now going on and a very tyrannical course pursued by those who are left behind, and men [are] conscripted and cleaned out as [though] raked with a fine-toothed comb; and if any are left, if they are called upon to do a little home guard service, they at once apply for a writ of habeas corpus and get off...if something is not done immediately for this country, we will all be ruined, for the

home-guards now will not do to depend on....[6]

In turn, this prompted Governor Vance to write once more to Confederate Secretary of War James A. Seddon, on April 11, 1864:

> I beg again to call to your earnest attention the importance of suspending the execution of the conscription law in the mountain counties of North Carolina. They are filled with tories and deserters, burning, robbing and murdering. They [the counties] have been robbed and eaten out by Longstreet's command, and have lost their crops by being in the field nearly all the time trying to drive back the enemy. Now that Longstreet's command is removed [and all of East Tennessee is in Union hands], their condition will be altogether wretched, and hundreds will go to the enemy for protection and bread....

THE 'BONNIE AND CLYDE' OF WATAUGA COUNTY

Historically speaking, many of the violent men who roamed the mountains were anonymous. They were known to those who sympathized with their allegiances, and in many cases they were known to their victims and their victims' families. But most of the violence happened to people who had neither the education nor the inclination to leave detailed written accounts, and by the time regional historians began writing down the orally preserved stories of wartime events -- not until the early 20th century, in many cases -- a great deal of information was lost forever, or had become smudged by time and countless retellings.

But of all the colorful and bloodthirsty characters who roamed the high country during the war years, none was remembered more vividly, and in more detail, than the outlaw Keith Blalock. His saga is the very stuff of mountain ballads.

Blalock was born on the lower slopes of Grandfather Mountain, the highest peak in the Blue Ridge chain, in 1836. He was christened L. McKesson Blalock, and was raised by his mother and stepfather, a man named Austin Coffey, who appears to have done a conscientious job of raising the boy. In later years, Keith always spoke of Coffey with affection and respect — as, indeed, did most of those who knew him.

The nickname "Keith" was acquired at some point during his adolescence. During those years, the most renowned professional

147

pugilist in the western counties was a man from Burnsville named Alfred Keith. Young Blalock gained a reputation for being quick and effective with his fists, and the nickname stuck so tightly that, eventually, no one bothered to call him anything else.

Austin Coffey was a staunch Union man; his stepson took that basic political creed and added to it an intense degree of personal, militant zeal. When war came, Keith weighed the alternatives. He could go into hiding for the duration — but God alone knew how long that might be; or he could make the long and hazardous trek to Kentucky to enlist as a Federal volunteer. Neither choice seemed very attractive, especially since Keith had just acquired a new bride: a slim, attractive, teenaged girl named Malinda Pritchard.

Keith finally came up with a plan. He would enlist in the Confederate Army and just wait until some dark night when he was close enough to Union lines to slip over and change sides. If he timed his defection to occur during or right after a battle, he would be listed as "missing" rather than labeled a deserter, and his young bride would be compassionately looked after by the numerous Confederate sympathizers in their neighborhood.

But Malinda enjoyed being with her vigorous young husband as much as he enjoyed her softer company. She didn't want to be left behind while he marched off on his great adventure, and she had enough spunk to propose a daring scheme that would enable her to share the adventure with him. She cut off her hair, donned trousers and a loose-fitting shirt that masked her adolescent breasts, adopted the name "Sam" Blalock, and enlisted as Keith's younger brother. She was about 16 at the time, and was later described by one who had served with her as "a good looking boy...weight about 130 pounds, height five feet, four inches."

Fortunately, the couple enlisted early enough to take advantage of the custom of putting volunteers from the same family into the same outfit — a luxury which the Richmond government dispensed with as soon as the enthusiasm drained out of the volunteer effort and people started to realize that it was not going to be a six-month war. "Sam" and Keith were mustered into the same company, shared the same tent, and ended up, bizarrely enough, as part of the regiment commanded by future- Governor Zebulon Vance: the 26th North Carolina.

Unfortunately for Keith's original scheme, the regiment was nowhere near Yankee lines. Instead, it was pulling garrison duty at Kinston, camped alongside a big patch of swamp. Short of swimming Albemarle Sound or trekking a hundred miles into Virginia, the Blalocks were stuck as Confederate soldiers, like it or not.

Keith didn't like it one bit, but he bided his time until he could think of something. Meanwhile, both he and "Sam" performed their routine duties well enough to arouse no complaint. And if anyone noticed that Sam never joined the other guys in the swimming hole, it was chalked up to some quirk of personal hygiene or shyness — no one ever suspected the actual reason.

Finally, out of boredom as much as conviction, one suspects, Keith Blalock took extreme measures: He waded deep into the swamp and rolled around naked in a murderous thicket of poison oak. As a result, he developed such a virulent rash that the regimental surgeon could not identify it for what it was, and, fearing some sort of loathsome, unknown contagion, granted him a medical discharge. At that point, "Sam" came forward and revealed her true identity, insisting that she be discharged with her ailing husband. This resulted in some delay, not because the regimental officers wanted to press charges — Vance seems to have been more amused than angered by the masquerade — but simply because the whole business was too irregular to be covered by existing paperwork procedures. Keith left Confederate service on April 10, 1862, about a month after he had enlisted, and as soon as the paperwork could be completed on Malinda, she too was mustered out. In the *Official Records*, the matter is noted thusly: "Mrs. L.M. Blalock — discharged for being a woman...."

After the couple returned to the mountains, Keith cured himself by taking long baths in brine. Keith's discharge was a legitimate one, and, by law, he should have been left alone. In time, the Confederate authorities would come to wish that they *had* left Keith alone, but the couple had arrived back home just as the hated Conscription Act went into effect. When the local Confederate draft officers noticed that Keith's affliction cleared up just weeks after the ink was dry on his discharge papers, they began to keep a close eye on him. Now that he was healthy, he was a prime young specimen once again. One day, a detachment of well-armed Confederate agents rode up to the Blalock cabin and informed Keith that he had two choices: reenlist and serve the duration of his original commitment, or be branded as a shirker and subject to the full penalties of the new draft law. They would give him a few days to think it over, they said. "We'll be back."

But Keith Blalock had not subjected himself to the physical discomfort of a monster case of poison oak just so he could be arrested in his own front yard. He and Malinda gathered weapons and a few essentials and fled up into the impenetrable forests on the slopes of Grandfather Mountain. In time, as the conscription net was flung throughout the region, other draft-dodgers joined them, forming the nucleus of a band. They lived, communally it would seem, in a rude hut on the high slopes of the mountain, eating wild berries, fish, and game.

In time, of course, the authorities found him. For the first time, a price had been put on his head. When the recruiting party showed up, Blalock and his men opened fire and repelled it, wounding one. Keith himself took a ball in the left arm, fled further up the mountain, and spent several hours huddled inside a large herd of penned hogs, waiting for the searchers to give up. Immediately after this skirmish, the couple fled into Tennessee, where Keith — inevitably, one feels — gravitated to the command of the feared and bloody-minded guerrilla leader, Colonel George W. Kirk. He became a trusted member of Kirk's operation, and frequently operated autonomously, with handpicked men, crossing into North Carolina many times either to gather intelligence or to conduct raids.

There were Confederate sympathizers who made it their special quest to track down Keith Blalock. His actions, from the start, had been so flagrant that he had inspired a kind of wild resentment among his former neighbors who remained loyal to the rebel cause. Two members of the Moore family, in particular, made it their ambition to bushwhack and kill Keith Blalock on one of his trips into North Carolina.

Keith knew all about this from his own network of informants, and he decided to get the drop on them first. He boldly rode into the state one day, Malinda and a few trusted gunslingers at his side, and attacked the Moores' house. During the exchange of gunfire that followed, Carroll Moore, patriarch of the clan, was wounded.

But one of his two sons managed to put a ball into Malinda's shoulder, which prompted Keith to break off the attack and flee back to Tennessee, where he could get medical attention for his wife. Thus ended Round 1 of the Moore-Blalock feud.

The family situation Keith had left behind in North Carolina was one of divided loyalties and torn emotions — typical of the rifts that split mountaineer society to its bedrock heart. Keith's stepfather, Austin Coffey, was a Unionist and made no secret about it. His brother McCaleb was not. Although the two men lived within sight of one another at Coffey Gap, on the old Morganton Road, they belonged to different sides. Their relationship was strained, although they tried to remain civil to one another. McCaleb had a son named Jones who was off serving with the Confederate Army in Virginia. There were two other Coffey brothers, too — Reuben and William — who were active Confederate partisans. They helped the conscription agents round up shirkers and the militia track down deserters. Family ties or no, these activities were enough to put them on an inevitable collision course with their nephew, Keith.

When Keith and Malinda had been chased from Grandfather Mountain into Tennessee, the party that had attacked them was led by a prosperous local Confederate named Robert Green. Green had one residence at Globe, in Caldwell County, and a nicer home at Blowing Rock. Keith may have been told that Green was the man who had shot him on Grandfather Mountain. Green's relatives claimed that he was not, but Keith Blalock kept his own personal hit list, and once a man's name was on it, that man was in peril.

Blalock and several of his men came across the border one day and laid an ambush for Green on the road between Blowing Rock and Globe. They had been well informed; after a few hours, Green appeared, calmly driving his wagon. When he saw Keith Blalock suddenly emerge from the trees, Green leaped off the wagon and began running down the mountainside. Blalock took careful aim with his preferred weapon — a big-bore Sharp's rifle, of the type favored by many buffalo hunters because of its enormous stopping power — and fired. He was aiming to cripple, not to kill, for he disdained to finish off Green when he had the chance. He walked down to where Green lay screaming on the bracken, inspected his handiwork, satisfied himself that a proper degree of revenge had been meted out, and walked away. Blalock's shot had cracked Green's thighbone in half.

The collapse of General Robert Vance's thrust into Tennessee, in January 1864, and the stunning impact of Colonel Kirk's raid on Morganton, emboldened Unionists on both sides of the border. One of the men who guided Kirk's column into the mountains was a friend and sometime comrade of Blalock's, Joseph E. Franklin. By the end of 1864, Watauga County was in a state of near anarchy. Keith Blalock appeared on raids arrogantly dressed in a full Federal officer's uniform, although the men he commanded continued to look more like Corsican brigands than soldiers.

It was in this tense, dangerous atmosphere that Blalock decided to make his move on his Confederate relatives. Accompanied by several of his men, he first visited the home of Reuben Coffey, but did not find him there. Next, they rode on to William Coffey's house and captured him. They marched him a short distance into the forest to a mill owned by James Gragg. Coffey was ordered at gunpoint to sit down on a hand-carved bench. Keith, with what can only be considered remarkable punctiliousness under the circumstances, refused to pull the trigger on his uncle; instead, he ordered one of his men, a fellow named Perkins, to carry out the execution. Perkins shot Coffey while he rocked back and forth nervously on the wooden bench. They left him where he fell.

It was either on the retreating end of this raid, or on another that came soon after, that Keith was again involved in a desperate gun battle with the Moore boys. This time it took place in an orchard that belonged to the Moore family, near Globe, in Caldwell County. Either Jesse Moore got the drop on Keith, or Keith just didn't shoot as straight on this occasion as he usually did. Keith winged Jesse Moore in the heel, and one of his men shot another one of the Moore boys in the thigh, but Jesse ignored his own pain and shot out one of Keith Blalock's eyes.

A grim cycle of retaliation was under way. In reprisal for Keith's activities, a party of Confederate vigilantes swept into Coffey Gap on February 5, 1865. Keith's Unionist stepfather, Austin Coffey, was off visiting his Confederate brother, McCaleb. The Confederate mob might have turned around and returned home, had not a Unionist neighbor named James Boyd pointed out where Austin

Coffey had gone.

Boyd then went back home. The last he saw of Austin Coffey, he was being led off by the band of Confederates, whose commander was named James Marlow. The detachment marched off toward Blowing Rock and camped for the evening in an abandoned farmhouse. After eating some food, Austin Coffey, a man of advanced years, dozed off beside the fireplace. It grew still inside the cabin. In a quiet voice, Marlow ordered a soldier named John Walker to kill Austin Coffey. Walker refused. Then a rough-mannered mountaineer named Robert Glass volunteered. Without the slightest hesitation, he leaned over, put his pistol close to Coffey's mane of white hair, and blew the old man's brains out.

Austin Coffey may have been a Union man, but he was not a man of violence. One regional historian described him thus, based on interviews with people who had actually known him: "He was a bighearted man, who had fed Confederates as well as Union men at his house."[1]

The Confederates dragged the body outside and hid it in a laurel thicket. It was not located until a week later, when a stray dog was found trotting along the road carrying Austin Coffey's hand in his teeth. A party of local people was able to backtrack the dog and locate the site of the killing.

Keith Blalock had in his band at this time a man named Levi Coffey. (What relation, if any, he was to the Coffey family of Coffey Gap is not clear from the records. The historian, in tracing these events, must take a deep breath when trying to keep track of all the family relations in these areas; the Coffey clan was quite large, and settled over wide areas of both Watauga and Caldwell counties.) A party of Confederate riders led by Benjamin Green (probably related to the Robert Green who had been maimed by Blalock earlier — the violence twisted round and round the same clan names, time after time) rode up under cover of darkness to the house where Levi Coffey was spending the night, courtesy of Blalock's network of Unionist sympathizers. Coffey woke up in time to figure out what was happening, and ran from the front door through a hailstorm of pistol balls, escaping into the trees despite a painful wound in the shoulder.

Keith Blalock now declared renewed war on the Green clan. First, he and his men paid a nocturnal call on Lott Green, near Blowing Rock. As it happened, Lott Green was expecting a caller that night so he didn't hesitate to open his door. When he beheld Keith Blalock and his band, armed to the teeth, he slammed the door and quickly bolted it. Fortunately for Green, he already had some visitors in the house that night, including his brother, a brother-in-law who was with the local Home Guard, and a relative named L.L. Green, who later became a Superior Court judge, but who was at this time only 17 years old.

Blalock had five other men with him, including the now recovered Levi Coffey and a deserter from a Georgia regiment named Edmund Ivy. When Lott Green slammed the door, Blalock loudly demanded that every man in the house surrender immediately.

"What treatment will you give us?" asked one of the men inside the cabin.

"As you deserve, damn you!" replied Blalock.

At that, the men inside opened fire from the windows. At least one of Blalock's men was hit, in the side. Blalock, realizing from the volume of fire that there were more men in the cabin than he had bargained for, ordered a withdrawal. The men inside Lott Green's cabin now had their blood up, however, and they tracked the bloodstains for more than a mile, finally cornering Blalock's band at John Walker's cabin. There was another wild shoot-out, and again, the oft-wounded but incredibly lucky Keith Blalock managed to escape. Edmund Ivy, the deserter from Georgia who had joined Keith's band, was not so lucky, however. He was cut down as he leaped from the back door, and he died on the spot.

The War Between the States ended too soon for Keith Blalock. When he learned about the murder of his stepfather, Austin Coffey, he swore that he would kill John Boyd — the man who had fingered his stepfather for the assassins — even if it took 40 years. It took considerably less. At dusk on February 8, 1866, nearly a year after the war had ended, Boyd was peacefully walking with another man near his home in Caldwell County. Blalock stepped from the bushes and said, "Is that you, Boyd?" Boyd sensed his danger and took a swipe at Blalock with his cane. Blalock caught the blow on his left arm, reeled back a few paces, and came up out of his crouch firing. His Sharp's rifle blew an enormous hole through Boyd, killing him instantly and very messily.

Amazingly, considering all the bad blood he had stirred up, Keith Blalock boldly returned to his home county after the war, settled down in his own neighborhood near Grandfather Mountain, drew his veteran's pension, dabbled in local politics, and lived a vigorous life until August 11, 1913. He was at that time 77 years old, in good health, and he did not die by an enemy's hand. He was pumping a handcar on a stretch of mountain railroad track when he overshot a steep curve and plunged into a chasm; the handcar landed on top of him, crushing him to death. His wife, Malinda, had passed away in 1901. Both had long since entered the realm of mountain legends.

THE LAST HOG

The mountain legend of "David" was not actually written down, apparently, until more than a century after it happened. But the oral storytellers of the mountains know their craft, and, even if some details (such as the main character's last name) have become blurred, and some others doubtless elaborated upon over several generations of retelling, the tale itself rings absolutely true to the time, place, and conditions of the mountain war.

It happened in late 1863 or sometime in 1864. If, as the story has it, Colonel George Kirk's Yankees were marching openly on the road, in uniform, it must have taken place in one of the border counties — Watauga, Haywood, or possibly Madison, the areas where Kirk's raiders seem to have been most active.

A rebel soldier named David was home on leave. He had been shocked at the appearance of the farm when he arrived: "The cornfield was nothing but a slantwise piece of ground torn up by its roots, with here and there a corn stalk lying dried and tramped on by soldier shoes."[1] The horses had all been "impressed," the cow stolen, and all the hay confiscated from the barn — maybe even to feed Confederate horses, but what difference did that make? The only resources left to the family were a couple of scrawny chickens and a single hog. The hog was being saved until the last possible moment, for that one pig would be the family's sole source of meat through the coming winter.

The soldier's wife, Clarinda, had saved a little flour for his homecoming. She busied herself preparing chicken and dumplings, while David played with his infant son, Matthew. As she worked, Clarinda kept praying that David would decide not to return to General Robert E. Lee's army. Every time she thought of facing the coming winter without him, she experienced a "sucked-dry" feeling in her heart, according to the storytellers.

David, Clarinda, and Matthew were just sitting down to their meal when they heard the unmistakable sounds of marching soldiers, approaching on the road that passed by the farm. David went to the door and peered out. There was dust hanging in the air by the berry bushes alongside the road, and through it he could see men in blue coats. David stepped back to where his rifle hung on wooden pegs from the cabin wall.

"Hide!" cried Clarinda, "Hide in the loft!" Just then, a chicken wandered up close to the front door. Clarinda scooped it up with one smooth motion, threw it squawking into a trunk, and slammed the lid. "That's one chicken they won't git," she said. Their other surviving fowl, panicked by all the approaching humans, had begun to run distractedly about the yard, wings flapping. It was too late to run out and grab the bird, for the blue-bellies were approaching the yard. "You and the young 'un eat," admonished David, as he climbed the ladder into the cabin's loft.

Clarinda began shoveling dumplings into the child's mouth as fast as she could. Above her, David lay on the floor, rifle at the ready, peering down through a chink in the floor boards. He could see the raiding party now: Why, hell, they looked just as hungry and worn out as Lee's graycoats back at the front. He felt curiously detached as he watched them straggle by — few of them had as yet given the cabin more than a cursory glance — and was somewhat surprised that he felt no ill will toward them. Not if they just kept on marching and left his home, his child, and his 17-year-old girl-wife alone.

But just then, the fattened pig — whose meat was to have seen the wife and child through another iron winter — came trotting out into the dusty sunlight to see what all the commotion was about. Bacon on the hoof, the animal was instantly grabbed and carried along in the middle of the Unionist column, squealing piteously.

Whatever live-and-let-live feelings David had were swept away in that instant; those Yankee bastards had just yanked the food from his family's mouths. And what self-respecting man would, or could, just lie there and watch such a thing happening? Certainly no mountain man.

Silently, David dropped outside through the loft window, ammunition pouch in one hand, rifle in the other. Then he sprinted for the woods. He tracked the Federals for a half-mile or so until they reached a level, pleasantly shaded spot, where they fell out and prepared to devour their loot. David could see it all from where he lay. These Yankees were mountain boys, too, and they knew how to butcher and dress a hog. One man grasped the struggling animal, straddling it and pulling back its head to expose its throat; another man, in rolled-up sleeves, leaned down and stabbed it efficiently and smoothly.

While the raiders were making their barbecue fire, David chose his ground: a tall sycamore tree with stout, even branches, the kind of tree that invites boys to climb. From his perch, David could see the smoke rising from the chimney of his cabin.

Settled in, his weapon loaded and cocked, David did something he could do better than any hunter in the valley: He uttered the characteristic call of the wild turkey — one of the wariest and most delectable forms of game to be found in these hills. At the sound of that call, some of the raiders sat up from where they had been lying in the shade, ears pricked. One fellow, standing near the spitted pig, took up his rifle with a grin on his face and said, "That's turkey, boys! Now we'll have a feast!"

The Unionist moved through the woods like an experienced hunter, but not as experienced in tracking wild turkeys as David was in imitating them. David waited until the man was close enough for him to discern the individual hairs on his beard, then fired. The Minie ball pierced the raider in the breast, and he fell, groaning softly. His comrades released a whoop of enthusiasm, thinking the shot had been fired at the turkey, not at their comrade by a bushwhacker.

A few minutes went by, then another Federal stood up and was heard to say, "Ol' Joe must've missed." He, too, came into the woods to answer the turkey's call, which David now repeated in modulated form, so that the sound seemed to come from farther away than the first calls. This second turkey hunter almost tripped over the body of the dying man beneath David's tree. David shot him at a steep angle, the ball slicing open the man's belly. With his mouth open like the gasp of a dying fish, the man slid down into a sitting position, back against a tree, his eyes already cloudy with death.

The next creature that entered the glade was the panic-stricken hen that had run away from David's front yard earlier. There are only two kinds of chicken behavior: stupid and crazy, and this bird was clearly as crazy as an outhouse rat. Dazed and staggering, it pecked dementedly at insects around the feet of the two dead men.

After a few more minutes, a third Unionist raider rose from the barbecue fire, a worried expression on his face. Taking his weapon, he too entered the woods. But he advanced with stealth, every combat instinct fully mobilized, adrenalin pumping.

David and the Unionist saw each other simultaneously. Their eyes locked in shock; David recognized the man as the one who had stolen his hog. David squeezed the trigger, but the hammer of his rifle hung fire. He yanked and jerked on the steel crescent, but the weapon would not shoot.

No such problem affected the Yankee's weapon. If his shot hadn't killed David, the fall would have, for some of the sharp, breaking branches ripped him up pretty bad.

The sniper was just a boy; so was the raider who had killed him. He stood in the glade now, surrounded by three corpses, his carbine smoking and a stupefied expression on his face.

"See!" he cried to his comrades, as they came running to investigate the commotion. "Oh, see what I have done!" In his voice was astonishment, pride, remorse.

One of the first soldiers into the glade, an old campaigner, ignored the corpses — he'd seen plenty before — and instead made a lunge for the chicken. Then he realized that the deranged hen had its head buried in one of the bodies and was hungrily gobbling up the intestines. No one wanted to add that particular bird to the menu. One of the soldiers cursed the chicken and kicked it, sending it squawking back into the trees, minus some feathers. The barbecued hog, however, was delicious.

Shoot-out On Beech Mountain

Not all the Home Guard units were comic-opera jokes. Some were comprised of loyal and zealous Confederates, mountain men just as hard and tough and savvy as their opponents, and aggressively led. One of the most effective Home Guard units was the Watauga County company that operated out of Camp Mast, near Boone. Its commander was Major Harvey Bingham. His policy was to call "Halt!" one time and then open fire. After several people had been killed by his men while attempting to get to Federal lines in Tennessee, retaliation squads were formed among area Unionists, sometimes led by associates of Colonel George Kirk, sometimes by Yankee recruiting agents. One of their favorite rendezvous points was Blowing Rock, at that time a kind of no-man's land which might be in Unionist hands one week, rebel hands the next.

One such retaliation squad, thought to be made up of men from one of Kirk's regiments, stole into Watauga in the spring of 1864. They robbed several houses — even stealing the blankets from children's beds — shot one man who got in their way, stole six horses, evaded the patrols from Camp Mast, and passed back into Tennessee by way of Banner Elk.

Major Bingham re-retaliated by mounting a raid into Tennessee. He captured one wanted man and drove off a herd of Unionist cattle. On the return march, his men captured a Yankee scout, and just below Banner Elk they blocked the road in front of a woman of known Union sympathies and relieved her of a mule-load of tanned leather, as well as her horse — despite her pleas that her children had bare feet and her fields needed plowing. There was some disagreement about whether to rob her or not, but it was finally decided that this action was a fitting retaliation for the blankets stolen from the children of the Confederate sympathizers that Kirk's marauders had visited earlier. Bingham's men, now weighed down with loot and beef, left the woman weeping in the road and marched on. They captured another suspected guerrilla at Lewis Banner's farm, then went back to the Boone Road and camped for the night.

Meanwhile, an enterprising Unionist scout named Jim Hartley, heading up a 15-man force that had been guarding one of the Tennessee passes near Blowing Rock, had been informed by one of his spies that the Home Guard was out and doing mischief. He decided to teach Bingham a lesson. By nine o'clock that night, Hartley's force was in position to see Major Bingham's campfires, and Hartley had formulated a plan for an ambush.

He selected a site at Bowers Gap, about a mile east of the militia's encampment, where the road was dominated by steep slopes littered with fallen trees. Hartley, with ten men, would take positions above the road; five of his men would do the same below the road. It was an ideal setup for a crossfire. Hartley would be outnumbered, but his plan was simply to deliver one deadly volley, then melt back into the terrain.

That night, Hartley visited the cabin of a sympathetic woman named Polly Aldridge, whose land overlooked Bingham's camp-fires. Whether she and Hartley were friends, lovers, or cousins is unclear (a man named Aldridge was in Hartley's command, but he may have been some relation other than husband). Clearly, how-ever, Hartley and Polly Aldridge were close, because Hartley told her all about his tactical plans — not the sort of thing one confided, in those days, to a casual acquaintance.

Major Bingham, of course, knew this landscape just as well as Jim Hartley, and he may well have suspected the possibility of an ambush at that very point on the road; it was just the sort of place Bingham himself would have chosen. For whatever reasons, Bingham did not do the expected when he broke camp the next morning. Instead, he led his men up an older, rougher path, across the eastern slopes of Beech Mountain.

Polly Aldridge spotted this movement from her cabin and went out to warn Hartley. There was no time for her to take a safe, circuitous route through the woods — she just marched boldly down the road, straight through the Home Guard column, and disarmed any questions by asking the men, in the most neighborly manner possible, "Did you happen to see my spotted cow down here anywhere?" As soon as she had passed beyond sight of the marching men, she cut off at an angle, ran full speed to Hartley's position, and informed him of the changed situation. One of Hartley's men was an old bear hunter who knew of an alternate route that would enable them to catch up with Bingham.

After an exhausting double-time march, Hartley's bushwhackers caught up with Bingham's column and deployed in time to bring the rear guard under fire. Their first volley killed one man and one horse. Hartley's forward elements now turned around, alerted to the danger from their rear, and there ensued a running battle all across the face of a high timbered knob. The number of men wounded, if any, is not known, but there was only one more fatality: a 17-year-old boy named Elliot Bingham, who had joined his relative's militia company only two weeks earlier. With the boldness of youth, he charged Jim Hartley single-handedly, calling out that he was determined to shoot him. But Hartley, like many Unionist scouts, was packing state-of-the-art weaponry — in this case, an eight-shot Spencer repeating rifle — and he dropped young Bingham with a flurry of shots.

One incident during this skirmish illustrates vividly the bitterly fratricidal nature of the war in the mountains. Jim Hartley's own brother, Cal, was fighting with the Home Guard. At one point, the two men were close enough to converse. Jim Hartley yelled: "Ha, Cal! Come here and shake hands with your brother!" Cal's response was to fire a shot that tore a hole in Jim's coat sleeve.

The young Bingham boy died, in his mother's arms, the next day. Jim Hartley himself, after the fighting had died down, helped wrap the boy in a blanket. Shepherd Dugger, a local historian who collected details about the event, still mourned Elliot Bingham's death 60-odd years later, writing of him: "He had helped us hoe corn throughout the past summer, in fields where he could watch for the enemy through the day, and at night, when the home guard, on foot, would not [be caught] thirteen miles from their camp, he would come into our house and play the fiddle, which made him a favorite with me, and his death is still a great sorrow."[1]

That's all there was to the incident that became known locally as the Battle of Beech Mountain: two men and one horse killed in a backwoods brawl on a windswept knob that was worthless at the time, but is now some of the priciest ski resort property in Watauga County. Nobody bothered to write official reports about such encounters. What little we know of them is contained in the informal, obscure, and often maddeningly incomplete stories of local chroniclers who, writing as they were for a local audience only, often left out details of time, place, and personal relationships which were common knowledge among their intended readers, but whose absence causes bafflement and confusion among modern researchers. All that can be said with certainty is that a Battle of Beech Mountain happened somewhere, in almost every mountain county, at least two or three times a month during the last two years of the war.

After this skirmish, Major Bingham seems to have experienced a change of heart. He continued to be diligent in his defensive duties, but his marauding expeditions against regional Unionists tapered off and finally stopped altogether. "If I believed in special providence," Shepherd Dugger wrote at the conclusion of his account, "I would say that he escaped that death trap in Bowers Gap by Divine strategy, because from the end of the war to his death he was one of the loveliest men the mountains ever produced."[2]

THE QUILT OF VIOLENCE

The intermingling of Unionist and Confederate loyalties, the absence of peacetime moral constraints, and the total breakdown of conventional law and order — all played out against a backdrop of deepening hunger and desperation — made the mountain counties of North Carolina hazardous and nerve-wracking places to live during the Civil War. The contrast between these man-made conditions of anarchy and the immutable beauty of the landscape only made things seem worse.

The situation appears to have been more serious in the mountains of Kentucky, Tennessee, and Virginia than it was in North Carolina — at least until the summer of 1863. After that, the cyclical feuding, raiding, and counter-raiding became equally intolerable in every part of Appalachia. In Lee County, Virginia, there was a posse of Confederate vigilantes that shot or hung anyone who even looked like he might be a Union sympathizer. A similar partisan band in Kentucky perfected a gruesome technique of slow hanging which permitted them to beat their victims even as they strangled to death. By mid-1863, the deserters' routes through that part of the Appalachians were marked by buzzard-eaten corpses hanging from trees, for the inhabitants were too frightened of the vigilantes to cut down the bodies.

Once desertion became epidemic, and the social stigma that once clung to it disappeared, the pattern changed somewhat. Whenever it seemed safe to do so, the deserters stayed at or near their own homes, attempting to grow their crops and take care of their families in as normal a manner as possible. When regular troops or zealous militia units were in the neighborhood, they went back into the deep mountains and slept in improvised shelters, and even in caves.

Of course, their habits were known to the Confederates, and the result was an increasingly deadly game of cat-and-mouse. Sometimes, the deserters ambushed those who came into the woods after them. And when the authorities could not find the man they were looking for, they often took out their frustrations on his home, possessions, and family. A man might come down out of the mountains to find his cabin burned, his corn stolen, his cow slaughtered, his children hysterical with fear, and his wife beaten (or worse). One brutal tactic the Confederates used with some success was to round up all the deserters' families in a given area, imprison them in camps, feed them nothing but bread and water (if that much), and then spread the word that the detainees would be released, and fed, only when the heads of the families turned themselves in.

Sometimes rebel agents would pose as deserters, or as escaped Federal prisoners — always, of course, in a county where they were not personally known — and seek help from the local Unionists. These people, in turn, learned to devise tests and rites to help establish the authenticity of any stranger's plea for assistance. Failure to unearth a "plant" would sooner or later bring down a swooping, barn-burning raid from the local Confederate authorities.

Given different circumstances, the roles of hunter and hunted could be reversed, for the deserters and Unionists had their informers, too. As conditions became more chaotic and brutal, people became, quite understandably, very paranoid, and were increasingly prone to simply turn and kill anyone they thought was after them. After the fall of east Tennessee to the Yankees, North Carolina Unionists became much bolder, for it became progressively easier to get help from Federal raiders such as Colonel Kirk.

To North Carolina Unionists, men such as Kirk, Jim Hartley, Keith Blalock, and Daniel Ellis became almost like Robin Hood figures, the very stuff of mountain legends, for they mostly preyed upon "rich Confederates," and they were wild and colorful characters. In reality, of course, they were much rougher and infinitely more squalid than the ballads sung about them. To their enemies, and to those neutral people unfortunate enough to be nearby when the raiders needed food and horses, these men were nothing more than vicious desperados. They struck equally hard at genuine rebel sympathizers, at those who had been forced to declare Confederate loyalty whether they felt it or not, and at those poor souls who still clung to the illusion of neutrality.

As the conflict deepened and the very fabric of mountain society became scorched with bitterness, rationalizations were found for every sort of barbarity. The Unionists' farms and families had been victimized by Confederate outrages, and the men responsible had shown little inclination to make fine distinctions of allegiance or mitigating circumstance — so why shouldn't they retaliate in kind? "Few Rebel homes and farms could feel completely safe from these guerrilla forces, whose definition of Rebel was often broad: anyone who had something worth stealing."[1]

As their cause suffered setback after setback on distant battle-fields, rebel partisans in the mountains became, if anything, even more brutal. The most horrific figure was a guerrilla named Champ Ferguson who operated mostly in the Cumberland Mountains, with occasion forays into the Virginia range of the Appalachians. Ferguson was pushed over the edge by atrocities committed against his wife and child, but the Jack-the-Ripper style of his executions (he slew more than 100 men, many of them bound or wounded, and on one occasion sliced open a victim and stuffed corn cobs into the wounds) indicates that he was probably a raving psychopath. Some of the worst outrages took place just across the North Carolina-Tennessee border, in Carter and Johnson counties, where no fewer than four Confederate guerrilla bands operated from late 1863 to 1865. One such band, led by a man named Wicher, moved through Carter County in a November 1863 raid that left more than a dozen Unionists murdered. A year later, in the autumn of 1864, a grim figure named Bill Parker led a Confederate band through Johnson County, killing at least a dozen men, driving hundreds of women and children from their homes, and burning numerous farms. A band of Unionist partisans took after him, tracked him down, and killed him a few weeks later.

But when one of these men died, his place was instantly taken by others. The killing, the pillaging, went on as before; nothing seemed to change as the war entered its last stage, except for the degree and frequency of barbarous behavior on both sides.

Due to the fragmentary nature of the records dealing with the mountain war, a truly orderly and comprehensive account of this conflict cannot be written. But just as mountain quilters patiently stitch together scraps of colorful material to form a coherent design, so too, perhaps, can we glimpse an overall view of this random pattern of violence by examining individual incidents. Indeed, the nature of the historical documentation permits no other method.

It is rare to find an authentic first-person voice in the existing documentation. By the time regional historians began writing down some of the family stories, it was usually too late to hear them from the lips of the original participants. But it was not too late to hear them from the sons and daughters of those who lived through those harsh times. One such account, which conveys the flavor of the period with unusual vividness, was taken down verbatim in the 1930s from the lips of an old Mitchell County resident named Doc Hoppas, whose grandfather, a Unionist, had gone off to fight for the Federal Army:

> It makes me mad to even think of the Home Guard for the way they done my daddy and grandmammy. When the war come, they drove off all the men into one army or the other, and then after a while they said they had to have a Home Guard to take care of the women and children. Hit was a militia they raised up, but they didn't take care of 'em. They tuck from 'em. They was the hatefullest, most thievin' bunch there ever was. Down at Jim Bailey's they come in and found a little cloth in the loom Aunt Polly was weavin' to make John some clothes and they cut it out and took it with 'em. If a family hadn't a thing to depend on but their own cow's milk, they'd kill her for beef right in the yard and leave 'em with nothin'.
>
> My daddy was Allison Hoppas that was the son of Abe Hoppas that's buried with Yankee soldiers at Knoxville. His daddy was Adam Hoppas that come from across the water in Ireland. When he come in this country he married Old Link's daughter and heir-ed all the Grassy Creek land from him, but he lost it again puttin' up money for slaves.
>
> My grandmammy seen hard times after grandpap we with the Union. She was a Buchanan, sister to Lewis Buchanan that was my wife's grandpap. This here militia knowed Grandpap was with the Union but they suspicioned he was home layin' out. One day they come and got grandma and said they'd make her tell where he was so they could get him. She told them the truth — all she knowed. He was

gone to the war and she hadn't seen him no more'n they had. They wouldn't believe her and kept at her until finally they dragged her out to the fence and lifted up the top rail where it sits...and put her fingers in between and walked on the rails. They thought then she'd have to tell, but she couldn't tell what she didn't know. When she was give out, and they got tired of that, they picked on my daddy that was just a little boy. He had a great big pet dog and they figured he'd tell anything to keep them from hurting his dog. Of course he couldn't tell neither. Then they said if he wouldn't they'd make him chop up his dog with the axe. And that's what they done. He had to hack him to pieces on the door stone to the house. When I heard him tell that when I was growing up, I turned Republican right then, and I been so ever since. Two of us children was Democrats and two Republicans, so we just killed each other's votes regular, come election....[2]

Allegheny County was so beset by bushwhackers in mid-1863 that its Confederate citizens appealed to neighboring Surry County for the loan of some militia. About 100 men answered the call and crossed into Allegheny, via Thompson's Gap in the Blue Ridge Mountains. Four of them were dispatched to Duncan's Mill to obtain supplies of grain. They were accosted by a well-armed band of outliers. One of the militiamen was captured and was found a few days later, kneeling in front of a tree stump where the outliers had permitted him to say a prayer before shooting him. In retaliation, the Home Guard detachment went out and hung the first Unionist suspect they encountered — guilty or not, it was never known. He was a fellow named Levi Fender, who lived a couple of miles from present-day Sparta. Twice, units of regular Confederate troops swept this area, capturing dozens of deserters and hanging a number of known or alleged robbers. But as soon as the regular troops left the vicinity, the outrages began once more. In October 1864, just a mile northwest of Sparta, another detachment of Home Guard was ambushed by outliers hiding in a dense thicket of ivy; the Guard suffered one man killed and four wounded.

Near Andrews, in Cherokee County, in the early autumn of 1864, a trio of outliers was bushwhacked and killed by local people, and the surviving members of the band swore vengeance against the leading Confederates in the area. On October 6, 1864, they took it. Just before noon, some 27 outliers — described by one eyewitness as "swearing drunk" — appeared at the home of a

Confederate named William Walker. (What, if any, relation this man was to Colonel Walker of Thomas's Legion is not known.)

After smashing all of the Walkers' china and glassware, the guerrillas took Mr. Walker off at gunpoint. Mrs. Walker, a lady of great pluck (as the Victorians would have said), followed their trail on horseback for two days without rest before she lost them and was forced to turn back.

When she returned, she discovered that the same men, or some of their colleagues, had returned during her absence, stolen everything of value from the house -- including some clothes that had belonged to a deceased infant -- and then had urinated or defecated on all the feather beds.

Left in a state of utter destitution, Mrs. Walker nevertheless pulled herself together and managed to raise their five sons singlehandedly. But it was unspeakably hard just to continue living. "I wept for three years," she later wrote, "and two pillows were so stiffened by my tears that they crumbled to pieces."

Her husband was never seen again. His bones still lie in some gloomy backwoods hollow.

In Haywood County, just south of Madison, the very heartland of disaffection in western North Carolina, violence was common during the last two years of the war. Dozens of people died or were crippled for life, and at least seven murder victims are mentioned by name in regional chronicles, although it is impossible now to determine which were Unionist and which Confederate. Of course, ordinary crime continued throughout the war, too, as demonstrated by the case of an axe-murderer named Solomon Groomes, who was strung up on the outskirts of Waynesville in 1862 for slaying a neighbor who had paid the wrong kind of attention to his daughter.

In Transylvania County, an apparently harmless citizen named "Old Billy" Deaver was shot down at his own front door by Confederate bushwhackers who mistook him for his son — a captain in a regular army outfit who had been successful in rounding up deserters in the area. And down on the Henderson/Transylvania county line, a farmer named Sitton was robbed by a band of intruders who forced him to fix them a full dinner, and then shot him for his trouble after they had eaten.

In what is now Graham County, between Yellow Creek and the

Little Tennessee River, lived two of the best-known outlaws in that part of the mountains. Both were named Kirkland, and both were graced with colorful nicknames: "Bushwhacker" and "Turkey Trot." Though every bit as bloody-minded as most of their breed, these men at least had a reputation for remarkable bravery. They led at least a score of nuisance raids against Unionists in Tennessee. Late in the war, a Federal captain named Lyon took a partisan force into North Carolina for the express purpose of eliminating the Kirklands. Both Bushwhacker and Turkey Trot were captured and executed, along with at least four more Confederate guerrillas. Before returning to Tennessee, Lyon's detachment made a side trip to Robbinsville. There, they assassinated a Cherokee who, at some time or another, on one of Thomas's incursions into east Tennessee, had earned a bad name for himself. Tit for tat, eye for eye, the killing went on until (and even after) General Lee's surrender at Appomattox.

One Watauga County clan that was all but swept away in the currents of retaliatory violence was the family of old Levi Guy. He had three sons who were active Union men: Enoch, David, and Canada. Among their neighbors were the Stouts and the Potters. Thomas Stout, patriarch of the clan, also had three sons: John, Abram, and Daniel. These families lived in a close-knit community in the beautiful pastoral country near the head of the North Fork of the New River. From early 1863 onward, the Stout, Potter, and Guy boys were involved in numerous depredations against their pro-Confederate neighbors.

Those neighbors soon devised an alarm system. Each house kept a horn; if attacked, someone would blow a signal to alert everyone else in the area — a kind of 19th-century Community Watch program. One night in 1863, a party of Unionist bushwhackers — thought to be made up of the three Guy boys and some of their bunch — surrounded the house of Confederate sympathizer Paul Farthing, near Beaver Dam. After demanding his surrender, the raiding party opened fire on the house, sending ball after ball crashing through the windows and splintering the log walls. Mr. Farthing returned fire from inside, while his wife blew lustily on the signal horn from an upstairs window.

Several Confederate neighbors heard the signal, armed themselves, and came over shooting. They drove off the attackers, but not before one of their own people was killed. A short time later, some Home Guardsmen descended on the North Fork of the New River and arrested Levi Guy. Guy protested he had only done what any father would do — feed his own sons when they were under his roof. That was not good enough for the Home Guard. They took Guy — described by one early chronicler as "an old and inoffensive man" — and hanged him from a chestnut tree in his own yard.

Naturally, the lynching of Levi Guy sparked more violence. The Potters and the Stout boys bushwhacked a Confederate sympathizer named Isaac Wilson while he was plowing his fields. A few days later, some Home Guard vigilantes, men from Ashe County as well as Watauga, swooped down and captured Canada Guy and a teenaged boy named Jacob May, who just had the bad luck to be there at the time. Although Canada Guy probably had nothing to do with the Wilson shooting, and Jacob May was probably innocent of any killings, both men were summarily hanged.

In retaliation for this, Paul Farthing's house was attacked again, and once again the assailants were driven off by vigorous resistance. One of the attackers was severely wounded and probably died later — just who it was, no one ever learned, but there was a big trail of blood on the road leading away from the Farthing place.

This spiral of violence peaked in the spring of 1864, when the Home Guard arrested old man Thomas Stout, whose sons were suspected of committing the Isaac Wilson murder. The Home Guard promptly turned him over to some of Wilson's relatives. The relatives marched the old man off toward Morganton, telling onlookers that they intended to turn him over to Confederate authorities at Camp Vance. But, predictably, Thomas Stout was never seen alive again. Two months later, a cowherd found one of his shoes on Rich Mountain. A search party, returning later that day, found his remains covered with brush and leaves, just a few yards from the oak tree where he had been hanged. The noose was still there, swaying in the wind.

This long-running feud was climaxed by an act that seems tinged with madness. In retaliation for Thomas Stout's hanging, some of his friends and relatives laid an ambush for a party of men who had come to the North Fork to bring in the crops for some of Isaac

Wilson's relatives. That's all the men were doing — harvesting crops — but some of them were Home Guard, and some of them might have been involved in the Levi Guy hanging. The bush-whackers fired a deadly volley from the woods; two men were killed and two more severely wounded, including one man who went blind from his injuries. Whether from bullets or bad luck, it is said by local historians that every single man who participated in the hanging of Levi Guy "speedily came to a bad end."[3]

The Farthing clan continued to be embroiled in this kind of internecine combat right up to the end of the war. Near the end of 1864, nine men robbed and shot James Farthing at his home on the lower Watauga River. Then the same band of outliers rode a mile upstream and attacked Reuben Farthing's house, but were driven off when another relative opened fire with a pistol from an upstairs window. On their way out, the band stole a number of the Far-things' horses. An 18-man Home Guard patrol went out after this gang. They managed to recapture some of the horses near Cran-berry, but on the way home, about seven miles from Reuben Farthing's house, they were ambushed by still another party of bushwhackers and lost two men before they could break out of the trap.

A story related many years later by Shepherd Dugger is a typical one, too. Shepherd was a young boy during the war, and his father was away at the front. A family friend named Lee Foster, too old for either the draft or the Home Guard, stayed at the Dugger farm, both to help out with the chores and to offer some measure of protection to Mrs. Dugger and her children.

One night in 1864, a neighbor named Anthony Keller came knocking on the Dugger's front door. He greeted Foster warmly and asked if Foster would mind taking his rifle and coming out on an errand — a bear had killed one of his hogs, Keller said, and he needed some help tracking and killing the brute.

The truth of the matter was somewhat different. Keller, it seems, was a rebel deserter. That fact was widely known — indeed, Keller had boasted of it often, and had even come home wearing his gray uniform in full sight. A Confederate sympathizer had just informed Keller that two Federal scouts had slipped over the mountains from Tennessee and were spending the night with a Union man named

Aaron Von Cannon. Keller saw this as an opportunity to insure his own safety. What he planned to do was to enlist Lee Foster's aid in sneaking up on the Von Cannon house and capturing the three men inside. Keller would then turn them over to the Home Guard in exchange for their promise to leave him alone. When Foster got outside, and learned the true nature of the "errand," he also saw that Keller had brought two other armed men along to help.

It almost worked. Keller and Foster surprised and disarmed the two Federal scouts from Tennessee, but Von Cannon was a light sleeper. He bolted awake, grabbed his rifle, and "ran across the level yard and up the hill, in fifty yards, and took protection behind the high stump of a broken-off tree." Keller told Foster and another man to arrest Von Cannon while he covered the two Yankees. Foster and the other man, quite sensibly, refused — they weren't in anybody's army, and Foster was an old man besides. Keller cursed them for cowards and swore he would do it alone. Then he reck-lessly strode up the hill toward Von Cannon's position.

Von Cannon, it so happened, was one of the best marksmen in the county. At a range of 40 yards, he easily dropped his attacker with a shot that entered just above Keller's right eye. Keller lived for several hours, groaning and thrashing constantly, until he finally expired inside Von Cannon's cabin at ten o'clock the next morning.

By that time, young Shepherd Dugger had run over excitedly from the Dugger place. Sixty years later, he still had a vivid memory of visiting the site where Keller had fallen: "A puddle of his brains was left behind, which the chickens consumed, leaving a large blood spot on the grass. I saw him laid to rest in a little group of graves on the high bank of the creek below the highway on the lands now belonging to J.F. Hampton of Linville."[4]

The two Federal scouts were released and allowed to go on their way. Von Cannon was taken, after a fight, by a squad of mounted Home Guard, and was sent to the hellhole of the Salisbury prison camp. He escaped through a tunnel, made his way to Tennessee, and donned the blue uniform. He was with Champion's command on the day Camp Mast was taken, and after the war he went west to Colorado, where he lived out the remainder of his years.

In antebellum days, Flat Rock, in Henderson County, was the

most popular resort community in the whole mid-Atlantic region. Rich plantation owners from the South Carolina lowlands had discovered the place in the 1820s, and many of them had built vast, gracious estates there. Every summer, when the 'skeeters and humidity and malarial fevers became intolerable along the coast, the planters' entire families, with ample servants, would pack up and head for the cool, invigorating landscape around Flat Rock.

The area's most famous estate was probably Rock Hill, now better known perhaps as Connemara, built in 1838 by Christopher Gustavus Memminger. Memminger, a self-made millionaire whose childhood years were spent in an orphanage worthy of Dickens, was the first Confederate secretary of the treasury and a passionate secessionist. He retired from the Confederate cabinet in June 1864 and went to live year-round in the great house at Rock Hill. Henderson County was by then so overrun with bushwhackers and deserters that Memminger had to turn the mansion into a fortress. Sandbags were piled around the bottom-story windows and loopholes were cut into the walls at strategic locations, so that every angle of approach could be covered by rifles. When raiders were active in the area, the otherwise defenseless people of the area went to Rock Hill and stayed there until the danger had passed — not unlike vassals taking shelter in the lord's castle.

Memminger attempted, during the last chaotic weeks of the war, to get President Jefferson Davis to proclaim Rock Hill as the new capital of the Confederacy — claiming, with some justification, that with even a fragment of Lee's or Johnston's armies, the mountain heartland could be defended for years.

In fact, there are persistent local legends claiming that Davis had the Great Seal of the Confederacy sent to Rock Hill by trusted courier, and that it lies buried, even now, in a secret place on the slopes of Glassy Mountain. If so, Memminger took that secret to the grave with him in 1888.

Henderson County's Home Guard was unique in that it included a Negro soldier — in full Confederate uniform, openly bearing arms. The man's name was George Mills, and he had become a legend in those parts because of his steadfast loyalty to his master, the prominent William Bryson. Early in the war, Bryson had dispatched Mills, then 18 years old, to look after his son, Watt

Bryson. Mills reached Bryson's regiment, near Malvern Hill, in time to be directed to young Watt's fresh corpse. A Yankee sharpshooter had put a Minie ball through his head only hours before.

Mills — an unescorted Negro slave in the heart of the Confederacy — then undertook to bring his young master's body back to the mountains. After buying an airtight casket, Mills traveled by train, and then by wagon, for many long days. Eventually, after a three-day trek across the Smokies from the nearest railroad depot, in Greeneville, Tennessee, he kept his promise and brought the boy home. Mills served in the Home Guard loyally throughout the war, was given his freedom, acquired property, and raised a large family. He later became a regular and much-talked-about delegate to the national meetings of the Confederate Veterans, and he drew a pension for wartime service until his death in 1926.

The most famous bushwhacking incident in Henderson County annals took place at Beaumont, the mountain mansion of Andrew Johnstone, located at Flat Rock. Built from mica-flecked local granite, Beaumont was (and still is) a regal, imposing residence of three stories and 18 rooms. The entranceway is especially striking: vast granite steps flanked by a pair of bronze lions.

Johnstone was a fabulously wealthy rice planter from the Santee region of South Carolina — a fine specimen of the planter aristocracy, and a man famous for his culture and elegant manners. He had first visited the Flat Rock area, at the behest of some other planters who had fallen in love with the region, in the early 1830s. Soon thereafter, he purchased 800 acres of prime mountain land and began erecting his dream house, which was completed in 1839. In 1847, he was instrumental in the construction of the first seasonal resort hotel in the area, still standing today under the name Woodfields Inn.

When the war started, Johnstone moved his entire family to Beaumont and resolved to live there year-round, in what he hoped would be tranquility and safety. It was not to be. Rich, well known, an aristocrat to his fingertips, and the owner of many slaves, Johnstone was the very embodiment of the "high-toned" secessionist that the pro-Union outliers hated the most. And on June 10, 1864, he paid a high price for his lifestyle.

At about 2:30 in the afternoon, six armed men entered the house, declaring that they were Confederate scouts. They asked, rather brassily, for a meal. Johnstone was suspicious, but eventually invited them in and ordered the kitchen staff to prepare some more food. While that was being done, the six guests took their ease, flirted with the young ladies of the household, and even played the piano with them.

One member of the family who scented trouble was Elliot Johnstone, a boy of 11. He took the precaution of stepping into an alcove off the dining room, loading his pistol, and placing it where he could get to it in a hurry.

When the tense but ample meal was finished, Johnstone told the men they could have some extra bread to put in their knapsacks. The burly fellow who seemed to be their leader said he would be happy to accept the kind offer. Then all six men rose from the dining table. Their leader peered out into the hallway to see if anyone was lurking there, then turned to his men and said, "Are you ready? Draw!"

Four of the strangers drew on Johnstone, and two went after young Elliot. The boy lunged for his own weapon just as one of the marauders' pistol balls gouged splinters from the door post beside his head. The other men fired at his father, wounding him in the stomach. Johnstone was convulsed with agony, but crawled across the floor in a spreading pool of his own blood, emptying his pistol at them. His hand was too unsteady for his shots to find their mark, however, and after firing the fifth and final round from his revolver, he collapsed.

He was avenged by his son, whose shooting was remarkably steady under the circumstances. Elliot emptied his pistol at the gunmen and wounded four of them. One, seriously hit, fell sprawling on the front steps. Out of ammunition, Elliot sprang forward and wrested the smoking pistol from the wounded man's fist and kept firing at the fleeing assassins, scoring at least two more hits.

The gunman who had fallen on the steps died a lingering death, screaming and raving with delirium. Another man, hit at least twice by Elliot's fire, made it as far as the fence around the mill pond before he died. Another left a trail of blood as far as the French Broad turnpike, where all trace of him vanished. Rumors spoke of a third corpse found in the forest, although whether it was the man who had left the blood trail or yet another outlier, was not known. Two others were also wounded in the fray, but managed to make good their escape.

Andrew Johnstone died that same afternoon. After two hours of terrible agony, he seems to have been granted release from his pain, and it is said that he met his death awake, composed, and with the greatest dignity. The outlaw who died on the lawn was buried beneath a marker topped with a stone devil's head.

For decades, Beaumont was reported to be haunted by the ghosts of those who died there on that bloody afternoon; some say it still is. The identity of Johnstone's killers was never determined. No one in the area recognized any of the dead men, and no identification was found on their bodies. It was as if they had materialized out of the mountain fogs for the sole purpose of committing their grim deed.

The bloodstains on the dining room carpet at Beaumont can still be seen.

Haywood County had its own "Spring Laurel" section, an enclave of militant Unionists known as Big Creek. It was nestled up in the northwestern corner of the county, against the Tennessee line and the lower edge of Madison County. Contact between the Unionists there and the strong Unionist clans in Shelton Laurel was frequent. Colonel Kirk's men, and various freelance raiders as well, had often found shelter, manpower, and fresh intelligence at Big Creek. By the spring of 1865, there were a dozen families in the Big Creek area, most if not all of them actively Unionist. The local Home Guard commander, Captain Robert Teague, had played cat-and-mouse with local deserters and had been fired on numerous times by snipers thought to have come to Big Creek.

During the closing weeks of the war, Teague succeeded in capturing three of these outliers: George and Anderson Grooms, and a fellow named Caldwell. Anderson Grooms was well known in those parts as a fiddler, and in happier antebellum days he had been much in demand at weddings and other social events. Figuring he was going to jail, Grooms asked if he could bring along his violin. Teague said he could. Roped together, the three captives were forced to march over Sterling Gap to the Chattaloochie side of Sterling Mountain, a distance of about eight miles.

Teague halted the party in deep forest. It was a cool spring morning, the fog still lingering like scarves of soft gray wool around the crisp evergreen-scented shadows in the creeks and hollows. All around, the mountains loomed in perfect stillness, mottled by passing galleons of clouds; hawks circled in the high clear light above.

"Play something for us, fiddler," commanded Captain Teague.

Anderson Grooms took out his instrument and tucked it beneath his chin. In moments, the sad, minor-key melody of "Bonaparte's Retreat" — Grooms's favorite song — filled the gloom beneath the trees. Everyone in the party listened, spellbound; Grooms surpassed himself that day, infusing the tune with such indescribable longing that even his captors were moved.

But not enough to bother marching their prisoners any farther. As soon as Grooms had finished his tune, all three men were lined up and shot. It is said that Grooms clutched his violin to his breast as he faced the muzzles of the firing squad. The men were left where they fell. Their kin from Big Creek came out at dusk and loaded the bodies into a sled drawn by an ox.

Even today, "Bonaparte's Retreat" is known in that part of the mountains as "The Grooms Tune."

ESCAPES
AND ENCOUNTERS

Some of the most vivid accounts of wartime conditions in the mountains came not from the native inhabitants, but from outsiders — Yankees, in fact — who came to the region with fresh attitudes, virgin eyes, and few ideological axes to grind. To them, the mountain region was as colorful, exotic, and dangerous as the bandit realms of Corsica. They were escaped Federal prisoners of war who made their way west in hopes of finding guides who would convey them to friendly lines. It was a sort of "underground railroad," but never as precisely defined as the similar system, long in place even before the war, which aided escaped slaves in other parts of the state. Several of the men who made this arduous journey wrote book-length accounts of their adventures in the mountains — especially valuable not only for their detail, but also for their freshness of viewpoint.

In the autumn of 1864, J.V. Hadley of Indiana and several companions, all officers, escaped from the infamous prison camp at Andersonville, Georgia, and made their way north toward the rumored sanctuary of western North Carolina. There — so said the prison grapevine — a fugitive Yankee should have little trouble finding shelter, food, and a guide to convey him to Federal lines in Tennessee.

The first leg of the journey, through rural Georgia and South Carolina, was arduous but relatively safe. To obtain food and shelter, all the escapees had to do was find an isolated slave cabin. The slaves were usually eager to help Yankees and often were able to snitch a first-rate meal from the "big house" for the hidden men. Just north of Greenville, South Carolina, however, Hadley's party survived their first narrow escape: Two Home Guard horsemen passed close by while they lay in a cornfield, as motionless as logs. After this experience, Hadley recorded, "We longed for the loyal whites of North Carolina, of whom we had heard so much all along the way. We felt that as soon as we placed South Carolina at our backs, our work would be almost done — that we would be nearly home."[1]

Indeed, the closer the escapees got to the North Carolina line, the more they heard about how sympathetic the white mountaineers would be, and about how widespread were the Unionist sentiments in the western counties. It was natural, therefore, that they experienced a sensation almost of euphoria on the November day they crossed into the Old North State, at a point about 60 miles from Asheville.

The first North Carolinian they encountered was a Negro who offered to hide them in a wagon full of corn shucks he was supposed to take to the city. The Tennessee Yankees, this black man claimed, were only 20 miles farther on. The four-man party of escapees debated whether to take the man up on his offer. Heated words were exchanged, then blows; the fistfight was apparently won by the men who felt the offer was too good to be true. In the end, no one went with the wagon. It was probably a wise decision, in view of the fact that there were no Yankee formations anywhere near Asheville at that time, and if the escaped prisoners had been caught with an unattended slave, their chances of being summarily executed would have been significantly increased.

The next night, they were chased over road and field by a large pack of ferocious dogs, which they finally eluded by wading half a mile through an ice-cold stream. Negro cabins were getting scarce, and they were already at the foot of the Blue Ridge Mountains. They were beginning to discover that the situation in western North Carolina was not quite as friendly as rumor had painted it. "Somehow or other, the 'good Union people' we had heard so much were always a little ahead."

After escaping the dogs, Hadley's party reached a small settlement on the road to Hendersonville which included one "rich-looking" house with some slave huts in the back. They spent the entire day hiding in the woods a quarter-mile away, and then approached the Negro cabins under cover of darkness. The first black man they encountered told them that the whole countryside

was aroused, because four Yankee fugitives had been spotted and
chased last night by somebody's hunting dogs. The young man
who told them this seemed rather slow-witted, but he did have a
brother named Reuben, who was, even at that moment, standing
guard at a nearby crossroads. Reuben's owner, a Home Guard
officer, had given him a musket and told him to watch for the
escaped Yankees. He would inform Reuben about their situation,
the dull-witted brother promised, and Reuben would come talk to
them as soon as he got off guard duty.

Would he indeed, or would he bring a company of local Confederates? Hadley and his comrades didn't feel too secure with this
arrangement, but since they were down to a handful of shelled corn
for food, and since they desperately needed reliable intelligence
about the route ahead, they had no choice but to wait for Reuben.

According to Hadley's account, Reuben proved to be a "mon-
strously large" man of about 40, a "laugh-and-grow-fat sort of
darky," who found it vastly amusing to be shaking hands with the
very fugitives he was supposed to be capturing. When one of the
escapees rather testily asked him what was so funny, Reuben burst
into renewed spasms of merriment and replied, "Why, you see, ol'
Massa — ha, ha, ha! — old Massa...has me tryin' to kotch you
gemmen, for two hours — ha, ha, ha! — why, sah, I'd radder kotch
my grandmother runnin' from de debbil!"

When quizzed about the threat posed by "ol' Massa's" Home
Guard company, Reuben snorted derisively and told Hadley that if
the four Yankee gentlemen attacked that company with nothing but
"a big rock" they would easily conquer the field. Hadley felt
relieved, but they were not about to attack, with rocks, a party of
men equipped with firearms. Reuben advised them against traveling by night, since that was when Confederate vigilance was the
greatest. He offered to show them a hiding place "that would
puzzle our shadows to find us."

After hiding them, Reuben brought them some meager but
welcomed food: sweet potatoes, cabbage, a little bread. Their route
from here on would be dangerous, he explained. It was six miles to
the gap that would take them through the Blue Ridge, and another
eight miles to Flat Rock, where there was an active Confederate
garrison whose main purpose was to apprehend escaped Yankees.

But that was down the road a ways. Closer to hand, it would be even trickier, for the road to the gap ran directly in front of the local Home Guard commander's house, just half a mile from their hiding place, and there was no alternate route. If they tried to march over the mountains, they would just get lost, and hunger would drive them to give themselves up. Reuben was sorry, but there was precious little food on the place just then, and he was unable to give them any additional supplies to put in their knapsacks.

At ten o'clock that night, as Hadley and his three companions were sneaking quietly past the Home Guard officer's house, they encountered a man on the road, not ten feet from where they were walking. He seemed even more frightened of them than they were of him, and sidled past without threatening them, stammering only, "W-who a-a-are y-you?" The leader of Hadley's party raised his walking stick and responded in a sepulchral tone of voice, "*Mooove oonnn.*" The stranger broke into a run and vanished through the Home Guard commander's front door.

Six miles farther, at Green River Gap, they almost walked over a sentry who was dozing by his campfire, a rifle with fixed bayonet across his knees. Hadley's party got as close to the river as they dared, wary of loose rocks with every step they took, and inched past the man less than 100 feet from where he sat, his back to the river. He did not waken.

Keeping off the road wherever the terrain made it feasible, the escapees drew close to Hendersonville, where Reuben had told them they might find some sympathetic Negroes. Unfortunately, not five minutes after they judged it safe to return to the road, they encountered not friendly slaves but four well-armed Confederates. The escapees had acquired some bits and pieces of Confederate clothing, and attempted to pass themselves off as rebel soldiers on furlough from a North Carolina regiment posted to Charleston. After a few minutes of nervous questions and answers, the leader of the Home Guard detachment drew his sword and announced that he intended to keep the four men until their story could be checked out. There seemed no alternative but to make a run for it, which Hadley and his three friends did, diving into the laurel thickets beside the road and heading straight up Glassy Mountain.

Their spirits, and their stamina, were dwindling fast. Now the whole of Henderson County would know of their presence, and they had no idea, since leaving the road, where the village even was. They had no food except for a few grains of shelled corn rattling in their knapsacks. They were crawling up a mountain in November, at least a thousand feet up, at four o'clock in the morning. The wind was coming at them from the northeast in gale-force gusts. An hour later, torrents of freezing rain lashed them. By seven o'clock in the morning, it was snowing. "It was a blue time," Hadley remembered:

> ...the merciless wind howled and swayed the stunted trees and lodged the driven snow in crusts on our sides and in our hair. Then Goode and Baker said they must have a fire or perish. Chisman and I said they could not have a fire, for the smoke would betray us. They gathered sticks and logs to the side of a cliff and would have fired them had we not prevented it by force. They piteously begged for fire, but we sternly refused them...in the extremity of human endurance there is neither conscience nor compassion; so we felt and so we acted.[2]

By early afternoon, the weather moderated. Wrapped in their tattered blankets, the fugitives slept for a few hours under wan autumn sunlight, their backs against a cliff. Sleep revived their spirits, but the food situation — "the keen tooth of hunger," as Hadley called it — was critical. Late in the afternoon, they spied cultivated land — a cabbage patch. Not seeing any houses nearby, they felt driven to take a chance. One of the party, an Irishman named Goode, crept down into the field and was in the process of hacking off the first cabbage when he was suddenly hailed by a white woman standing at the opposite end of the field. Goode scampered away, but the lone woman was soon joined by three others, and all of them kept calling out to him -- in a friendly and inviting manner.

There was a panic among the refugees as the four women came closer to their hiding place. But a hasty discussion of their alternatives made a conversation with the ladies appear to be their best option; after all, four women alone could not capture them, but could only run off and tell of their presence — which was already known, in any case. Here was a perfect opportunity, it seemed, to test the reality of all those rumors about Unionist loyalty in the mountains. Hadley himself was deputized to start the conversation. As the women approached, he put on a smile and stepped out into the open.

"Halloo, girls! Don't be frightened — we won't hurt you."

"Who are you?" the women asked.

"We are soldiers," Hadley replied.

"What kind of soldiers?"

"Confederate, of course."

"Well, you ought to be engaged in better business," admonished one of the women.

"What business can we be at?" asked Hadley.

"Picking huckleberries."

"Why, I believe you're a Yankee," said Hadley.

"No, I ain't," replied a woman, "but I'm no Secesh [secessionist]."

"How's that?" Hadley asked. "Not a Yankee and not a Secesh? What are you?"

"I believe in tendin' to my own business and lettin' other people's alone," she said.

"But would you have the Yankees overrun the South, steal our Negroes, and rob us of our property?"

"Yes," the woman replied, "if you don't quit this fightin' and killin'. You all fetched on this war. For a few niggers you've driven this country to war and force men into the army to fight for you who don't want to go, and you've got the whole country in such a plight that there's nothin' goin' on but huntin' and killin', huntin' and killin', all the time."

The four fugitives looked at each other as if to say: Well, if we're ever going to trust anybody, here they are. Hadley then related a true account of their adventures and asked for any assistance the women might give them with regard to food, shelter, and obtaining the services of a guide to Knoxville. The youngest of the women, a 16-year-old girl named Alice, ran to their cabin and procured some buttered cornbread — sheer ambrosia to the fugitives' palates — and a couple of big, juicy apples.

The women were named Hollingsworth. There were five sisters in the family, and one brother; the latter had deserted for 18

months, but had grown tired of the outlier life and was now back in
the ranks, taking his chances in the trenches outside Petersburg in
Virginia. Their mother and father were old and somewhat feeble.
The entire family worked as tenant farmers for Charles G. Memminger, former Confederate secretary of the treasury, whose mansion
stood only a mile away.

The women hid Hadley and his men inside a farm building,
where they were able to make soft, warm beds in a big pile of corn
shuckings. Food was brought to them regularly, and when the coast
was clear they were even permitted to sleep in the house, in real
beds. With their basic survival taken care of, the escapees' thoughts
naturally returned to the matter of finding a guide. There was a band
of outliers living in the mountains nearby, the women told them,
men who had survived two years of being hunted. They were a
fairly desperate bunch, rough and ruthless and well-armed, but they
might be just the right people to serve as guides, if they were
willing. The two older Hollingsworth ladies volunteered to seek out
the sister of the outlaw band's chieftain, a local man named Jack
Vance, and find out what the prospects were of engaging his services.

This took longer to arrange than Hadley would have wished, for
the band was gone off to the Georgia part of the mountains on a raid
and would not be back for a week. In the meantime, Hadley and his
comrades were made comfortable in every respect, even enjoying a
certain amount of (presumably) chaste flirtation with the five young
women. Hadley could think of no way to repay this family except
by writing a note, addressed "To any Federal soldiers who may
come this way," praising the family's loyalty to the Union, describing their services, and commending them to the protection of
whatever officer first read the document. Each of the fugitives
signed it with his name, rank, and unit.

Finally, the outlier's sister, whom Hadley called Eliza Vance,
came and told them that her brother was back in the vicinity, and
she was ready to take them to him. After a six-mile hike through the
wilderness, Eliza began to shout: "Halloo Jack!"

Two large men, carrying guns, appeared suddenly in the depths of
the foliage. One of them stepped forward a little ways.

"What're you doing here, Eliza?" he asked.

"You know," said Eliza. "We've brought the Yankees over from the Hollingsworth's."

"How do you know they're Yankees?"

"Why, they say they are."

"They are liars," said the suspicious outlier. "They are nothing but damned spies, and we'll feed 'em to the bears on this very mountain." Gesturing to the fugitives, Jack Vance ordered, "You! Come here!" As they hesitantly shuffled forward, he cocked his piece and leveled it at them. "Who are you and what are you doing here?"

Hadley told him the truth: that they were four Federal officers, recently escaped from the prison camp at Andersonville, looking for a guide to take them into Tennessee.

When Hadley had finished, Jack Vance snarled, "Every word you utter is a lie."

But the fact that none of the four strangers was armed seemed to mollify the bandit just a trifle. He conferred with his brother and sidekick, Lem Vance, and then announced, "Well, we feel our safest course would be to put you to sleep, but we have decided to try you a little further." The fugitives were then made to swear on the barrel of Jack's rifle that they were indeed what they claimed. Afterward, Lem stepped forward and handed them a canteen from which all six men took a drink, ritualistically. Hadley thought later that the canteen had held whiskey, but he was really too nervous at the time to take note of it. "We were more concerned about the contents of the muskets than of the canteen."

Then the haggling commenced. When and if the outliers became convinced that Hadley and his companions were what they purported to be, a trip to Knoxville might be possible. The price would be $400 in gold, payable on arrival. The escapees agreed; $400 or $4 million — what difference did it make at that point?

They agreed to meet the outliers the next morning at a place called the Devil's Boot. Jack's mother would bring them breakfast there. This old lady, when she appeared in the morning, proved to be as talkative and as neighborly as her son had been taciturn and threatening. From the mother, Hadley learned a lot about the son and his band. They had been on the run for two years, and not once in all that time had they slept in a bed or eaten at a table. She seemed to be as proud of her sons, and of the other eight men in the gang, as she would have been were he a decorated hero in a regular army. The fact that his actions had caused a reward to be put on his head, and might one day also cause a noose to be put around it, seemed not to faze her at all. Anybody who had sympathy for the South deserved what they got, she insisted. Any lawlessness was justified, if directed against the hated "Secesh," especially the right to plunder them:

> Since the Confederates had driven them from their home-pursuits, they would turn the war to their advantage, and make Rebels and Rebel sympathizers pay for their time. She and they expressed inveterate hate for all Rebels, and, right or wrong, scrupulously regarded everyone a Rebel who had any valuables or lived in a painted house.[3]

There was a big cave deep in the mountains where Jack and his men stashed their loot and slept during inclement weather. They had a vast amount of silverware, Hadley noticed. In fact, the cave was illuminated by dozens of costly silver candelabra, now tarnished black, which had once cast their glow over the dining rooms of the South Carolina gentry's summer mansions. In addition, there were chests of money and jewelry, an unabridged dictionary, a couple of big family Bibles, and — as the satisfaction of some bizarre whim or other — a life-size oil painting of George Washington. It must have cost the original owner a considerable sum, but, when Hadley viewed it, the painting was hopelessly encrusted with mold.

Hadley's detailed descriptions of Vance and some of his men offer a unique glimpse of the mountain guerrilla:

> If the reader should be curious to know the general appearance of these men, I would say, first fix in your mind an untutored man, thirty-five years old, six feet high, weight one hundred and eighty pounds, in a suit of coarse, homemade clothes; his skin dark, but not as dark as his long hair that grew down almost to his eyes, nor as dark as his beard that covered most of his face; his black eyes set deep in his head, under a pair of heavy, closely knitted brows, and, though seldom fixed directly at you, his glare withering when it did come. Imagine his wool hat full of holes, his Springfield rifle, bright as steel

can be, lying across his left arm, with his right hand on the hammer and trigger, and it will do for a picture of Jack Vance.[4]

Vance's henchmen were, if anything, more colorful. One of them wore a striped turban decorated with eagle feathers, and another was quite outrageous: his fur coat was made from the hide of an adult bear, tailored so that the sleeves were formed from the beast's forelegs. The paws hung down over the man's hands, terminating in sets of massive claws. The head and face of the animal had been treated so that, if the owner desired, he could pull them over his head as a kind of cowl. The bearskin wasn't this fellow's only affectation, either. Around his neck, gathered into a great bow-knot in front, was the spotted skin of a rattlesnake.

As anxious as Hadley and his friends were to get underway for Knoxville, they had to wait on the outlaws' pleasure, and Vance had no intention of leaving his home turf until he had robbed a local Confederate of a $102 cache of silver the man was supposed to be hiding on his land. The outlaws were biding their time until this gentleman returned from business elsewhere; when he did, they would rob him. Then, and only then, would they be willing to start for Knoxville.

Hadley remonstrated with Jack, offering to add another $102 to the promised fee awaiting him in Knoxville, if only they could get started. "No, sir," growled Jack, "We're not goin' to leave these parts till I git that 102 dollars from that damned Rebel, and if you-ens is in a hurry, and don't want to wait till we-ens is ready, why jist put out any time you please, and let this be the last of it."

The raid did not go quite as planned. The Confederate escaped after Vance's men prematurely fired a volley into his house. The man's wife, though roughed up and threatened by the outliers, refused to tell them anything. As long as they were there, however, Vance and his boys decided to treat themselves to a little recreation:

> Having failed to get the money, they were determined they would not fail in some barbarous fun; so they brought the Negroes, whom they had taken from under the bed, into the sitting room, in presence of the ladies [of the house], and made one pat and the other dance for their amusement. They goaded them on for a straight hour, without one

> moment's cessation, and when, from exhaustion, they would moderate their activity a little, the heartless bystanders would bring down their guns and command them to "go into it, or we'll shoot you on the spot." Thus they kept them at it till they both sank to the floor.
> Tired of this, they plundered the bureaus and the cupboard and retired.[5]

News of this attack stirred up the region like a stick poked into a ant hill. The Flat Rock detachment of regulars went into the field, together with all the available Home Guard in the vicinity. This, in turn, had the effect of forcing Jack to get moving on the Knoxville trip.

When they finally did set out, the combined party experienced great difficulty crossing the French Broad River. Part of the bridge was down, and they had to cross the gap by clinging to a floating log and going into the water one at a time. The march was resumed, on the far bank, in soaking-wet clothes.

Some miles farther along, however, they found shelter at Jack Vance's brother-in-law's cabin. Here, Hadley found the essence of backwoods isolation. The nearest neighbor was six miles away, and there were so many children, arrayed in ages from one to 21, on pallets that almost filled the one-room cabin, that Hadley likened the interior to "a juvenile asylum." There was a fairly good supply of food, including a wild hog that one of Jack's boys managed to shoot out in the forest. In spite of his dislike for the uncouth Jack, and in spite of the Dickensian sleeping arrangements and general scratch-ankle squalor of the place, Hadley was impressed by the frontier hospitality that was extended to them by this family:

> The entire table-service consisted of six plates, two of them tin; three knives worn to a point; two forks with broken prongs, and one large antediluvian dish. No cloth, no chairs, but stools; no cups and saucers, but as substitutes for the latter the [ersatz] coffee was served in small round gourds, neatly dressed. There were no apologies, no embarrassment, no complaint about hard times. The cheery host and hostess went merrily chatting about the table, cutting and helping plates with that air of natural, easy, generous welcome that made their simple breakfast refresh their guests in a degree not found at the tables of the formal rich.[6]

Not long before sunset the following day, the party reached the

foot of towering Mount Pisgah. A tall column of smoke, indicating
more than just an isolated campfire, was seen rising from the
summit. Reconnaissance by the outliers revealed its origin: A
patrol of Cherokees from Thomas's Legion was dug into the
mountain top, on guard against just the sort of thing the fugitives
were trying to do. It was clear to Hadley that, as tough and ornery
as Jack Vance and his cut-throats might be, the prospect of tangling
with the Indians was enough to put the fear of God into them. After
a 20-minute discussion among the outlaws, Jack told Hadley that
this was the end of the line; there was no good alternate route, and
no way in Hell they were going to get past that Indian outpost. The
fugitives offered more money. Jack made a counter offer, telling
them they could return and stay with the gang until spring, when
they would try again. That prospect did not hold the slightest
appeal for the Yankees — in some ways, it promised even greater
danger than forging ahead. When further arguments and passionate
entreaties proved useless, the outlier band just turned around and
headed for home, leaving the four escapees stranded in the middle
of enemy territory, with no food, money, or maps.

Then one of Hadley's party spotted a strip of cultivated valley
land and a few threads of chimney smoke, at a distance of six or
seven miles from where they stood. Whoever lived down there, that
tiny settlement seemed to offer the only hope of procuring a new
guide. So down they went, sliding through the tangles of laurel,
into thickening shadows at the base of Pisgah's great darkening
bulk.

If the village had a name, Hadley never learned it. Apparently it
was called after the stream that ran through the place: South
Hominy Creek. The first dwelling they came to was "a rude little
cabin, quiet as a tomb." A stooped and deeply wrinkled old man
was engaged in his business near the front door. One of Hadley's
party had acquired almost a complete Confederate uniform by this
time, and he offered to step out and accost the old gent, hoping for
enough conversation to enable the refugees to read the political
coloration of the little settlement. The approach to the old man —
whom they soon learned to call "Uncle Jimmy," just like everyone
else in the neighborhood — was direct; they had nothing to lose at
this point.

"Grandpa, are you a rebel or a Union man?"

"What, sir?" croaked the old mountaineer, coming upright to the accompaniment of popping joints.

"I want to know whether you are a rebel or a Union man."

"What do you want to know that for?"

"Oh, I have heard you called both, and, as I was passing, I just thought I would ask you."

"Well, sir, if it will do you any good to know, I will tell you that I was born under the old Government, I have lived eighty-two years under it, and I am an old man now, and I want no better to die under. If this is not enough, I will add further, if you are a rebel soldier, you will relieve me by passing on."[7]

Ironically, although the escapees were now convinced that Uncle Jimmy was a staunch Unionist, they had a hard time convincing Uncle Jimmy that they were Union men, too. The timing of their appearance could not have been worse. Earlier that month, two strangers had appeared, very much as Hadley and his men were doing, and had passed themselves off as rebel deserters. They had begged hospitality and protection, and the community had extended both. The two men stayed for a week and a half, long enough to learn who was who in the local resistance. Then, one morning, they vanished, without a kind word to any of their hosts. Earlier on this very same day, at the time Hadley's party was making its way through the thickets on the other flank of Mount Pisgah, the two "deserters" had reappeared at the head of a column of Confederate militia. There had been a fierce gun battle only five or six hours before Hadley and his companions showed up at Uncle Jimmy's cabin; although nobody was killed, a number of boys on both sides had been badly wounded before the Home Guard withdrew. The village was understandably on edge, and it took a lot of arguing for the escapees to persuade Uncle Jimmy that they were authentic. At first he was stubborn, insisting that they just move on and find another village to molest. He was also rather spunky in his defiance, saying at one point, "I am too old to be punished and too smart to be deceived."

Finally, one of Hadley's party dug his officer's commission out of his pocket and showed it to the old man. Fortunately, Uncle Jimmy could read, and after he'd puzzled out the letters and their import, he thawed considerably toward the strangers.

Yes, he admitted, there was one man — "one of the boys" — who had made the trip to Knoxville on at least two prior occasions; he might be willing to help them. His name was Henry Davis, known to the locals as Kim. In the morning, Uncle Jimmy would take them to meet him, high up in the mountains.

When Hadley and his comrades observed Uncle Jimmy at this first meeting, he had seemed old, slow, quite frail, and brittle. The next morning, to Hadley's astonishment, the old mountaineer's fragility vanished once he got up into the high country. "Though he swayed like an old tree loose at the roots, he had a wonderful capacity for getting over space. I do not think he walked a step the whole distance; it was a half-run all the way. With his body bent forward at an angle of forty-five degrees, he went as rapidly through the mountains as a trained youth, stopping only now and then to look or listen, with an upturned ear."

"Kim" Davis made a totally different impression than Jack Vance. He seemed intelligent, his moral sensibilities unblunted by his months as an outlier, and his attitude toward the four strangers was considerably more friendly. It was also cautious, of course, and he, too, questioned them at length, and with a subtlety that impressed Hadley: "Their procedure was eminently cunning and sagacious, and it is hard to believe that men could have told them a falsehood and escaped discovery." When Davis had satisfied himself that the men were indeed Federal officers and not enemy agents, he explained his own motives for wanting to help them. And he did not ask for money:

> Yes sir; I have made up my mind that I would like to go North, if I had any assurance of getting through the Northern army into the country, where I could throw away my gun. I am tired of this war, this man-killing, out of the army as well as in the army. I have but little stake in the contest anyhow; I have no negroes to save, nor much property to protect, and I'm so tired of hunting men's lives and hiding to save my own that I don't want to go into either army at this date. Your offer [of money] is most liberal, but if I go with you it will be as a companion, and not as a servant. This is the only condition to be considered: that you guarantee to me that when I have conducted you to Knoxville, you will conduct me north of the Ohio River, and protect me from the army.[9]

As before, however, there would be a delay. Davis told Hadley and his friends that he needed a week to attend to some personal business in Haywood County. Actually, he didn't — he was just using the week to further test the four strangers. While Davis was out of sight, they were closely but unobtrusively watched by his friends. Evidently, their reports were favorable, for when Davis reappeared, he freely confessed the ruse, and vowed to keep his word.

He did. It took a week of brutally hard trekking for the entire party to reach the outskirts of Knoxville, which they finally did on December 9, 1864, but it was a cooperative effort, utterly without the tension of the time the fugitives had spent with Vance and his brigands. Davis proved to be a superb guide. Not once did they encounter terrain that was impassable, nor did they encounter a single Confederate patrol. Hadley's description of the day they reached Federal lines is worth quoting in full:

> ...There was the park of army-wagons. There was the tented field. There were Federal soldiers on parade. We stood a moment in silence, and looked congratulations at each other. We did not fall down and give up the ghost; we did not go into ecstasies. We did not hug each other; we simply felt good and went on.[10]

Kim Davis eventually settled in Hadley's home state of Indiana. He went back to North Carolina in September 1865 to visit his parents, and while there he ran into one of the "deserters" who had infiltrated the South Hominy Creek settlement and betrayed the people who had taken them in. The man approached him with his hand stuck out and a smile on his face, saying, "Hello, Davis! The war's over! How are you?" In reply, Davis pulled out his revolver and began shooting. Fortunately, he missed, and Davis spent only three months in jail for assault, rather than a considerably longer term for manslaughter. After serving his sentence, he said goodbye to his family, returned to Indiana, and settled there for good.

J.V. Hadley himself returned to the Carolina mountains many years later, in 1897, irresistibly drawn back to the scene of his youthful adventure. He found all five of the Hollingsworth sisters still alive, happily married, and surrounded by large families. Jack Vance had faded into backwoods obscurity, but his brother, Lem, was pulling a life sentence in the state penitentiary for murder. Hadley was not surprised.

A fairly large number of men, several hundred in all, escaped from the infamous confines of the Salisbury prison camp in North Carolina and made the same trek to Tennessee. The grapevine about the "underground railway" was especially active in Salisbury — the city was, after all, in the foothills, close to the mountain country, and there was considerable Union sentiment among not only the townspeople, but also among some of the prison staff as well, including both guards and officers. Inside the walls, it was possible to obtain the names, addresses, and passwords of area Unionists who made it their business to assist escapees.

A dramatic account of travel on the underground route from Salisbury was published, only months after the war, by Albert D. Richardson, a correspondent for the *New York Tribune* whose noncombatant status had not prevented him from being captured and treated like any other prisoner of war.

With the help of purloined documents, Richardson and several companions bluffed their way out of the Salisbury prison camp on December 18, 1864. They were aided in their escape, and given directions to friendly hosts in the Salisbury area, by a Confederate lieutenant named John Welborn, who was a member of the secret Unionist movement known as the Heroes of America (see Volume I).

For the first 50 miles of their odyssey, they followed the track of the Western Carolina Railroad from Salisbury to Statesville. Then they turned northwest, aiming for Wilkes County; the area around Wilkesboro had such a reputation as a Unionist stronghold that it was known by the nickname "Ol' United States." This first leg of the journey was a route well known among the prisoners; it was also, of course, well known by the guards and to the militia detachments that patrolled the area, looking for escapees. Inside one of the "safe houses," the fugitives were able to relax in some degree of comfort. If nightfall caught them in the open, their best course was to make contact with the likeliest-looking Negroes they could find. There might be little the slaves could do other than provide a chunk of cornbread and a bed of straw, but not once in any escapee's account is there an instance of a slave actually turning a refugee over to the Home Guard.

Beyond Statesville, however, things started to get dicey. With every westward mile, there were fewer and fewer Negroes. Richardson and his party were more fortunate than most, because one of the escapees had contrived to steal a complete Confederate uniform. Since this man could speak without a Yankee accent, he was able to scout ahead and, sometimes, obtain provisions simply by walking into a store and paying for them. Just north of Statesville, this member of the party entered a country tavern, ordered a meal — part of which he hoped to take back to his freezing comrades — and was pleasantly surprised when the old man who ran the establishment stealthily gave him the secret recognition signal of the Heroes of America.

As soon as indentification had been established, the tavern keeper closed his shop, brought out three mules, and guided the refugees five miles down the road to the house of his brother, another staunch Union man. Richardson and his companions were able to spend the night warm and dry and well supplied with apple brandy. The only compensation their hosts required was absolute secrecy.

That was the pattern, all the way into the mountains. One Unionist would shelter the party and either lead them or direct them to another Unionist, farther on. By Christmas Day, Richardson's group had reached Wilkes County, where they stayed in a barn owned by the patriarch of a multi-branched, old-time mountain clan. Richardson kept rough notes of the experience, which he expanded into a detailed account only weeks after reaching safety. As a trained reporter, he could take down considerable information very quickly, and one of the things he took down verbatim was a long speech by the 70-year-old Unionist, which gives us an intimate picture of the friend-versus-foe conflicts that were common in most of the mountain counties:

> The Home Guards are usually pretty civil. Occasionally they shoot at some of the boys who are hiding, but pretty soon afterwards, one of them is found in the woods somewhere with a hole in his head! I suppose there are a thousand young men lying out in this county. I have always urged them to fight the Guards, and have helped to supply them with ammunition. Two or three times, regiments from Lee's army have been sent here to hunt conscripts and deserters,

and then the boys have to run. I have a son among them; but they
never wounded him yet. I asked him the other day: "Won't you kill
some of them before you are ever captured?" "Well, Father," says
he, "I'll be found a-tryin'!" I reckon he will, too; for he has never
gone without his rifle these two years, and he can bring down a
squirrel every time from the top of yon oak you see on the hill....[11]

The food shortage, which by the end of 1864 existed all over
North Carolina, was especially bad in the mountains. In areas
where there had been no recent foraging by either guerrillas or
Confederate expeditions, Richardson found reasonably ample
supplies of pork and cornbread — a diet which, he averred, was
tailor-made for heavy physical labor — but such a shortage of
manufactured goods that the inhabitants fastened their clothes
together with thorns instead of pins. In other places, the countryside had been scoured bare, and the fugitives were lucky to find a
meal of parched corn.

Richardson found evidence, too, of a shift in loyalties among
citizens who had started the war as flag-waving rebels. One
slaveholder near Wilkesboro, reputed to be a zealous secessionist,
actually sent an invitation to the escapees when he heard through
the neighborhood grapevine that they were near, asking them to his
house for food, clothing, shelter, and some civilized conversation.

Yes, he admitted, he had at first supported the Revolution (as he
called it), but now he rued the day he had persuaded his two sons to
enter the Confederate Army. One was rotting in a Yankee prison
camp, and the other was an outlier, living in the woods, constantly
on the run, in danger, unable to visit home except on rare dark
nights when the militia was known to be elsewhere.

As for the mountain families who had supported the Union from
the start, Richardson was amazed at their dedication: "They
earnestly questioned us about the North! How they longed to
escape thither! To them, indeed, it was the Promised Land. They
were very bitter in their denunciations of the heavy slaveholders,
who had done so much to degrade white labor, and finally brought
on this terrible war."[12]

The Richardson party avoided Wilkesboro itself, creeping
around the town on the night of December 29, walking through
deep snow and leaning into a wind so strong, so bitingly cold, that

breathing itself became difficult.

At dawn the next morning they reached the banks of the Yadkin River and began searching for the cabin of Ben Hanby. Here, they had been told farther back down the route, they could find shelter. Richardson's account of how they found the place conveys a vivid impression of the prevailing suspicion, not to say paranoia, that characterized all meetings between strangers at this period of the mountain war:

> We reached the Yadkin River just as a young, blooming woman, with a face like a ripe apple, came gliding across the stream. With a long pole, she guided the great log canoe, which contained herself, a pail of butter, and a sidesaddle, indicating that she had started for the Wilkesboro market. Assisting her to the shore, we asked:
> "Will you tell us where Ben Hanby lives?"
> "Just beyond that hill there, across the river," she replied, with scrutinizing, suspicious eyes.
> "How far is it to his house?"
> "I don't know."
> "More than a mile?"
> "No," (doubtfully), "I reckon not."
> "Is he probably at home?"
> "No! He is not! Are you the Home Guard?"
> "By no means, madam. We are Union men, and Yankees at that. We have escaped from Salisbury and are trying to reach our homes in the North."
> After another searching glance, she trusted us fully and said: "Ben Hanby is my husband. I wondered, if you were the Guard, what you could be doing without guns. From a hill near our house, the children saw you coming more than an hour ago; and my husband, taking you for the soldiers, went with his rifle to join his companions in the woods. Word has gone out to every Union household in the neighborhood that the troops are out looking for...deserters."[13]

That night, after supper, Richardson got his first close look at the part-time guerrillas of Appalachian North Carolina:

> At evening a number of friends visited us. As they were not merely Rebel deserters, but Union bushwhackers also, we scanned them with some curiosity; for we had been wont to regard bushwhackers, of either side, with vague, undefined horror.
> These men were walking arsenals. Each had a trusty rifle, one or

two Navy revolvers, a great bowie knife, haversack, and canteen. Their manners were quiet, their faces honest, and one had a voice of rare sweetness...he and his neighbors had adopted this mode of life, because determined not to fight against the old flag. They would not attempt the uncertain journey to our lines, leaving their families in the country of the enemy. Ordinarily very quiet and rational, whenever the war was spoken of, their eyes emitted that peculiar glare which I had observed, years before, in Kansas, and which seems inseparable from the hunted man.[14]

At one point in the evening's conversation, Richardson's guests explained to him the customary mode of warfare in this part of the mountains:

When the Rebels let us alone, we let them alone; when they come out to hunt us, we hunt them! They know that we are in earnest, and that before they can kill any one of us, he will break a hole in the ice large enough to drag two or three of them along with him. At night, we sleep in the bush. When we go home by day, our children stand out picket. They are our wives bring food to us in the woods. When the Home Guards are coming out, some of their [Unionist] members usually inform us before hand; then we collect twenty or thirty men, find the best ground we can, and, if they discover us, we fight them. But a number of skirmishes have taught them to be very wary about attacking us.[15]

Although Richardson and his party were lucky enough never to come under fire, he dwelt among the mountain Unionists intimately enough to hear numerous personal stories in detail. He came away from the experience convinced that the level of violence in the western counties of North Carolina was much more serious than the outside world realized:

During our whole journey we encountered only one house inhabited by white Unionists which had never been plundered by the Home Guard or Rebel guerrillas. Almost every loyal family had given to the cause some of its nearest and dearest. We were told so frequently — "My father was killed in those woods" or "The guerrillas shot my brother in that ravine" that, finally, these tragedies made little impression on us.[16]

The final miles to the Tennessee line were grueling. Along one stretch of road, the party had to cross the same creek 29 times in the space of 12 miles, usually on rude log bridges, but several times simply by wading through the ice-flocked water. On January 2, 1865, they crossed the New River, and at 4 p.m. the following day, they entered Tennessee -- only to discover that rebel guerrillas were even more active on that side of the state line than in the counties they had just passed through. Once, they even had to detour around an area where an estimated 80 Confederate bush-whackers had set up a vast ambush for Colonel George Kirk. But since everybody in the neighborhood already knew about it, Kirk avoided the trap with ease.

At the first Unionist village Richardson encountered, he learned that there had been plenty of local action recently. A rebel guerrilla captain, whose band operated on both sides of the state line, who had slain several Union men in their own homes, and who took sadistic pleasure in abusing women, had stolen $200 from a man named Jones. In turn, Jones had put out the word: The money was to be returned or the rebel was a dead man. The rebel partisan, of course, did not return the money, so Jones stalked him, found him at home, and called him out. Both men "slapped leather" in the best Wild West tradition, and the rebel chieftain fell dead on the threshold of his own home. Richardson also learned about the summary execution, by local Unionists, of another "particularly obnoxious" rebel guerrilla who had simply vanished some weeks earlier. His bleached bones had been found deep in the forest just a few days before Richardson arrived. The guerrilla's money and watch were untouched, still in his coat pocket, but the skull looked like it had been battered with a ballpeen hammer, and 21 bullet holes were counted in the coat alone.

The last lap of Richardson's long journey was marked by numerous narrow escapes. Even in this final season of the war, rebel guerrilla activity on the Tennessee side of the border seems to have been quite intense. Richardson and his party finally reached Federal lines near Knoxville on January 13, 1865. The straight-line distance between Salisbury and Knoxville is about 200 miles, but Richardson estimated that, because of the twisting roads and rough terrain, not to mention their frequent detours around potential danger spots, they had actually walked 350 miles. And every man in the party had been sick and undernourished at the start.

For the last and most dangerous stage of his journey, Richardson was lucky enough to gain the assistance of the legendary Unionist guide Daniel Ellis — known to the rebels as "The Old Red Fox." Ellis, a wagon-wright and mechanic by trade, was a native of Carter County in east Tennessee, and was in his mid-30s. He had been one of the original "bridge burners" in November 1861, and had since become one of the most successful "pilots" in the border country. Some accounts credit him with escorting more than 10,000 people from Confederate territory to Union lines, first from east Tennessee into Kentucky, and then from North Carolina into Knoxville. He was also a bonafide Federal recruiting agent, and he made trips for that purpose into North Carolina, sometimes going more than 20 miles deep into rebel territory and bringing back parties of volunteers numbering from 40 to 500.

No man was more hardened to outdoor life than Dan Ellis. In four years of all-season trekking, he developed unequalled skills in camouflage, woodcrafts, evasion, and small-unit tactics. He carried a Henry rifle with a magazine capacity of 16 rounds, as well as two Navy Colts and a Bowie knife, and he saw to it that the men he worked with were similarly well-armed, usually with Spencer repeating rifles. During the last three years of the war, Ellis alone, or parties of men under his command, engaged in dozens of skirmishes with the Home Guard, rebel bushwhackers, and even, on one or two occasions, Confederate regulars. The volume of fire Ellis's men could generate with their Spencers, combined with their unmatched ability to turn the landscape to their own advantage, enabled the scout and his men to either win or escape, time after time. There was a standing price on his head of $5,000 (in real money, not Confederate notes), and many rebel guerrillas who thought they were good went out to get him, only to find they were not nearly as good as he was.

Though slightly wounded several times and painfully injured on dozens of occasions by falls and other accidents, Ellis survived the war and wrote an autobiography. It is modestly entitled, *Thrilling Adventures of Daniel Ellis, the Great Union Guide of East Tennessee for a Period of Nearly Four Years During the Great Southern Rebellion.* No contemporary chronicle of the mountain war thunders with greater melodrama, nor runs with such rivers of gore, as does Ellis's narrative. The historian must approach it cautiously, however, for Ellis is almost hysterically biased. He records, in gruesome detail, dozens of appalling atrocities committed by Confederate guerrillas (usually described as "howling fiends from the nether pits of Hell," or something similar); but not once, in all 429 pages, does he so much as acknowledge that Unionist partisans such as George Kirk were committing the same outrages against innocent Confederate families with equally sadistic gusto.

Nevertheless, some of Ellis's descriptions of massacres are corroborated, in all their hideous detail, by other, less one-sided chroniclers. Ellis may have been a braggart and a windbag, but he was not a liar. And no other contemporary gives a more searing impression of the sheer horror of what was happening in the Appalachian guerrilla fighting.

Not all of the refugee parties from North Carolina, for instance, were as lucky as Albert Richardson's. In the winter of 1863, Ellis relates, a party of 57 Unionists, fleeing from Wilkes County, North Carolina, were en route to seek Ellis's help in reaching Federal lines. They were cornered at Greasy Cove, Carter County, by a rebel partisan chieftain named Wilcher. Most of the party managed to escape by fleeing wildly into the woods, but 11 men were trapped and massacred with methodical sadism. Some were bayoneted to death, others clubbed to a pulp with rifle butts, and one wounded old man was held spread-eagled against the ground while the bushwhackers dropped rocks on his head until his brains squirted out. Ellis's narration of this incident, though lurid in the extreme and curdled with hatred, can probably be trusted. He was only a few miles away when it happened, and he obtained the details from eyewitnesses who hid in the woods and watched the horrors as they unfolded.

And there is one episode in Ellis's book that above all others captures the bitterness and cruelty of the mountain war -- in a way that is only suggested by more timid writers. Although the specific location was in the Cumberland Mountains, not far from Powell's Valley and Baptist Gap, where the Cherokees of Thomas's Legion took their first scalps, it could have happened anywhere in the mountains:

While I was engaged in filling my canteen from the crystal

fountain, my nose was saluted with a most horrible effluvium. I immediately began to look around for the cause of the noxious odor which had so suddenly visited my nostrils, expecting every moment to see the putrid and decaying carcass of a dead hog or some other animal, when, horrible to relate in a civilized country, I saw the fleshless skeletons of three human beings hanging [from] a stooping sapling. I went up nearer and examined them; there was no fragment of clothing to be seen, and the flesh had all decayed from their bones. Their hair had fallen off of their heads and was lying beneath their feet upon the ground. The bones of two of them were still all united together, forming two whole skeletons of the former living men; and from the backbone of the other one having separated just below his ribs, the leg and hip-bones had fallen to the ground. I presumed that he had been shot through the backbone, which had caused his frame to separate where it did.

They had been hung with hickory bark, which had been peeled off of some hickory sprouts growing near...I at once guessed that they were poor fugitives who had been captured while they were trying to get through the lines. I did not tarry long at this spring, for I well knew that the fate which had been allotted to these poor men would most unquestionably be meted out to me if I should fall into the hands of the rebels. When I got a short distance down the road, I met with a woman coming down the road, and, after the usual salutation, a short colloquy ensued between us as follows:

"How came these men to be hung upon that tree?"

She replied, "They were a parcel of Lincolnites that our boys captured at that spring while they were getting water." "That is a horrible sight, madam. Is that the way that the Lincolnites are disposed of when they are so unfortunate as to be captured?"

"Yes; and they receive no mercy whatever from our boys. If you will go down the road about one hundred yards you will find a parcel of them that were captured here a short time ago, and were shot immediately, and were thrown behind an old log, and covered up with leaves and chunks."

"How does it happen that so many men are captured in this neighborhood?"

"Why, there is a company of soldiers stationed on Clinch River, and they have selected the best hunters in the country to watch the roads and mountain paths to catch men who are making their way through the lines."

"Well, that is the most diabolical sight I have ever witnessed in all my life."

"Oh, that is not a strange sight to me, by any means. I have seen the hat and shoes taken off of many Lincolnites, and have seen them kneel to pray before being shot."

"And did it cause you no emotions of pity to witness such a terrible spectacle?"

"No, none whatever. That is the very way that men ought to be treated whenever they are caught running away to Old Abe. All of them ought to be killed."

"But do you think that the poor men whom you have seen murdered so unceremoniously were really guilty of any crime for which they deserved to be killed?"

"Yes, I have no sympathy for them whatever. I believe it is perfectly right to kill them whenever they are caught. I have a husband and two brothers in the Southern army, and every man who is unwilling to fight for the Southern Confederacy, who may be caught in the act of running off to Kentucky, ought to be hung or shot."

This pugnacious virago was quite talkative, and I do not think that she was more than twenty-five...she was young in age, but old in wickedness...I would have asked more questions, but I was afraid to remain any longer in this dismal valley, where the bones...of dead men seemed to give no terror whatever even to a woman. I therefore bid this loquacious female rebel good-day, and hastened on toward the rough mountain....[17]

PART 4:
THE BLOOD
OF SHELTON
LAUREL

Whenever the vandal cometh

Press home to his heart with your steel, And when at his bosom you cannot,

Like a serpent, go strike at his heel. Through thicket and wood go hunt him

Creep up to his camp fireside, And let ten of his corpses blacken,

Where one of our brothers hath died.

-- S. Teackle Wallis, "The Guerrillas: A Southern War Song," 1864.

'BLOODY MADISON'

Back in 1861, you couldn't get into Madison County except by passing through a gap — usually a gap with a daunting, if not ominous-sounding, name: Devil's Fork Gap, for instance. Roughly fist-shaped, its knuckles resting against the high ridges of the Smoky Mountains, Madison County is a landscape defined by many high places and one low place: the great French Broad River.

The French Broad is old and gnarled, and over centuries it has cut a deep granite-ribbed canyon for itself through the ancient hills. Fierce and foaming and wild at its headwaters in the high cliffs, the river gradually broadens and becomes more civilized as it flows northwest into Tennessee. Some of the flavor of that land can be sampled from the names of the deep-cut, black-crystal creeks that feed the river: Spillcorn Creek, Shut-In Creek, Wolf Laurel, Crooked Branch, and — best known of all during Civil War times — Shelton Laurel. The whole heartland region of Madison County is sometimes referred to simply as the Laurel Valley. The mountains that hem in the Laurel Valley have music in their names, too: Sandy Mush Mountain (60 feet shy of a mile high), Sugarloaf Knob, Max Patch, Little Bald, Big Butt, and — no one today seems to know why, exactly — Sodom. One returning Confederate veteran was heard to cry out, in May 1865, "God bless dear old Sodom!" much to the puzzlement of the Yankee outsiders who were standing nearby.

Trees there were in such abundance that the axes of three generations of settlers, building and heating exclusively with wood, had made little impression on the forests of spruce, juniper, hemlock, pine, red and white oak, chestnut, maple, black walnut, poplar, and hickory. In between the trees grew dense thickets of rhododendron. There were whole hillsides, and gullies, and vast emerald groves so full of twisted laurel that the landscape seemed misplaced from a tropical rain forest. Even today, in places where developers have not bulldozed the land into submission, you can find vast stretches of wilderness covered with vegetation too dense to walk through. On one camping trip to the region back in the early 1960s, the author had to pass through a rhododendron grove so dense that the only way to make progress was to tunnel through with machetes, clambering from branch to branch without setting foot on the earth more than a half-dozen times in an hour.

What nature makes primitive, she also tends to make beautiful. Multi-hued violets splash the meadows in the spring, topped, for a heart-achingly brief period of bloom, by windblown snowclouds of dogwood. In the summer, the rhododendron blossoms, as do the flame-colored azaleas. And in the autumn, the colors of the trees, combined in perfect synesthesia with the lonesome aroma of woodsmoke drifting from a cabin at the end of some long cove of molten gold, is poignant enough to call songs from the very stones.

The rural settlements were tiny, back in 1861, and some of them bore strange names: Duel Hill, Grapevine, Faust, Luck, Trust, Skillet Lick, and even a cabin-cluster simply named Joe. The only towns of any size were Marshall, the county seat, and Mars Hill. Tiny as they were, the towns were home to people whose relationship to the land was subtly different from that of the rural mountaineers. Towns attracted individuals who, for whatever personal reasons, were discontented with the traditional ways of life they had inherited in the hills, people who were hungry for contact with other people who hailed from different places and different milieus — people, in short, who wanted more influence over their own destinies than was available in the close-to-the-soil traditions of the backwoods hollows, where nature called the shots and men often took more pride in their endurance than in their self-betterment.

There were 20 or so families living in the Shelton Laurel section at the start of the war. They had been there ever since the land was first wrested from the Indians in the 1790s. They stayed in spite of their poverty and in spite of the fact that, as the original families grew and spread into the more remote valleys, the good parcels of land became smaller and smaller. Families were large — six or seven people to a cabin — and their life expectancy was short. In the 1860 census, there were 137 Sheltons listed, and only four of them were older than 40.

For these families, the sense of physical isolation was very real. The only major "highway" through this part of the mountains was the French Broad turnpike, parts of which were barely passable on muleback. The side roads, most of them, doubled as part-time stream beds. And even under peacetime conditions, the poverty of the area was flinty, pitiless. "[The inhabitants] seem to have solved the problem of how to live on nothing," wrote one traveler through the region, "for besides their wretched little break-neck cornfields, they have no visible means of subsistence."[1]

But running like an armature through the whole region was the pride the Shelton Laurel inhabitants felt at having willfully removed themselves from the outside world. The rough configuration of the land made that easy to do. The price was a monolithic ignorance of the outside world, and an awareness that the outsiders felt a certain measure of hostility and contempt toward the hardscrabble rural folk. Against that was pitted the backwoods farmers' sense of right and wrong, powerfully inculcated by heritage and immeasurably reinforced by the basic social fact that everyone they knew — everyone — shared the same narrow values.

Shelton Laurel gained its reputation as a Unionist stronghold quite early in the war when a Federal officer, sent in to mobilize anti-Confederate partisan activity, both recruited men there and used the place as a hideout between raids. His name was David Fry, and he had first gained notoriety during the bridge-burning attacks of November 1861. Fry's objective had been the Lick Creek bridge. Leading his guerrillas boldly, Fry had overpowered all the bridge guards and carried out his incendiary mission. The action was distinguished by the brutality of his treatment of the captured bridge guards, some of whom were beaten just for the fun of it. After torching the Lick Creek bridge, Fry had gone on to raise hell up and down the rail line between Chattanooga, Tennessee and Marietta, Georgia, ripping up tracks, cutting telegraph wires, and even stealing a couple of locomotives for transportation before eventually escaping into the mountains and making his way back to the valley of Shelton Laurel.

That was not his only base, of course. Like all good guerrilla leaders, he never stayed complacently in one place for too long. Fry led his small band on numerous forays during the winter of 1862, falling on isolated Confederate households and relieving them of their horses, guns, and valuables. He was also extremely active in recruiting Union sympathizers and establishing "safe house" locations.

He made one attempt to lead his men into Kentucky, promising them the benefits of formal enlistment once they had made it to Federal lines. But Confederate patrols, stirred to wariness by Fry's own depredations, were too numerous to elude, and the guerrillas were forced to return to their mountain base.

Late in the winter of 1862, the Confederates went in after Fry. Warned by sympathizers, Fry hastily set out with about 20 men and tried again to get through to Kentucky. He was captured, clapped in irons, and packed off to prison in Atlanta. The Confederate command in east Tennessee basked in this small victory for a few weeks, then decided to launch a punishment raid on Shelton Laurel for the treasonable crime of having sheltered Fry and his men.

The punitive expedition, comprised of Tennessee troops, left Greeneville on April 7, 1862. Its orders were troublesomely vague: "Put down any illegal organization of men that might be found there." The closer the troops got to Shelton Laurel, the tougher the march became, through laurel thickets too dense for a man to walk through upright; then up, always up, straggling splay-footed across the sides of steep-walled valleys. Several times, on the days of April 8-10, the column was fired on by snipers hidden in the underbrush.

At the end of their three-day "search and destroy" mission, after three days of physically grueling exertion and constantly the target of snipers, the Tennesseans had killed 15 men while suffering three casualties themselves. They were utterly worn out and were both amazed and depressed by the bitter, open hostility of the region's inhabitants.

So much resistance had been encountered that a larger sweep was mounted the following week. The commander of the Tennessee state militia deployed a large force around the whole Shelton Laurel valley, first blocking all the passes and then systematically beating the brush from one end to the other. These tactics netted more than 30 outlier prisoners and gave rise to a rash of on-the-spot oath-taking ceremonies. What mountaineer would refuse to swear allegiance to the Confederacy while staring down the muzzles of a dozen rifles? The loyalties thus obtained were every bit as transitory as you might imagine, and within weeks after the militia's departure, raids were again being mounted against Tennessee Confederates by men from the Shelton Laurel valley.

Whence came this pervasive and stubborn adherence to the Union? Partly it came from history, or, more precisely, from a set of historical attitudes that, like so many other aspects of mountaineer culture, had become frozen in time two or more generations before the start of the Civil War.

Many of the first settlers in rural Madison County were veterans of the Revolutionary War. They had come to the hills seeking a chance to realize, through their own hard work and determination, the ideals instilled by that experience. Moreover, many of them had come to the mountains not from across the Piedmont in a lateral direction, but in migratory patterns at right angles to that axis, and from the North. Hundreds of families, for instance, had started from Pennsylvania and had simply followed the north-south valleys farther and farther, until finally they found a place where the landscape matched their dreams and they decided to put down roots.

Increased isolation from outside influences, starting in the early 19th century, meant that the attitudes these original settlers brought with them tended to be transmitted intact and unaltered to their descendants. These people had had little chance to develop a specifically "Southern" attitude, and they had so little physical and cultural contact with the outside world that they could relate to it only by means of attitudes passed down from within the family, or from within the valley where they lived. These attitudes conveyed a dim but still vibrant memory of places and institutions in the North, in the Union, and they had nothing whatever in them of "Dixie." The Deep South, to these people, was as remote and alien as the surface of Mars.

Even more than in other mountain counties, the division in Madison between Unionists and secessionists grew out of some fairly stark conditions of class antagonism. And, while it would be

213

a distortion to apply a strict Marxist interpretation to what was happening in 1861, it was, in truth, a socio-economic class division whose potential for conflict would have been grasped rather quickly by someone like Mao Zedong.

The handful of people who were slaveowners, and the larger number who actively supported secession, were the most influential people in Madison County. These were the office holders, the merchants, the closest thing a raw frontier county had to an elite class. Like their poor rural neighbors, these men were mountaineers because they loved the country for its beauty, its potential, and its ambiance of individual liberty. But that was about all they had in common. The wealthy gentleman-farmer might occasionally get his fingernails dirty at harvest time, but he didn't have to break his bones digging granite boulders out of a briar-choked patch of ground just so he could grow a few more scrawny ears of corn to feed a litter of barefoot children.

The secessionists were the closest thing Madison County had to a leisure class, the only inhabitants with meaningful connections to the outside world and to the Southern economic system as a whole. Every antebellum year that passed deepened the chasm that separated them from the hardscrabble farmers out in the Laurel Valley, whose families kept getting larger and whose real wealth kept dwindling, even as their cultural and physical isolation grew more hermetic.

Conflict in this region, then, would largely arise between the minority of well-to-do families that stood to gain from a Southern victory, and the majority of fiercely independent poor people who resented them and looked upon them as petty tyrants and haughty aristocrats. This was a theme that populist politicians had played upon with great success in the decades preceding the war. "The slavocrats," said one such politician in the 1850s, "look upon a white man who has to labor for an honest living as no better than one of their negroes...these bombastic, high-falutin' fools have been in the habit of driving negroes and poor helpless white people until they think they can control the world of mankind."[2]

It must also be said that the Unionists of Madison County were in no way abolitionists. The fact that there were relatively few slaves in the area did not deter the mass of poor whites from actively despising Negroes in principle and voicing no love for the prospect of their liberation. It was the slaveowners' economic clout that the mountaineers hated, along with their seeming arrogance and "high-falutin'" ways, not the institution of slavery per se.

Unionism in counties such as Madison, then, was woven from a number of stubborn fibers, including hillbilly prejudice against urbanites, and the eternal antagonism of the poor and powerless against the wealthy and the influential. All of this was colored by a historical class-memory of the Union which may well have become somewhat vague after the passing of three generations, but which nevertheless remained an almost primal sense of orientation. For many Unionist mountaineers, the issue was not adoration for the Union so much as it was animosity toward the individuals who personified the idea of rebellion against it. This was a volatile matrix of conditions and attitudes; all it took was the addition of a lot of guns and an overriding excuse to use them, and you had the ingredients for a brutal and merciless conflict. The war provided an excuse to settle old neighborhood quarrels as well, and many a man who had spent years brooding over some real or imagined injustice done him by another family down the road, had little trouble convincing himself that, since the objects of his hatred were "damned secesh" or "black-hearted Lincolnites," it was now morally legitimate to go out and start killing them. It was both a personal and a social vendetta carried out beneath an umbrella of ideology (a pattern that was new to America then, but that has become, in our own time, much more common).

As with all internecine conflicts, loyalties could be slippery as well as steadfast, a matter of expediency and circumstance even more than conviction. This was surely the case with the many, many mountain families that just wanted to be left alone and take no part in the fray on either side. They were not, of course, permitted to do that — nothing infuriates a zealot more than someone who refuses to take a side.

And yet, many of Madison County's yeomen farmers "felt mighty Southern when the war come along" (as one man put it) and enlisted for the rebel cause. For some young men, enlistment probably seemed a means to experience glory and adventure, to be in on a quick and thrilling victory. When they saw how bloody the adventure was, and how elusive was both the glory and the victory, hundreds of them went back to the mountains as deserters, forming common cause with the Unionists, even if they did not subscribe to Unionist ideals. Another motivation that spurred the first wave of volunteers was the claim that the Confederacy was fighting to resist tyranny from the outside. Many hot-hearted young men were willing to accept that aspect of the cause. And, it may safely be surmised, many of the poor whites who enlisted did so out of a belief that a Lincolnite victory would unleash a radical racial upheaval in which the liberated blacks would cut into the already scarce economic opportunities available to the poor white farmers. Such men fought not to preserve slavery, but to fend off what they perceived as a serious threat to what little security and property they had managed to acquire.

Such a melange of motives would surely have been found among the men of the 64th North Carolina Regiment, 60 percent of whose troops came from Madison County. The name of the 64th would always be linked, by integuments of blood and shame, to the wartime history of Madison County. It was, from the start, one of those hard-luck outfits. Even its official historian (Captain B.T. Morris, writing in Clark's *Histories of the Several Regiments and Battalions from North Carolina in the Great War, 1861-65*) can find nothing better to say about his unit than "we did the best we could" — not exactly words to carve in marble.

Organized in August 1862, with a core of volunteers fleshed out to a full ten companies only after some draconian conscription drives, the 64th was plagued by desertion from the day it left the mountains for service in east Tennessee. This included one mass desertion of 300 men which might have set some kind of record, even for the mountain war. The 64th's officers were from the better-off class of mountain families, and there was little love between them and their reluctant hillbilly soldiers.

But for those soldiers who did not desert, who did their duty and remained, however unhappily, under arms for the Southern cause, the men who did leave were the objects of both scorn and envy — two dangerous emotions indeed, under wartime circumstances. The deserters had only done what all of them wanted to do: They had left behind the boredom and the danger and the subhuman living conditions and had gone *home*. And the men who remained in their units must have wondered, daily, why they didn't go home, too.

The war brought no glory to the 64th. Aside from garrison duty in Knoxville, a chore of staggering dullness, they spent virtually all their time chasing bushwhackers through the border counties. They were shot at constantly, now and then losing a man, once in a while killing or capturing someone, but mostly just enduring a routine that combined enormous physical discomfort with just enough mortal danger to keep them from ever truly relaxing. The "enemy," for the men of the 64th, was everywhere and nowhere. It was the kind of duty that would generate murderous frustration a century later in thousands of American soldiers in Vietnam; and, as was also the case in Vietnam, it made them so gnarled with anger and resentment that, when they actually got a chance to come to grips with the enemy, they sometimes killed the wrong people the wrong way. At the time, most of them didn't give a damn.

"When an officer finds himself and men bushwhacked from behind every shrub, tree, or projection on all sides of the road, only severe measures will stop it," wrote Captain Morris, in describing the 64th's experiences.[3] Morris went on to write:

> No one except those who have tried it can realize what those who do this kind of service have to endure...Our enemies were at home — knew all the roads, byways and trails, and were much in heart over the success of their arms elsewhere...we slashed them every time we had a chance at them [but] They never gave us a fair fight, square-up, face-to-face, man-to-man....[4]

Morris wrote detailed accounts of several anti-bushwhacker operations. A typical one went like this:

> Henry Perkins had leave of absence to visit his family. He lived in Green River Cove, in Polk County, about sixteen miles from [our] camp. When he arrived at home and had been there but a short time he walked out in the yard and was shot down; he saw the man that shot him and told who he was. He was a vile fellow who made it his every day business to bushwhack every detail that passed through the country. Word was immediately conveyed to camp and at the proper time[,] leaving camp in the evening so that our movements should not be known, we travelled nearly all night, arriving before day and

having been informed that he was a frequent visitor at a house near the river where some bad women lived, we put our men in ambush to wait for daylight to develop something. Just at the break of day the women came out of the house and began a general search as if suspicious of something...they made all the racket they could make and it did seem as if our trip was vain. Two of our men who had not been discovered, walked up a little branch only a short distance from the house, when suddenly a little dog commenced barking. The man we were seeking sprang to his feet and made an effort to get his gun, but was too late. They fired into him[,] one ball cutting an artery...and in a few minutes he was dead. Thus ended the life of a man who only a few days before had taken the life of his next door neighbor and that without cause. From this time on that section was more quiet....[5]

On another occasion, during sweeps through Transylvania County, Morris sent out a patrol of ten men. Bushwhackers spotted them and mounted an ambush at a narrowing of the trail where a great slab of mountain granite hung out over the path. The guerrillas took up positions on top of this formation, where they could fire over the lip of the rock and down the throats of anyone on the road, but were themselves almost impossible to hit because of the angle of the overhang. The patrol was allowed to get within 50 yards of the ambush before it was sprung: a murderous blast from shotguns as well as rifles and pistols. One man was killed, and every other man in the patrol was wounded — one man no less than six times. The bushwhackers may have suffered one casualty, but no one ever found out for sure.

It was that kind of war for the 64th North Carolina. And it wore down their officers as much as it tested the men. In command of the regiment was Lawrence M. Allen, who had originally tried to raise his own "legion" but who, lacking William Thomas's clout in Richmond, had to be satisfied with an infantry regiment instead. Again, Captain Morris is refreshingly blunt about his former commanding officer: "Colonel Allen ...was not an attractive man — rather otherwise — but he was chosen leader because he was known to be brave and fearless."[6] Allen was one of the few slaveowners in Marshall, and by the time the war broke out he had accumulated a considerable personal fortune from real estate dealings. He was also a powerful figure in regional Democratic politics. He had ambitions to high office. He had, in short, a vested interest in the

status quo, and that made him a passionate Confederate. He was
also recklessly greedy. At one point during the regiment's tour of
duty in east Tennessee, Allen was under investigation for perpetrating a sleazy little scam in which he allegedly arrested men for draft
dodging, and then extorted money in return for letting them go
free.

His second-in-command was Lieutenant Colonel James A.
Keith. The son of a Baptist minister who had done well for himself,
Colonel Keith was ambitious enough to have become one of
Madison County's richest men by the time he was 35. He had
influence and book-learning as well as wealth and property. He had
big plans for himself and for the town of Marshall; he was exactly
the kind of local citizen who jumped at the chance to organize his
own company of local troops, as soon as he heard that war had
been declared.

At age 35, James Keith was gaunt and rangy, with high cheek-
bones, pale skin, a fierce black beard, and long, rather straggly hair.
He looked like a mountaineer, moved like a bobcat, spoke with the
Elizabethan twist of an old-time Southern highlander, and had
dangerous-looking shadows in the depths of his blue-gray eyes.

When he appeared before the Confederate commander-in-chief
of east Tennessee, General Henry Heth, Keith was smoldering with
anger over the news of the ambushes that had just taken place in
Madison County. Heth must have realized at a glance that if he
turned Jim Keith loose against the outliers of Shelton Laurel -- at
the head of a unit like the 64th North Carolina -- there was going to
be some hard killing.

THE SALT RAID

By the end of 1862, the people of Madison County had a new enemy: hunger. Conscription had stripped the region of its labor force; harvests had been skimpy, weather bad. The vicious cycle of raids and retributions had diminished the number of usable farm buildings, the supply of horses and edible livestock, and the inventory of farm equipment — what had not been stolen was breaking down, and there were no spare parts for repairs. What grain supplies there were, by the winter of 1862, had become the exclusive property of flint-hearted speculators, who asked usurious prices for what they held and preferred to sell to government agents, at inflated prices, rather than to hungry housewives.

The worst hardship, by far, was the lack of salt. In this age before refrigeration, salt was just about the only way to preserve meat, and there was no substitute for it during the slaughtering season of mid-winter. If farmers did not have salt, they had no meat to sell, and no meat to eat. In North Carolina, the salt shortage was deadly, for the state had no internal source of supply except for the coastal distillation plants, and very little of that output ever got through the pipeline into the western counties. By the end of the winter of 1862-63, the price of a sack of salt had climbed from $12 to $100. Meager supplies were trickling into the small warehouses in the mountain counties, and they were tightly controlled by Confederate agents in the towns; the poor people out in the hill country got nothing. This was a calculated, pitiless policy, de-signed to punish them for their Union sympathies and to create additional pressure on deserters to come in, give themselves up, and "do their duty" — just so their families could get enough salt to survive the winter.

It was a dire need for salt that drove a band of Shelton Laurel

221

men into the town of Marshall one achingly cold night in early January 1863. Nobody made an accurate count, but most estimates put the number of men in the party at about 50, and a good portion were deserters from the ill-starred 64th North Carolina. If they could get enough salt, their families had a chance of surviving the winter; and if anybody tried to stop them...well, they had little sympathy to spare for the safe, warm, relatively prosperous Confederate sympathizers in the village.

Home on leave that week was Captain John Peek, also from the 64th, and a close relative of the wife of Colonel Lawrence Allen, the 64th's commander. Captain Peek was awakened by the unaccustomed sound of men scuttling through the iron-hard winter night. He dressed, armed himself, and went outside to investigate. He discovered the outliers breaking into the salt warehouse. One of their sentries shot him in the right arm, leaving him crippled for life, while the others helped themselves to all the salt they could carry, as well as a supply of blankets and cloth.

If the incident had stopped there, nothing else might have happened. But it didn't stop there — it just got personal. Egged on by some of the deserters from the 64th, the raiders proceeded to Captain Allen's house and broke in. The colonel wasn't home; ironically, he was with his regiment, guarding a salt depot in Bristol, Tennessee. Mrs. Allen was home, however, along with some servants and the Allen's three children, two of whom were critically ill with scarlet fever.

Once inside, the looters terrified everyone in the house, shouting and cursing, breaking open trunks and closets with blows from an axe, and helping themselves to whatever took their fancy: jewels, clothing, shoes, cash. They didn't even spare the children -- bursting into the room where two of them lay sick, the raiders stole some of the kids' clothing which laid near their beds. The sick youngsters were horribly upset by the incident, and their condition worsened as a result.

The raiders, loaded with all they could carry, still weren't finished. After leaving Allen's house, they paused to halfheartedly ransack a few dwellings on the edge of town. Finally they disappeared into the ringing darkness of the winter-black mountains.

Word of these outrages got back to the 64th in a day or so. Their

hearts knotted with anger, Colonels Allen and Keith approached
the commanding officer of the district of east Tennessee and asked
for permission to lead a punitive expedition into the Shelton Laurel
valley.

At the head of the chain of command was General Henry Heth, a
West Pointer whose Civil War career — largely through no fault of
his own — had been lackluster and dogged with failures. By 1863,
about the only thing propping him up was his personal friendship
with General Robert E. Lee. His military career before 1861, by
contrast, had been solid, verging on distinguished, and had included some fairly challenging tours of duty in the far West, where
he had formulated some heavy-handed theories about guerrilla
warfare based on his experiences fighting Plains Indians.

Heth had replaced Kirby-Smith as commander of east Tennessee. It was an assignment no Confederate officer wanted. The place
was crawling with Unionists, the day-to-day situation was confused, fluid, exasperating. Altogether, nine men held the post in the
space of 18 months, with predictably ruinous effect on policy and
morale. The job needed a man of acute political sensitivity and
subtlety; in Heth, it received a man embittered by the unjust
setbacks his recent career had suffered, and a man whose early
military assignments had been in places where diplomacy and
finesse had usually been pushed aside in favor of brute force.

Heth knew about the delicate political situation in the mountains, but chances are he no longer cared much about what happened to the inhabitants, on either side. The whole job was a
burden, an abomination, and one which he hoped to be free of
within a matter of weeks.

At his postwar trial, Colonel Keith insisted that Heth had said to
him: "I want no reports from you about your course at Laurel. I do
not want to be troubled with any prisoners, and the last one of them
should be killed." Keith then produced two witnesses who backed
him up. Heth, of course, denied ever issuing such a bloodthirsty set
of orders. However, he did admit to telling Keith that, if he fought
a battle with the salt raiders, he did not have to take prisoners, for
those men had forfeited their right to be treated according to the
code of war. Heth would not admit to issuing any orders that
permitted the abuse of women and children, or the cold-blooded

murder of people whose surrender, as prisoners of war, had already been accepted.

Realistically speaking, Heth did not need to issue any such orders. He knew perfectly well that the absence of orders to the contrary — that is, specific, detailed, written instructions forbidding the mistreatment of women and children or the killing of captives — left the door wide open for all sorts of horrors. His experience with partisan warfare in Mexico, and his campaigns against the Plains Indians, could not have left him with any illusions on that score. You can search all the transcripts and letters and newspaper accounts in vain for one comment from Heth that displays the slightest sign of guilt or remorse for what happened in the Laurel Valley; by his handling of the original orders, he was clearly an accessory, yet he managed to rationalize the whole business so that he probably lost not five minutes' sleep over it.

THE KILLING

Governor Zebulon Vance was sufficiently alarmed by the reports from Marshall to order out the regional militia, under General William G. Davis, headquartered at Warm Springs. The worst was feared: that the salt raid portended a general uprising of Unionists in the region, as well as a systematic offensive against Confederate families, warehouses, bridges, and railroads, on both sides of the border with Tennessee. Rumors flew thick and fast, including one seemingly reliable account of 500 well-armed and disciplined Unionists already in the field — a force equal, if not superior, to anything the Confederates could throw into the area on short notice.

So while Colonels James Keith and Lawrence Allen were readying the 64th North Carolina Regiment for its grueling march into Madison County, other Confederate units under General Davis — including militia units from as far away as upper Georgia, ten companies of cavalry, and Colonel Thomas and his Cherokees — were beating the bushes from the Georgia line to Greeneville, Tennessee, looking for signs of that pending uprising.

They didn't really find any. The salt raid had been an isolated, local affair. The existing outlier bands — not nearly so numerous in January 1863 as they would be a year later — just went deeper into the hills and hid out until the heat was off. Only in Madison County, in the Laurel Valley, did one of Davis's companies make significant contact. This unit captured 20 outliers, most of them deserters from the 64th North Carolina, after a firefight in which a dozen men were killed.

Meanwhile, two columns of the 64th North Carolina were converging on Shelton Laurel. One column, under Colonel Allen, was entering the valley's mouth, and the other, under Colonel Keith, was coming in from the higher side, over the Bald Mountains. Both officers had personal reasons for wanting to come to grips with the outliers. Keith had lost a young nephew in the

225

guerrilla fighting, and Allen had just had his home pillaged and his family terrorized. It was, for both officers, a time for revenge.

If the troops of the 64th North Carolina hadn't already been in a foul mood when the Laurel Valley campaign started, they surely were by the time they got within sight of the place. The Smoky Mountains are no place for a prolonged march in January. The wind, funneling through the passes and sweeping up the long brown valleys, scoured their flesh like sandpaper. The low, curdled sky bled thick snow into their path; and the wind poked it at their skin, working the fat, icy flakes into every opening, no matter how small, in their layers of clothing. The men's feet were perpetually wet. During the last 48 hours of Keith's approach march, 25 of his men came down with frostbite -- and a bad case of frostbite, in 1863, meant the surgeon would whittle off part of your foot with a knife, and with nothing but rotgut whiskey for anesthetic.

The first sign of the enemy was eerie, blood-chilling: horn-calls from deep in the forest, echoing down the valley as sentries signaled the approach of the rebel columns. As the 64th drew within range of the first settlements, rifle shots rang out in the hard, gray air. Shot after shot was fired by men, and boys, whom no one could see, hidden deep in the winter-black twists of rhododendron groves, hidden up in the evergreens on the steep, hog-backed ridges, hidden in snipers' nests of gray rock mottled with curds of snow, all but invisible against the gray, snow-mottled sky. The infantry fired back, of course. But at first, when the range was long on both sides, the men of the 64th experienced the torment of firing blindly at an enemy who could see them, and who had their range with some exactitude, but who was himself invisible. There were some casualties, although the records do not say how many.

Then, as the range closed and the Confederates could bring their horses, their numbers, and their superior firepower into play, they began to see some results. Allen's column killed eight men as it closed on the valley, and at a place near Bill Shelton's farm, something like a real skirmish took place when approximately 50 outliers tried to make a stand. Pinned by volley fire, and sharply attacked by a small force of cavalry, the mountaineers fled the field, leaving six bodies sprawled in the snow. Satisfied that things were going well, Allen posted pickets and made camp for the night.

A little while later, Keith's column arrived from the opposite direction.

Whatever Colonel Allen's crimes and shortcomings, and they were considerable, it is hard not to feel pity for what he had to endure that night. After Allen had fallen into an exhausted slumber, a courier rode into camp, bearing for him the bitter news that his six-year-old son had died that day of scarlet fever, his condition greatly aggravated by the terrorism of the salt raiders a few days earlier. And that was not all, said the courier: Margaret, his four-year-old daughter, was not expected to live, either. At first light, Allen headed home with a four-man escort and galloped through the hills as fast as the terrain allowed. He was shot at dozens of times as he left Shelton Laurel, one Minie ball passing through the withers of his horse. He reached his house in time to hold his daughter while she died.

Lawrence Allen buried his children the next morning, and 24 hours later he was back at Shelton Laurel, where he found that news of his personal tragedy had already reached his command. Allen was not liked by his men — most of them detested him, actually — but under the circumstances, they could not help sympa-thizing with his personal grief and absorbing from him an extra charge of hatred. Whoever fell into their hands now was to be pitied.

By the time the final sweep got underway the next morning, most of the outliers who had actually participated in the salt raid on Marshall had had enough sense to flee the valley. The first dozen or so suspects taken ended up in the hands of Keith's adjutant general, a fellow named Bailey, who did the proper thing by bundling them off to the jail in Asheville or to the conscript collection center in Greeneville. These prisoners, and the three men who voluntarily surrendered to the authorities in Marshall that day, were the fortu-nate ones.

As for the rest who fell into the hands of the 64th that day, "the mood of the soldiers was brutal, for they were in an environment guaranteed to terrorize both soldier and victim and to obscure the distinction between them."[1] They did not, of course, find the menfolk right away, but they found their families, and that was the next best thing, because the families always knew where the guerrillas were.

> They claimed they did not know, but they had to know. They had to
> know to justify what you were doing to them. Some talked, some did
> not. Almost no one died from what you did, but you had made them
> pay. Then, as you left, you killed the livestock so that the enemy
> would have no provision and maybe you burned the barn or the
> house itself. Then you ride or walk away and hate them all the more
> for what they were making you do, for what they were making you
> be, for making you find that sometimes you liked it — Jesus God —
> sometimes you liked it.[2]

The women, including an 85-year-old grandmother, were
whipped or hung by the neck, their toes barely scraping the ground,
until they were nearly dead, then let down for more questioning. An
experienced man could tell how long to leave them in the air —
there was a certain shade of blue that crept into the skin just this side
of death — so that the sensation of almost dying could be repeated
over and over again, as many times as it took, not unlike the "uncon-
trolled drowning" techniques practiced by modern interrogators the
world over. A 70-year-old woman named Sally Moore was flogged
with switches until the skin on her back burst open. An infant was
placed in the open, in lashing clouds of snow, and its mother tied to
a tree just out of reach; if she talked, if she told where her man was,
the brave Confederate soldiers of the 64th would untie her and
permit her to take the screaming child inside. Otherwise, they could
both stay where they were until spring. Mary Shelton, wife of one
of the suspected salt raiders, was severely flogged and repeatedly
hung until her face turned blue; she later went insane and had to be
cared for, by Shelton relatives, for the remainder of her life. Rape is
not mentioned in the investigative reports, but it surely happened —
men who would not hesitate to flog a 70-year-old grandmother are
hardly likely to draw a fine moral line at more intimate forms of vio-
lation.

The net result of all the "questioning" was a haul of 15 suspects;
maybe a half-dozen of them had actually been in on the Marshall
raid. The rest included elderly grandfathers and adolescent boys,
such as David Shelton, who was only 13 and could not possibly
have been involved in the salt raid.

"Don't matter how goddamned young they is," growled the men of the 64th; "piglets grow up to be hogs." More than one sniper they had captured in their anti-bushwhacker patrols had been too young to shave.

Once the 15 suspects had been gathered together and securely roped, Keith strode up and down through the swirling snow and spoke to them. They were going to be marched into Tennessee, he told them, to Knoxville, where they would stand trial for their crimes.

They did not leave at once, however. Instead, they stayed in the Laurel for a couple of days while Keith and Allen scoured the hillsides, unsuccessfully, for more suspects. During that period, two of the Shelton Laurel prisoners managed to escape. (As soon as the Confederates left the valley, the escapees turned into fighting guerrillas again.) On or about January 18, 1863, the other 13 began their march into what they thought would be captivity. They started out on the Knoxville road and had no suspicion of what awaited them only a few miles from their homes.

The column halted at an open meadow near one of the many creeks which feed the great French Broad River. It was a virtual amphitheater, a place where every mountaineer lurking in the nearby hills could see what was happening. There would be nothing hidden about the vengeance of the 64th North Carolina.

There was no preamble. Colonel Allen had ridden on elsewhere, but he had worked out the details with Keith before his departure; the two men had even selected the spot in advance. Suddenly, the column simply halted, and -- before the prisoners realized what was happening -- five of them were pulled out of line and pushed, or clubbed, to their knees. When they raised their heads, they were staring into the muzzles of a row of rifles. Some of the men Keith ordered into the firing party refused to go. He told them what officers like Keith usually tell their men in such situations: Either you join the firing squad, or you can take your place with the prisoners and share their fate.

One of the kneeling men, a 60-year-old grandfather named Joe Woods, cried out, "For God's sake, men, you're not going to shoot us?" When their silence answered his question, Woods begged, "At least give us time to pray!" Observing Keith with his sword drawn, preparing to give the order to fire, another prisoner yelled, more in anger than in fear, "You promised us a trial!"

One or two of Keith's men may have aimed off to the side or over the heads of the kneeling men, for the sake of their own consciences, but not enough did to make any difference. The volley ripped the stillness of the cold mountain morning. The impact of the huge Minie balls puffed clouds of snow-powder from the garments of the victims — white before the spurting red — and four of them died instantly. The fifth man was severely wounded in the gut. He was a spectacle, flailing wildly at the stony ground, screaming with pain and begging for mercy. He received a ball in the brain, which in his case probably was a kind of mercy.

Another five prisoners were dragged to that patch of bloody ground. The youngest, David Shelton, pleaded for his life; then, when he realized it was no use, he begged the firing squad to at least not shoot him in the face, nodding at the body of his father, whose features resembled a split watermelon. The soldiers did as he requested, but only succeeded in shattering both of his arms. The boy staggered toward his executioners, blood rivering down his sides, crying, "You've killed my old father and my three brothers, you've shot me in both arms, I forgive you all this — I can get well. Let me go home to my mother and sisters!" A couple of Keith's men stepped forward and dragged the boy, still pleading, back to the killing ground and gave him the coup de grace. The last three prisoners died stoically.

The cleanup was tinged with madness. One of the firing party momentarily lost his wits and began clapping out the minstrel tune "Juba"; he began dancing a jig on top of the shallow mass grave, shouting, "I'll dance the damned scoundrels down to and through Hell!" Some of his comrades laughed wildly at these demented antics, while others turned away in disgust. Now and then, one of the victims would moan or show some other sign of life, a spasm of dying muscle in the hand or foot. When that happened, the call would go up: "Where's the man with the hoe?" Then a soldier armed with heavy-bladed hoe would step forward and chop at the heads and legs of the victims until they lay still.

It was bitterly cold and the earth was hard as stone, so the grave was much too shallow for all it contained. When the surviving families crept out of Shelton Laurel the next morning, they found that wild pigs had come out of the forest during the night, uprooting the grave and devouring part of one corpse's head.

When Governor Vance heard about the massacre, he was outraged to the depths of his soul. He was from that part of North Carolina; he knew the hearts and temper of those people, and he knew it would not have been possible for a Yankee saboteur to conceive of any action more certain to arouse Unionist sympathies, and armed resistance, than this kind of atrocity. Vance commissioned the respected Judge A.S. Merrimon to investigate the incident. Responsibility for the killings quickly devolved on Colonel Keith, primarily, with Colonel Allen a close second, and General Heth as head of the chain of command. Vance vowed that he would hound Keith "to the gates of Hell" in order to bring him to justice -- but it didn't quite work out that way.

Keith had as many defenders as he did enemies, and the political complications of Reconstruction made it impossible for him to be tried in an expeditious manner after the war. He did spend two years in jail, but, fearing that he was about to become a victim of "Judge Lynch," he escaped, on the night of February 21, 1869, from his Buncombe County cell, probably with some outside assistance. His whereabouts thereafter are not known with any certainty, but he never dared return to Madison County. He sold his land there in 1871, through a lawyer's office, and may have ended up in Arkansas.

Colonel Allen's case was elaborately covered up by the Confederate Army hierarchy. In the end, he was administered a wrist-slap: six months suspension without pay.

Allen, too, moved to Arkansas after the war, and quietly farmed for 20 years. Then he got some kind of itch and headed west. In 1885, in a hotel cafe in Arizona, he was drawn into an argument with a boorish Yankee at a nearby table. When the man insulted Southern women ("no better than New York streetwalkers"), Allen threw his coffee in the man's face and challenged him to a duel. The two men settled their argument on Washington's Birthday, 1885, in a field outside of Sonora, Mexico, with Colt .44s at 60 paces. The honor of Southern womanhood, on that frontier morning, was well and truly defended: although wounded himself, Allen slew his opponent.

Allen eventually returned to North Carolina and published a self-glorifying pamphlet entitled "The Partisan Campaigns of Colonel Lawrence M. Allen, Commanding the 64th Regiment, North Carolina Troops, During the Late Civil War. Valiant Deeds of Heroic Patriotism. Self Sacrifices for the Southern Cause. His Rapid Promotion. Terrific Contests With the Notorious Bush-whacker Kirk. Duel in Defense of Southern Womanhood."

Lawrence Allen died in bed. But for 20 years after that grim morning in January 1863, the mothers of Madison County still quieted their vexatious children by telling them: "Allen and his soldiers will get you if you don't behave!"

PART 5: COMES THE DELUGE – STONEMAN'S RAID

With halter, and torch, and Bible And hymns to the sound of the drum

They preach the gospel of Murder, And pray for Lust's kingdom to come.

To saddle! To saddle! My brothers! Look up to the rising sun,

And ask the God who shines there, Whether deeds like these shall be done!

-- S. Teackle Wallis, "The Guerrillas: A Southern War Song," 1864.

Winter 1865 — Things Fall Apart

Colonel William "Little Will" Thomas returned from Richmond sometime in late November 1864, armed with the broad new powers the War Department had granted him on November 9. His reputation cleared and his command intact, he seems to have recovered some of his former energy. All through the winter of 1864-65, Thomas and his officers recruited new troops, on both sides of the state line, and welcomed back a significant number of deserters as well as men who had been wounded in Virginia and who were now sufficiently recovered to resume active duty.

Thomas's Legion now comprised more than half of General James Martin's total regional resources, and as the number of men on its muster rolls approached 1,000, he took the long-overdue step of reorganizing the unit along rational lines. The Legion was re-grouped much as it had been during its better days back at Strawberry Plains. Its scattered companies and detachments were once again formed into a regiment and a battalion; James R. Love, now recovered from the effects of the Shenandoah Valley campaign, once again assumed command of the regiment, and Colonel Stringfield of the battalion. The four Indian companies were also grouped into a battalion; as always, Thomas himself would be in tactical command of them. A battery of light artillery was even located and transferred to the Legion, under a South Carolinian named James Barr. The battery was a dubious asset, however, for the men's morale was shaky and the weapons themselves in such bad shape, most of the time, that Barr could count on having only one or two guns in firing condition on any given day.

General Martin also took decisive action to end the bickering between colonels Palmer and Thomas. New spheres of responsibility were created: Thomas was now in charge of defending Haywood County and everything west; Palmer had responsibility for all the counties north and east of Haywood.

Martin had done a good job of bringing some degree of order to the Confederate defenses. By year's end, on paper at least, he had trebled the number of regulars available to defend the mountain counties to nearly 1,500 men -- discounting, of course, as any sensible general would, the problematical Home Guard companies. But the loyalty and reliability of the regulars, too, were open to question. News came slowly to the people in the mountains, but by the end of 1864, it was abundantly clear that the Confederacy was crumbling all around them.

Even so, Confederate partisans were not entirely passive during that final winter. In February, Stringfield wrote a dispatch from his headquarters in Valley Town (about halfway between Murphy and Quallatown) to Thomas, at his headquarters in Quallatown, expressing concern that "these frequent raids into Tennessee" would draw Yankee retaliation far stronger than anything Stringfield was prepared to cope with. The wording of his dispatch implies that these raids were probably unauthorized, guerrilla-type forays, one semantic step beyond mere banditry, rather than legitimate operations undertaken by regular troops. This would explain why no details about them have survived.

Whatever the raids amounted to, Stringfield had good reason to worry. Already, in January, a regiment of Indiana cavalry had galloped across the border, captured a few of Stringfield's pickets, and dashed back out again before anyone could fire a shot.

Stringfield was also worried about the condition of his troops. He wrote to Thomas on several occasions, urgently requesting not only such amenities as shoes and knapsacks, but such basic commodities as powder and shot. His men, he stated, were reduced to carrying their ammunition in their pockets. Not only that, but the average supply of ammunition per man amounted to five or six rounds — not enough ammo even for policing against the bushwhackers, never mind repelling any kind of serious Federal incursion.

One such incursion was already in the planning stages even as Stringfield fretted on paper to his commanding officer at Qualla-town. On February 1, George Kirk, at the head of 600 men, marched out of Newport, Tennessee and crossed the Great Smokies on their northern flank, at Sterling Gap. His primary objective was Waynesville. A single company of Home Guard blocked his path, but Kirk easily brushed them aside after a brief and apparently bloodless exchange of fire.

Waynesville was "easy pickin's," and Kirk turned his men loose to do what they liked with the town for nearly a whole day. The invaders tore through the little village like barbarians on a rampage, stealing anything they wanted, but paying especial attention to jewelry and silver. Many citizens were terrified and more than a few were beaten, but nobody seems to have been killed. In one act of pure, pointless vandalism, however, Kirk torched the home of a local Revolutionary War hero, Colonel Robert Love. The town jail received the same treatment, and all of its Unionist and deserter inmates were liberated; some of them joined Kirk's unit on the spot.

After the town had been thoroughly pillaged, Kirk marched away, in late afternoon, on the road to Balsam Gap. There, he camped for the night. After dark, a company of Haywood County militia, augmented by some irate local farmers, crept close to Kirk's position and fired a massed volley in the general direction of his campfires, hitting few men, but making a strong impression all the same. When Kirk's men replied with a blistering barrage from their Spencer repeaters, the locals prudently melted back into the forest.

Meanwhile, a lathered courier had ridden into Quallatown, where Bill Stringfield had gone to assume command of the whole district while Colonel Thomas was away in Asheville on official business. Stringfield rallied all the troops within his immediate reach — about 300 men, half of them Cherokees — and went forth to do battle with the mountain people's old nemesis. He would spend the next 72 hours in the saddle, trying first to find, and then to hurt, Kirk as much as he could. Even the Indians were hot to have a crack at Kirk. As Stringfield later wrote, "The Cherokees are good haters as well as fighters."[1] And Kirk's men, over the years, had given them plenty of reasons to hate.

Kirk had been more startled than hurt by that one nocturnal volley, but it clearly signaled that his position was known and that the countryside was turning out against him. Where there had been 100 angry mountaineers at midnight, there might be 500 by morning. He therefore decided not to forge ahead through Balsam Gap, but to double back through Waynesville and try passage through Soco Gap, a march of about 20 miles.

However, a small portion of Stringfield's command got there first: a detachment of sharpshooters under Lieutenant Robert T. Conley. From elevated and concealed positions on the slopes overlooking the pass, they opened a brisk fire on the head of Kirk's column. Kirk, realizing his men were too bushed from their march to storm such a position, ordered another retirement.

Kirk finally passed through Balsam Gap, without interference, on February 6 (not March 6, as Stringfield stated in his account, written many years later). He moved through the hamlet of Webster, then turned at the Tuckaseegee River, heading for Quallatown. He may have been after Colonel Thomas himself, but instead he met Bill Stringfield and his 300 men, positioned behind the trees at Soco Creek.

This was sacred ground for the local Cherokees. Here, the great Tecumseh had held council with their chief, attempting to persuade the tribe to join him during the War of 1812. And here, George Kirk almost met his Waterloo. Facts about this battle are infuriatingly scant. But everyone who bothered to mention it at all declared that the Indians fought with great enthusiasm and that, for a brief period of time, it looked as though Kirk had marched himself into a deadly trap. One can surmise, from looking at the maps, that Kirk must have found himself bushwhacked on a giant scale, with fire directed against him from elevations on three sides. Stringfield's summation of the battle is taciturn to the point of sourness: "...but for the want of ammunition [my men] would have badly worsted, if not destroyed, Kirk's entire force."[2]

It seems obvious, following Kirk's movements on the map, that on this occasion he had pushed his luck too far. There were only three or four routes he could have taken to get back to Tennessee from Waynesville: back the way he had come, or through the passes in the transverse Balsam Mountain chain. By all rights, he should have been in deep trouble on the morning after the Waynesville raid. The Confederates had a perfect chance to box him in, they had the advantage of the high ground, and they should have had numerical superiority. Yet what should have been a repeat performance of Braddock's defeat a century earlier fizzled out the moment Stringfield's men started to exhaust their ammunition — which must have been pretty soon, if most of them started the battle with only five or six rounds in their pockets. Although specific details are, again, maddeningly absent from the historical records, it appears that there were other Confederate companies in the area — which could have and should have helped bring Kirk to bay — but which actually sought to avoid engaging him, either by dawdling on the march until he was on his way back to Tennessee, or by showing up but simply not fighting.

Whatever the reasons, General Martin was disgusted by the ease with which Kirk disengaged at Soco Creek and made it back over the border. A few Indians trailed his column and sniped at it, but there was no more organized resistance. And the Unionist press in Tennessee once again trumpeted the triumphs of George Kirk. True, he had suffered more loses than he was used to (a dozen killed and twice that number wounded would be a reasonable estimate), but he had sacked Waynesville, killed at least 20 of the defenders, captured 20 more, liberated some Unionist prisoners, and brought back 150 stolen horses. (The last figure may have been an exaggeration, but if it wasn't, it represented a serious blow to the mobility, as well as the economic security, of many Confederates in Haywood County.) This raid, along with the increasingly ominous news from elsewhere in Confederacy, had a stimulating effect on Unionists inside the state as well as partisans across the border. As Stringfield summed it up: "...the enemy everywhere became more active and aggressive. The end was now rapidly approaching...."[3]

Things were no better in the counties north of Asheville that February. The Confederacy lost one of the few "strong points" it still controlled in the northwestern end of the state, and lost it in a manner that was even more humiliating than the way in which Kirk had managed to evade serious harm.

About the only military post of any note in the counties north of Asheville was Camp Mast, located at Sugar Grove, a few miles west of Boone. The camp was garrisoned by Home Guard companies from both Ashe and Watauga counties, and the post was manned in rotation: one company would pull active duty for a week, while the other company was at home minding the crops and looking after their families. Ringed by some elementary earthworks and an abatis of fallen timber, the camp was no Gibraltar, but it was strong enough to qualify as a fortified, "permanent," Confederate presence. No one expected it to have to repel an attack by Yankee regulars, but it was deemed adequate for holding off bands of Unionist outliers.

By February 1865, however, the Unionists in the region had grown bold enough to undertake a fairly ambitious operation against Camp Mast. A Federal recruiting agent from Indiana, John Champion, had concocted a daring plan to take Camp Mast, and its garrison of the week, out of the war. Setting up temporary clandestine headquarters at Banner Elk, Champion used the existing Unionist network to spread the word that he was looking for volunteers. Within 24 hours, a force of about 100 pro-Union men had assembled, not all of them armed, but all of them willing. In his first speech to the band, Champion made it clear that he would not tolerate any plundering; any man who had come just looking for a chance to rob his neighbor could leave now. Twenty disgruntled mountaineers did just that. The rest proceeded, via Valle Crucis, and reached the area outside of Camp Mast just before dawn, on or about February 5.

Champion bluffed his way to a cheap victory. He spread his meager force in a circle around the camp and ordered every second man to build a campfire. When reveille sounded inside the perimeter, the cold and sleepy Home Guardsmen stumbled out of their huts and saw the surrounding hills ablaze with what appeared to be the campfires of a multitudinous army. It was the oldest trick in the book, but it worked. An emissary was dispatched to the camp under flag of truce and immediate surrender was demanded. After some spirited discussion, the garrison put the matter to a vote. Only a dozen men voted to fight, even though the fortified camp could surely have held out against Champion's puny and poorly armed force of part-time bushwhackers.

Majority rule won out, and the camp surrendered, without a shot being fired, at 9 a.m. As the garrison filed out and stacked arms, they were flabbergasted to see not a regiment of Yankee cavalry, but a grinning mob of their Unionist neighbors, armed with a motley assortment of squirrel rifles and shotguns. The post's regular commander, Major Bingham, was the sort of diehard Confederate who would have offered resistance, but it so happened that he was away that night, in Jefferson, for a conference with another Home Guard commander. Was Champion just lucky on that particular date, or had someone inside the camp tipped him off? Chances are, the latter; the fact that one of the Watauga County Home Guard officers was later seen riding into Tennessee at Champion's side lends credibility to the quisling theory, and furnishes yet another example of the treacherous loyalties in the mountains.

A lot of the local inhabitants came out and cheered Champion and his partisans as they marched the Home Guard prisoners into captivity. "On the road from Valle Crucis to Banner Elk," wrote one contemporary historian, "[there] was but one family of Confederates...and for these people to see this long-dreaded militia marching as prisoners, was a greater show for them than a road full of lions, tigers, and elephants...."[4] Captain Champion treated his prisoners well, and many of them spoke warmly of him after the war. Anyway, most of the men who surrendered at Camp Mast were just as happy to be out of the war as the civilians they had been harassing were to see them gone. Ironically, when Captain Champion returned to his routine duties in the mountains of Tennessee, he made the mistake of entering a house without first making sure who was inside, and was murdered by a band of Confederate guerrillas hiding within.

All things considered, February 1865 was not a good month for General Martin. Not only did his men throw away their one good chance to wipe out George Kirk, but he had lost one of the few "secure" positions he had north of Asheville. News of Kirk's raid, and of Camp Mast's ignominious surrender, fueled the fires of regional discontent to a new temperature. From all parts of the mountain district came reports of increased Unionist activities. The Heroes of America, the so-called "Red String Society," after years of working underground, was now holding open meetings and defying the local Home Guard commanders to do anything about it. Up in Yancey County, near Burnsville, an entire battalion of men deserted in one day. And, as if things were not already bad enough, General Martin also had an open mutiny on his hands.

It was another case of mountaineer stubbornness colliding head-on with outside authority. Governor Zebulon Vance had finally been apprised of most of the facts concerning his brother's capture, and he had belatedly concluded that the fault was not Will Thomas's, but Lieutenant Colonel Henry's. In late January, the governor did the logical thing: He sacked Henry and replaced him with Colonel George Tait, former commander of the 40th North Carolina Regiment. When Tait arrived in Asheville on February 11 to take over his new assignment, he was promptly beaten to a pulp by his men, one of whom bashed him in the head with a large rock. As soon as he could walk again, Tait wired Vance: "I cannot command a mob...." and headed back to Raleigh.

The mutiny caused headlines in the state capital. Henry's mountaineers were vilified as traitors and there were sanguine calls for the old Roman practice of "decimation" to be reinstituted for Henry's entire command. In reply to the furor, one of the regiment's officers wrote a letter of explanation to the *Raleigh Standard* which read, in part: "Gov. Vance, without the knowledge and consent of Lieu. Col. Henry or any of his officers or men, appointed a Mr. Tate[sic] Colonel over all heads, senior and junior. This man Tate had neither hand nor influence in raising the 14th Battalion [the unit's original designation]. He is an Eastern man and is now by despotic power...forced upon a body of good and weather beaten soldiers...."[5]

The fallout from the incident was even worse than the incident itself. By March 1, General Martin could report to the War Department that there had been 130 desertions from Henry's old unit, as well as another 40 or so departures from the 64th and 62nd North Carolina regiments, the two other regular units that comprised Palmer's brigade. Martin did not attempt to gloss over the military realities in the mountain sector:

I regret...I have nothing to report but disobedience of orders, neglect of duty, demoralization of the people, and the desertion of both officers and men. The enemy has been able to impress the whole country with the belief that all this part of the state is to be given up by our forces, and in consequence every man is doing as little for our cause as he possibly can, hoping by this course, undoubtedly, to be able to save his property when the enemy takes possession....[6]

By the beginning of March 1865, there was a Federal tidal wave forming on the western side of the Blue Ridge Mountains, and not even the mountains would be able to hold it back.

ERUPTION FROM TENNESSEE

This time, by God, George Stoneman was going to free some prisoners or know the reason why. And if he were ever going to do it, it would have to be soon — any fool could see that the war was entering its last stages.

He was 42 in early 1865, and he had a lot to prove. Born in a tiny western New York village called Busti, Stoneman had graduated from West Point in 1846, along with classmates Stonewall Jackson and George McClellan. His military career up to the start of the Civil War had been solid, if not particularly distinguished, involving service on the fringes of the Mexican War and a decade or so of routine Indian-bashing in the Southwest. When the war broke out, he was a captain, but his friendship with McClellan soon helped nudge him into the rank of brigadier general in 1861, and major general in 1863.

His big chance to make a name for himself came in 1863, during the Chancellorsville campaign, when General "Fighting Joe" Hooker devised a plan that called for sending a cavalry corps of unprecedented size — some 10,000 sabers — in a massive raid against General Robert E. Lee's communications. The operation would be timed for maximum impact just before Hooker attempted his main flanking assault against Lee. So on April 29, 1863, Stoneman set off at the head of virtually the entire cavalry force of the Army of the Potomac.

Although it wasn't a disaster in the sense of huge casualty lists, the raid proved to be a serious tactical blunder on Hooker's part. Stoneman's cavalry tore up some railroad track outside Richmond

245

and provoked considerable alarm in the Confederate capital for a few days, but one of his columns — its commander paralyzed by fear of nonexistent rebel cavalry on his flanks — did almost nothing, and the damage inflicted by the column under Stoneman's direct command was, at most, a temporary annoyance. Lee did not bite the bait. He simply ignored Stoneman and concentrated on whipping Hooker, who found himself utterly bereft of cavalrymen just when he needed them most. And at the conclusion of his foray, Stoneman found himself relieved of a combat command; he spent a year or so shuffling papers in a Washington bureau. So much for Stoneman's First Raid.

He went into the field again with General William T. Sherman. Throughout the war of maneuvers between Sherman and General Joseph E. Johnston during the march on Atlanta, the Federal cavalry lost every significant engagement in which it was embroiled, despite the fact that the Union troopers were better armed and equipped than their adversaries. Yankees just didn't take to horse-soldiering as readily as their Southern counterparts (although, as General Philip Sheridan was to dramatically prove, they were surely capable of learning from their mistakes). Sherman, for his part, was so disgusted with his cavalry that for most of the campaign he used them as dismounted infantry.

Finally, though, there came into view a seemingly golden opportunity for Sherman's horse soldiers, and he turned them loose. If the Federal cavalry could ride around the besieged city of Atlanta — with one column of 3,500 sabers under General Edward McCook, and one column of 6,500 troopers under Stoneman, each converging from a different point on the compass — and knock out Lovejoy Station, they would effectively cut off General John B. Hood's last reliable line of supply and probably force him to abandon Atlanta without a fight.

Stoneman importuned Sherman for the chance to do something more. He wanted to keep going, beyond that first objective, all the way down to Macon and liberate the wretched inmates of the Confederate prison camp at Andersonville. Andersonville had already become an emotional issue in the North, as reports filtered out about the barbaric conditions there, and Stoneman's request was one that Sherman, in all conscience, could not refuse. Besides, there seemed to be a reasonable chance of success -- if the railroad was cut at Lovejoy Station first, that is.

Stoneman departed on his mission on July 26. But then he decided, strictly on his own, that McCook's men could handle Lovejoy Station by themselves. Rather than take part in that attack as planned, Stoneman led his men on a Custer-like plunge for glory, straight to Andersonville.

About the only thing this whole operation proved was that, despite their inferior armament, the Confederate cavalry could still ride rings around their Yankee counterparts. Ten thousand rebel horsemen, under the overall command of the hotspur General Joseph Wheeler, fell upon each Yankee column in turn. The Confederates killed or captured 2,000 Union cavalrymen, sending the rest falling back to Sherman in complete disarray. The railroad at Lovejoy Station was not severed, the 30,000 Yankee prisoners at Andersonville were not liberated, and George Stoneman was captured, along with 700 of his men, near Macon. Worst of all, it wasn't even one of Wheeler's regular units that captured Stoneman, but rather some Home Guard cavalry acting in concert with the main Confederate force. So much for Stoneman's Second Raid: It ended as a burning professional humiliation for an officer who had at least as many virtues as he had defects, and one which Stoneman spent the rest of the war trying to atone for.

Finally, in the closing weeks of the conflict, he was given a chance to wipe out those earlier blots on his record. Converging circumstances were about to make it possible for Stoneman to go down in history — or in the footnotes of history, at least — as the leader of Stoneman's Last Raid.

Stoneman had spent the autumn of 1864 in east Tennessee, that graveyard of professional military reputations, performing routine duties with routine competence. Photos taken of him at this time reveal a gaunt, tall (six-feet-four with his boots on), rangy man, glowering out at history with those smoldering Old Testament eyes that one sees in so many officers' photos of the period. In a haunted sort of way, he was a handsome man, with a firm mouth that was framed rather than obscured by his glossy, coarse black beard. He had large, slender, big-knuckled, articulate hands that looked as though they had been designed either to pound out octaves on a concert piano or to wield a cavalry saber.

Stoneman had watched the war slipping away from him, as each passing month brought a quickening of events. One by one, the Confederacy was losing its last strongholds. Mobile, the last important cotton port in rebel hands, fell in late 1864. In December, the brave but bull-headed Hood hurled the Army of Tennessee against strongly fortified lines during the Franklin-Nashville campaign, and achieved no more than General Ambrose Burnside had at Fredericksburg -- that is, the utter ruination of a magnificent army to no earthly purpose. Near the end of the year, Sherman stormed Savannah, Georgia. In January, Fort Fisher in North Carolina was overwhelmed, and the Confederacy lost Wilmington, its last link with Europe, its last source of imported strategic goods. Lee was still hanging on at Richmond, but he was getting by largely on the strength of his reputation; his army was stretched thin, wracked by massive desertions, and always on the verge of starvation. There were hundreds of tons of supplies accumulating in depots in North Carolina and western Virginia, but the Confederate supply service — grossly inefficient in its best days — had broken down, along with most of the locomotives and rolling stock.

By March, Sherman was about to link up with General John M. Schofield at Goldsboro, North Carolina, after which his forces would be far stronger than anything Joseph Johnston could hope to throw against him. And west of the mountains, in the Tennessee theater, the new commander of the Army of the Ohio, General Thomas, was preparing two major cavalry operations designed to tighten the noose around the throat of the shrinking Confederacy. One of these cavalry forces, under Major James H. Wilson, would be launched against the remaining rebel strongholds in Alabama; the other, under George Stoneman, would stab through the mountains of North Carolina and form, in effect, a hammer to Sherman's anvil.

Stoneman's previous commanding officer in Tennessee, General Schofield (who had just been transferred to the coast of North Carolina), had faith in the man's abilities. In December, Schofield had offered Stoneman a chance to redeem himself for his humiliation in Georgia. Stoneman had submitted a plan that was bold but well considered, not the scheme of a rash and reckless man at all.

He proposed to take a large body of horsemen on a deep, two-tiered raiding operation against some very sensitive rebel targets. First, he proposed to strike into southwestern Virginia, against the vital rail line between Bristol and Wytheville. Second, as long as he was already in the neighborhood, he would make a side trip to the saltworks at Saltville — which would be like stabbing a pin into Richmond's spinal cord. Then, rebounding off that objective, he would strike south into North Carolina, cross the edge of the Blue Ridge Mountains, and sweep down into Salisbury. His objectives there were twofold: liberate the 10,000 Yankees rotting in the Confederate prison camp at Salisbury, and destroy the large accumulations of war supplies being stockpiled there. The Confederates were stockpiling the supplies at Salisbury to keep them from falling into Sherman's hands, and also to form a strategic cache for Johnston or Lee, should either or both of those generals attempt to move their armies into western North Carolina.

In submitting his memorandum for this operation, Stoneman added a personal note: "I hope you will not disapprove...as I think we can see very important results from [this plan's] execution. I owe the Southern Confederacy a debt I am very anxious to liquidate, and this offers a propitious occasion...."[1]

On December 6, 1864, Schofield gave Stoneman the go-ahead for the first phase of this scheme, but put the Salisbury raid on hold until the overall situation in Virginia and western North Carolina became more clear. The timing of Schofield's permission was critical to Stoneman's career. Just one day earlier, on December 5, Schofield had received a telegram from the Secretary of War, ordering him to relieve Stoneman of command. Schofield decided to sit on the order and did not even inform Stoneman of its existence -- in effect, sticking out his own neck in order to give Stoneman a final chance to redeem his professional reputation. His faith was justified, for Stoneman's strike into southwestern Virginia was vigorous, disciplined, savagely destructive, and remarkably cheap in terms of casualties. Not until after Stoneman had returned from leveling Saltville did Schofield inform him of the directive of December 5. He also informed him that, because of the dramatic success of Stoneman's latest raid, he had prevailed upon the War Department, with General Ulysses S. Grant's personal concurrence, to have that order revoked.

Stoneman still wanted a chance to prove what he could do in the way of a strategic, rather than merely a tactical, operation. In the final days of the war's last winter, things were shaping up to give him a chance. In February 1865, as a reward for his successful foray in December, he was promoted to the post of commander of the district of east Tennessee. Meanwhile, General Grant was becoming more and more impressed with the devastating results Sherman was obtaining on the cheap: Old Tecumseh was closing in on Columbia, South Carolina, and all Confederate eyes in that region were watching the advance of his locust-like columns toward North Carolina. With all that attention focused in the east, Grant saw possibilities in reactivating Stoneman's plan for a massive cavalry raid from the west. With every available regular unit massing to oppose Sherman, the rebels would not have much left in the mountains to defend against a knife thrust in the back.

The plan's first version envisioned a strike by Stoneman from southeastern Tennessee into the northern corner of South Carolina, an agriculturally rich area that had not been affected by Sherman's campaign. On the way back, Grant reasoned, Stoneman could visit Salisbury, liberate the prisoners, burn the stockpiled supplies there, and scoot back to the Tennessee border before the Confederates would have a chance to block his retreat. By the time Stoneman actually collected his forces, however, Sherman had already captured and laid waste to Columbia, and had cut a tornado-like swath through the middle of South Carolina, against negligible opposition. There no longer seemed much point in flogging that strategically dead horse, so the Stoneman operation was slightly altered.

Instead of striking at South Carolina first, Stoneman would initially pass through the mountains along the New River Valley, do whatever damage he could in the upper northwest corner of North Carolina, then cross into Virginia and destroy all he could reach of the East Tennessee and Virginia Railroad. The strategic importance of that railroad was immense. It was one of Lee's two remaining supply lines, and it lay along his best route of retreat when the inevitable happened and Grant levered the Confederates out of the trenches in front of Richmond and Petersburg. After destroying this vital line in Lee's rear, Stoneman would then turn south, plunge into the Piedmont region of North Carolina, and tear up as much as he could of Lee's other major line of supply and retreat: the Greensboro-to-Danville railroad. Salisbury would, again, be the final major objective of this revised plan.

At Stoneman's disposal would be a force of approximately 6,000 horsemen, virtually all the cavalry available in east Tennessee. Stoneman's second-in-command would be the able but ruthless Brigadier General Alvan C. Gillem. Until now, Gillem had commanded a brigade of three east Tennessee regiments, the 8th, 9th, and 13th. There were mountaineers from both Tennessee and North Carolina in all of these units, but the 13th, especially, was comprised almost wholly of hard-bitten men from the disputed mountain counties. Stoneman called them his "Cossacks." In the weeks to come, Gillem's Tennessee regiments would acquire a reputation for brutality and brigandage fully equal to that of Sherman's "bummers" in the eastern part of the state. Hundreds of Gillem's men were natives of North Carolina who had been driven out of their home counties for their Unionist beliefs, and these men were burning for a chance to settle some old scores. A perceptive officer from the 15th Pennsylvania Cavalry -- the same hard-riding unit that had swooped down on General Robert Vance with such thundering success -- had something to say about Gillem's men. In a diary entry dated April 19, by which time he had had plenty of opportunities to see the 13th Regiment in action, he wrote:

> These Tennesseans in their present condition do not add any strength to the Union forces. In the beginning and during most of the war they had suffered terrible cruelties at the hands of the rebels. They had been hunted and shot down as unworthy of any humanity being shown them. Their homes were burned and their families driven away, and all because they were loyal to the flag, but now that the tables were turned and disloyal families were at their mercy, they repaid what they had suffered by an indiscriminate pillage. The result was a demoralized command, out of which little military duty could be had, and their General knew they were in no condition to fight an organized force, no matter how small.[2]

Stoneman's other regiments, however, were first-class: the 15th Pennsylvania, the 10th and 11th Michigan, the 11th and 12th

Kentucky, and the 12th Ohio. And the aggressiveness of Gillem's troopers was considered a greater asset than their dubious ability to face regular troops in a stand-up engagement. That kind of battle was just not expected to happen. General Grant's intelligence estimated the number of Confederate regulars in Stoneman's entire area of intended operations at 1,500 men. The Home Guard units, by this time in the war, were considered so worthless that nobody seriously factored them into the planning. Besides, Stoneman was under strict orders to "destroy but not to fight" unless he absolutely had to.

The raiding force was organized into three brigades of three regiments each, commanded, respectively, by Colonel William Palmer (the same intrepid Pennsylvanian who had gotten the drop on both Robert Vance and Will Thomas), Brigadier General Simeon B. Brown, and Colonel John K. Miller. In the interests of mobility, the force was ordered to travel light. There were only two pack mules per company: one for ammunition, the other for cooking utensils. Officers were limited to the personal effects they could pack into their own saddle bags. Each man was issued ammunition (from 63 to 100 rounds, depending on his company), a quartet of spare horseshoes, and a handful of nails. On the day the shoes and nails were issued, Captain Weand of the 15th Pennsylvania noted in his diary that "this smacks of a hard campaign." Stoneman's support elements were also stripped to the bone: a dozen ambulances (all of which broke down before the campaign was half over), four supply wagons, and a four-gun battery of artillery.

A number of Stoneman's troopers are known to have carried Spencer repeating carbines, giving them an additional edge of firepower over any force they were likely to meet, but exactly how many men carried Spencers is impossible to say. Despite its proven superiority, the Spencer was never officially adopted by the U.S. Army. (If it had, the Civil War might have ended at least a year earlier, for the South lacked the technology required to manufacture repeating rifles.) The only way a unit could acquire Spencers was to purchase them from the manufacturer. Some companies took up collections, and others were outfitted by their commanding officers, who sometimes paid for the guns out of their own pockets.

Stoneman's troopers were handsomely, indeed rather romanti-
cally, clad. The officers wore double-breasted frock coats with
canary-yellow stripes down their trouser seams, and the men wore
sky-blue overcoats with capes of yellow flannel, which could be
pulled over their heads during inclement weather.

There was some delay in starting the operation, because Stoneman first had to replace all the horses lost in the Saltville raid in
December. This took much longer than he anticipated, due to the
general shortage of good mounts in the Knoxville region — the
result of three and a half years of horse stealing and hard riding by
both sides. General Grant prodded Stoneman with telegrams,
urging him to get cracking. Stoneman replied, on March 1: "You
cannot be more anxious to get me off than I am to go...."[3]

Finally he was ready. All nine regiments, well mounted and in
good spirits, concentrated on March 23 at Morristown, Tennessee,
where the loyalist citizens gave the men a rousing farewell, lining
the streets and cheering as the cavalrymen rode through town. Once
the horse soldiers left the foothills and entered the mountains,
however, the march became a hard one, despite the assistance from
local Unionists. Captain Weand penned a vivid description of this
stage of the campaign in a diary entry dated March 27, 1865:

> ...Moved early to find something for our horses to eat, and found a
> short feed for them on the south bank of the Watauga River.
> Marched eighteen miles, and bivouacked on the mountain pass near
> the top of Stone Mountain at 4 A.M., on the 28th. Our march this
> night was one that those who participated in it will never forget. The
> road at times ran close to dangerous precipices, over which
> occasionally a horse or mule would fall, and in like manner we lost
> one of the artillery caissons, but no man was hurt. Many loyal
> citizens built fires along the road and at dangerous places, and also
> at difficult fords over the mountain streams. Looking back as we
> toiled up the mountain, the scene was grand and imposing as the
> march of the column was shown by the trail of fire along the road.
> Occasionally an old pine tree would take fire and blaze up almost
> instantaneously, looking like a column of fire...the sight of it repaid
> us for the toilsome night march.[4]

On March 28, at Sugar Grove in Watauga County, Stoneman's
force crossed into North Carolina. Riding point as his advance

guard was a detachment from the 12th Kentucky. The column passed just north of Banner Elk, but if anyone from that village spotted the bluecoats, they gave no alarm, for Banner Elk was a stout Union enclave. (Of the 14 Banner Elk boys who had enlisted to fight in the war, 13 had gone to the Federals.)

Boone lay directly in the invaders' path, however, and it was there that the first shooting erupted. Every account of the skirmish differs in detail, and (not surprisingly) no two accounts give the same tally of casualties.

What apparently happened was this. The local Home Guard company had received scant warning, and an entirely false impression, of the approaching enemy. The few loyal Confederates remaining in the ranks of the Watauga County Home Guard were still smarting about the way they had been bushwhacked by Jim Hartley's little guerrilla force at Beech Mountain, and they were sick and tired of the public derision that had been heaped upon them after the way Captain Champion had suckered the garrison of Camp Mast (nearly one-half of all the Home Guard troops in both Ashe and Watauga Counties) into surrendering. They needed an opportunity to redeem their pride, but this wasn't it. Whoever brought word of Stoneman's approach conveyed a faulty impression that the invaders were just another bunch of scruffy raiders from the Tennessee border country.

Local historian Shepherd Dugger, who interviewed several participants while the events were still fresh in their memories, got the distinct impression that nobody in the little Home Guard detachment had any idea they were about to take on 6,000 Federal regulars. When the point detachment of Kentuckians came into view, the Home Guards assumed it was the entire enemy force. If they had known the truth, the Confederate veterans assured Dugger, no man in his right mind would have squeezed a trigger.

In fact, the entire skirmish may have been started by the accidental discharge of one of the Home Guard rifles. It was not much of a battle, at any rate. There was a volley, probably just one, from the Home Guard, and one of Stoneman's men was hit, possibly killed. Hearing gunfire, the rest of the head of the Union column closed up fast and rode into Boone blazing away. Aghast at this sudden flood of blue uniforms, the vast majority of the Home Guard soldiers immediately took to their heels, some men not returning home for days. But once the shooting had started, it took some time for it to stop. Before it finally did, the little village of Boone was pretty well shot up.

As the Federal cavalry poured into town, a lady named Mrs. Councill, holding an infant in her arms, stepped out on her front porch to see what all the ruckus was about. She narrowly escaped death when a cluster of carbine rounds tore splinters out of the doorframe on either side of her head. A relative of her husband, a man named Jacob Councill, was not so lucky. He was out plowing his fields when some of Gillem's men rode by in pursuit of the fleeing Home Guard. Councill's field hand, overjoyed at the prospect of liberation from slavery, ran to the closest Yankees, got their attention, pointed to his master, and described him as "an infernal rebel." Despite his protestations of innocence (Councill had never borne arms for the Confederacy), Gillem's men shot him dead where he stood.

At least three members of the Home Guard died in the initial shooting. But a few, instead of running into the woods, dug in their heels and offered examples of brave but utterly futile resistance. One die-hard rebel named Calvin Green blew off an arm of one of Stoneman's troopers as they were chasing him through town; Green was in turn shot and left for dead, although he eventually recovered from his wounds. The most spirited resistance was offered by a 15-year-old boy named Steel Frazier, who was frantically chased by a six-man squad of Federals through the backyards of Boone. Frazier managed to kill two of the Yankees before escaping, rather miraculously, into the forest at the edge of town. Sixty-two of Boone's inhabitants were taken prisoner during that wild morning, and at least five wounded men — from which side, it is impossible to say — were treated by Stoneman's surgeons later that night.

General Gillem wanted to teach the recalcitrant inhabitants a lesson, so he burned down the county jail, and, with it, all the historical records of Watauga County. It was an act of pure vandalism, and he was angrily reprimanded for it by General Stoneman. Meanwhile, the captured Confederates were marched off under guard to Tennessee and sent on to the Federal prison camp at Camp

Chase, Ohio. The war ended soon and their captivity was mercifully brief, but since many of them were men in their 50s and 60s, several are known to have perished.

Aside from torching the county jail, the Federals did little pillaging during their brief stay in Boone. They did tease the inhabitants, though, by assuring them that their old friend George Kirk would soon be coming. Kirk's assignment in the campaign was to guard the back door for Stoneman. Kirk and a large detachment of the "Home Yankee" Second North Carolina Mounted Volunteers arrived on April 6. He made his headquarters at the home of the same Mrs. Councill who had so narrowly escaped death during the street fighting of March 28, and his men behaved like a pack of Huns, trampling the flowerbeds, urinating in the yard, relieving various citizens of such burdensome possessions as watches, coins, and rings, and leaving hunks of half-eaten meat to putrefy in the street — no one dared clean up the mess until after Kirk had moved on. He also cut loopholes in the county courthouse, so it could be used as a strongpoint if necessary, and he left a garrison of 200 men at Watauga Gap, strongly fortifying the place with log blockhouses.

After studying the maps and gleaning a lot of firsthand intelligence from area Unionists, Stoneman decided to divide his command before pushing beyond Boone. There simply was not enough forage left in the county for 6,000 men and horses traveling on the same road. Colonel Palmer and his brigade were ordered to proceed to Wilkesboro, through Deep Gap in the Blue Ridge; the other two brigades would march to Wilkesboro by a more roundabout route, through Flat Gap. Stoneman elected to ride with Palmer's column, which also contained the artillery.

At about 9 p.m. on March 28, Brown's and Miller's brigades, with General Gillem, reached Patterson's Mills, on the Yadkin River not far from Lenoir. Here, in the so-called "Happy Valley" section of the Yadkin Valley, the horsemen found not only ample forage for their mounts, but also a good supply of bacon for themselves. Brown's brigade ate its fill and rested until midday the following morning, when it resumed the march. A small guard was left to assist the following brigade — Miller's — in obtaining its share of the forage. Afterward, on Gillem's direct orders, Mr.

Patterson's mills were burned. Once again, Stoneman had angry words with his overzealous second-in-command, for Patterson was about as close to neutral as anyone still alive in the mountains. Furthermore, Patterson supplied large amounts of his output to Federal purchasing agents from east Tennessee; by burning down his mills, Gillem was, in effect, taking bread from the mouths of loyalists across the border. Gillem didn't see things that way: "neutralist" was a label he did not recognize anymore.

Stoneman's whole command was reunited on March 29. That same night, the 12th Ohio overran Wilkesboro with little shooting and no casualties. The next morning, in search of forage, the 15th Pennsylvania, 10th Michigan, and 12th Ohio regiments crossed to the north side of the Yadkin River. But before the remaining part of Stoneman's force -- including both Stoneman and Gillem -- could reach the ford, spring rains caused the river to rise. The last stragglers who tried to cross had some trouble; one man and several horses drowned in the attempt. A veteran Pennsylvania trooper named Howard Buzby, mounted on his faithful horse "Camelback," was ordered to remain on the Wilkesboro side of the river and to inform General Stoneman about what happened. This gave Buzby a chance to observe and later recount the strange tale of an impromptu "review" of Gillem's column, held in the middle of a cold downpour by an apoplectic General Stoneman.

The tale starts with Buzby waiting miserably in the rain for more than an hour, the river rapidly rising. Finally General Stoneman rode up. Buzby rode over, saluted, identified himself, and gave the general his message. Stoneman then rode with Buzby to the river's edge and beheld the Yadkin in full, foaming, cry; if it had been bad 90 minutes ago, it was impassable now, for the water had risen at least another foot.

"How long since they crossed?" asked Stoneman.

"About an hour and a half, sir," Buzby replied.

According to Buzby, Stoneman then turned the misty air blue with his language. Many years later, Buzby wrote, "Swearing does not look well in print, nor sound well in talking, so what he said, you will not know." One can only guess.

Buzby then volunteered to take "Camelback" across, confident that his steed was up to the task, but Stoneman refused to let him try. Instead, he ordered one of his own staff into the water. This officer did not get ten feet beyond the bank before both horse and rider were in serious trouble. When they finally managed to struggle back up the muddy banks, Stoneman flew into a rage. He began cursing everyone and everything in sight, including — perhaps especially -- General Gillem, whom for some reason he blamed for everything.

"I...thought Gillem's last day had come," recalled Buzby. "In fact, I thought everybody around Stoneman would be killed. He fairly roared like a lion...."[5]

His rage at the elements vented, Stoneman apparently resigned himself to waiting for the river to go down. To give himself something to do, he ordered the incredulous Gillem to pass his men in an impromptu "review." Gillem must have blanched at the order, for his men were in no condition to parade before the commander in chief at that moment.

For one thing, a good many of them had tethered their regular mounts and were riding along in a procession of stolen carriages, fiacres, wagons, and at least one stagecoach. This colorful but unsoldierly procession, Buzby reported, was at least a mile long. For another thing, since many of Gillem's men were local mountaineers, they were well aware of the fact that Wilkes County was (and still is) the home of some of the finest moonshine whiskey made in the state of North Carolina, and during the last day or so, a surprisingly large quantity of it had been unearthed along the route of march. As a result, most of Gillem's men were reeling drunk, and they looked to have been that way for some time.

So as Gillem's men straggled past in the pouring rain, many of them barely able to hang in the saddle, Stoneman's face darkened even further. When the procession of omnibuses and carriages began to lurch by, Buzby recalled, a "carriage of the George Washington type" rolled past completely filled with passed-out soldiers, "their boots sticking out in all directions." Stoneman began to sputter incoherently. He threatened, at one point, to have some of Gillem's men shot, but in the end contented himself with hauling a number of officers out of the column and demoting them on the spot.

The civilians on the north side of the Yadkin River, by contrast, were surprised at the good behavior of Palmer's men. A gentleman farmer named James Gwyn recorded in his diary:

> ...We were all very agreeably disappointed; those who passed the [farm of] Mr. Hickerson acted very well indeed, took only cattle & horses & mules & did not even enter our houses, or do violence to our families, & destroyed nothing but a little corn and oats which was thrown out to their horses. I kept out of the way thinking I might be taken off...but I need not have...they would not have molested me....[6]

While the two river-separated parts of Stoneman's command kept in intermittent communication by means of signal flags, Palmer proceeded to Elkin, arriving there on April 1. There he found a cotton factory staffed by 60 girls and women, who welcomed the Yankees with what seemed like unfeigned good will, as well as a warehouse full of such welcome comestibles as honey, molasses, butter, chestnuts, and prime-grade tobacco. Palmer's entire column soon appeared to be wreathed in cigar smoke.

Stoneman appeared across the river a little later that day, at Jonesville, on the bluffs opposite Elkin. After another exchange of signals, it was agreed by the commanders of both columns that the river was still too high to risk fording on horseback. Stoneman told Palmer to proceed to Rockford, farther downstream. By the time he got there, the river had fallen enough to permit Stoneman to unite his whole force once more, on the morning of April 2.

When the people living near Elkin had seen the last Yankees depart, the invaders gave every appearance of following the course of the Yadkin to where it makes a big bend to the south. It seemed obvious to anyone who knew regional geography that Stoneman must be on his way toward the only significant military objective in the vicinity: Salisbury. That was the conclusion drawn by Confederate officers in the region, anyway. General Pierre Beauregard, in command of the motley Confederate garrisons scattered from Greensboro to Charlotte, hastily rounded up a sizable force of men, together with more cannon than Stoneman had, and rushed them to Salisbury, fully expecting a head-on battle with Stoneman somewhere between that city and the south bank of the Yadkin.

Had Stoneman tried to take Salisbury at this time, there's little doubt that he would have had, at best, only an even chance of penetrating Beauregard's defenses -- and less of a chance if he had delayed long enough to give the Confederates time to really fortify the approaches. But hours, then days, went by, and there was no sign of Stoneman's force. It was as though the Yankees had vanished into the Yadkin mists.

Then the telegraph wires began to hum with news: Stoneman's regiments were swarming all over the railroad line south of Lynchburg, firing bridges, bending rails, and burning supplies. It looked as though the Yankees' march through North Carolina had been just a brief flanking movement through the mountains, a maneuver to enable them to fall on Lee's supply lines in southwestern Virginia. The Confederates in North Carolina breathed a sigh of relief.

It was a very premature sigh.

INTO
THE PIEDMONT

Once his entire command was over the Yadkin River, General Stoneman lost no time striking due north through Surry County. Just above Mount Airy, the Federals overtook and easily captured a large wagon train full of supplies. After taking what they pleased, they burned the rest. For many years afterwards, the place where this happened — near Dalton, North Carolina — was marked by a big pile of blackened wagon-wheel rims.

For the second time, as he entered Virginia, Stoneman and his force crossed the Blue Ridge, this time at Fancy Gap. A few shots were fired at them by the Home Guard in Hillsville, but other than that, they encountered no opposition. By the morning of April 4, the entire raiding force was encamped in that village.

It was a sensitive time for 6,000 Federal cavalrymen to suddenly appear in this area. Only 48 hours earlier, General Lee, his lines stretched to the breaking point, had abandoned Richmond and started a withdrawal to the southwest. This was the only route of march that offered even the possibility of continued resistance. He was hoping to link up with a sizable force of rebel troops -- about 4,500 infantry and 2,200 cavalry under General John Echols -- that had been garrisoned in the southwestern corner of Virginia. The wagon train Stoneman's troops had captured was part of this area-wide concentration, and Stoneman's sudden thrust into the middle of it would have intensely disruptive consequences.

After evaluating the latest intelligence and carefully studying his maps, Stoneman decided to break his command into separate raiding detachments, give each one a realistic objective as well as the freedom to tackle targets of opportunity, and then turn them loose to raise all the hell they could.

Five hundred men, under Colonel Miller, left first, following the railroad southwest to Wytheville. They destroyed two bridges and a substantial cache of supplies, including five tons of gunpowder. The Confederates in the Wytheville area reacted like disturbed hornets, however, and Miller had to cut his way through a desperate attack by rebel cavalry, losing 35 men in the engagement — Stoneman's highest loss for any single encounter.

Meanwhile, Stoneman took the rest of his command to Jacksonville, which was already bedecked with white flags by the time he arrived. From there, he peeled off another raiding party of 250 men from the 15th Pennsylvania, under the command of Major William Wagner. Wagner's orders were to follow the railroad in a northeasterly direction and do all the damage he could, while avoiding any pitched battles, if possible.

Wagner's little force would have an effect all out of proportion to its size. By the time he set off, on April 4, Robert E. Lee's options had dwindled still further. Lee had hoped to concentrate his troops at Danville, Virginia, where Jefferson Davis had set up temporary headquarters, and where hundreds of rebel stragglers had been put to work throwing up fortifications. But the rapid progress of General Sheridan's cavalry and General Ord's infantry had made it impossible for Lee to reach Danville without fighting his way through. He was left with only one option: withdrawal toward Lynchburg. But when reports reached him of Wagner's activities, he interpreted them to mean that Wagner was the advance guard of a major Federal force closing in on Lynchburg. With the enemy blocking him to the south, hotly pursuing him from behind, and now concentrating ahead of him as well, Lee found himself boxed in. Five days after Wagner's men struck out on their raid, Lee surrendered at Appomattox.

Wagner's first objective was the railroad town of Christiansburg, about midway between Lynchburg and Wytheville. He hit the town so hard and so fast that the telegraph office was captured before the Confederate on duty there had time to send out the news. This gave Wagner a chance to do some impromptu intelligence gathering, for he had had the foresight to bring his own expert telegraphist, a young fellow named John Wickham. Wickham began tapping out inquiries to Lynchburg, but then thought better of it: If the rebel operator on the other end knew his stuff, he would be able to tell the difference in "touch" between different telegraphists, and his suspicions would be aroused. So instead, the Yankees forced the Confederate telegraphist to send messages dictated by Wickham.

For a while, the ruse worked. For the first time, the Federals learned that Lee had evacuated Richmond and was in full retreat. Wickham pushed his luck, then, and started asking pointed questions of the Lynchburg operator. Where is the largest rebel force between us and Lynchburg? What news do you have about Yankee movements?

There was a long pause in the click-clacking. Finally there was this signal from Lynchburg: "I believe I am talking to the Yankees now...."

Having gathered the most important news anyway, Wickham dropped all pretenses and took over the key himself, explaining who he was. In the words of a Federal soldier who was present at the time: "The Lynchburg man let out with all the 'cuss' words he was able to recall...especially was his blasphemy heaped on the poor operator who had been forced to send the messages. But here Wickham stopped him, and wired back that he should not blame him, as a fellow with a pistol at his head is apt to say just what the fellow who holds the pistol wants him to say...."[1]

By mid-afternoon, April 5, Wagner had reached Salem, Virginia, which he found to be empty of rebel troops and virtually cleaned out of supplies. He burned a few wagons, but soon learned that the last train, crammed with troops and military stores, had pulled out only five minutes ahead of his troopers. Wagner pressed on and encamped at the Peaks of Otter area at about ten o'clock that night.

Wagner realized, from the news he had conned out of the telegraphist in Lynchburg, that the war was all but finished. A humane officer, he was reluctant to carry out any more destruction than was absolutely necessary. His men had taken control of two magnificent bridges over the Big Otter and Little Otter rivers, both spanning gorges over 100 feet deep and one of them nearly 1,000 feet long. It seemed a shame to destroy such splendid feats of engineering, when, in only a matter of days, they were sure to revert to peacetime use. Wagner waited almost 24 hours, until nightfall on April 7, hoping that orders would arrive which would free him of having to commit this pointless act of destruction.

When the orders did not come, he carried out his standing orders like the good soldier that he was, and told his men to fire the fence rails they had stacked on the bridges for kindling. By 11 p.m., the two bridges had fallen, in cascades of giant embers, into the waters below.

The next day, April 8, Wagner's force came to within a few miles of Lynchburg, but his scouts reported that the city was still too full of rebel troops to risk an assault. Content that he had performed his mission — indeed, he had performed more of it than he really wanted to — Wagner turned around and rejoined the rest of his regiment, narrowly avoiding contact with a 1,500-man force of Confederate cavalry that was lying in wait for him at Henry Court House. Since being detached from Stoneman's column, Wagner and his troopers had ridden almost 300 miles through hostile territory.

Success attended the other raids as well. The 11th Kentucky met no resistance when it captured and burned the New River bridges and tore up 20 miles of railroad track. The 10th Michigan did the same to the bridges over the Roanoke River. By the time Wagner's detachment rejoined the command, Stoneman's troopers had knocked out a 150-mile stretch of railroad and burned a half-dozen critical bridges, effectively paralyzing any last-minute Confederate concentration or resupply efforts. It was now time for the Federal raiders to leave Virginia and complete their work in North Carolina. Moving along different routes, the command headed toward a rendezvous point at Danbury, North Carolina. Only one regiment encountered any hostile forces during the return march: Colonel Palmer ran into a detachment of Wheeler's cavalry near Martinsville, Virginia, losing one man killed and five wounded in the skirmish.

By the time Stoneman's forces reached Germantown, North Carolina, on April 10, the Federals were encumbered with hundreds of Negroes who had attached themselves to the column as it passed through the countryside. Since Stoneman still needed to move fast and be able to deploy in a hurry in case of trouble, this "tail" of refugees had become a tactical liability. Detaching a small troop of guards for the ex-slaves' protection, Stoneman now sent them all off toward east Tennessee, where more than a hundred of the able-bodied males enlisted in the 119th U.S. Colored Regiment, one of the units that was busily fortifying the mountain passes behind Stoneman's original route of entry.

Germantown, incidentally, did not favorably impress the Pennsylvanians, who naturally compared it to the Germantown in their home state. They found the North Carolina town to be dirty, unpainted, and torpid: "Laziness is apparent all over it," wrote Captain Weand in his diary, on April 10.[2]

From Germantown, on April 10, Colonel Palmer's brigade was again detached and sent to the Winston-Salem area, with orders to destroy any targets of military value he could find. Upon learning that Stoneman was not only back in North Carolina, but on the very outskirts of town, a deputation of two dozen leading citizens marched out from Salem to meet the Yankees, waving white handkerchiefs. They were not well received, however, because a hot-headed Confederate picket had fired at Palmer's advance guard a little farther down the road. Consequently, despite their white handkerchiefs, the good burghers of Salem were nearly trampled down by a squad of irate Yankee horsemen. Corporal Smith D. Cozens, a Philadelphian who was riding with Palmer's advance guard that day, described the incident in detail:

> We reached the top of the hill, and right in front of us lay the town in plain view, about a mile and a half away, and at the bottom of the hill, a Rebel picket post of five or six men. We all saw them at once, and they us. I can remember so distinctly [my comrade] Overholt's remark, "Cozens, there's the Johnnies!" ...instantly I whipped out my revolver and said, "Come on, boys!" and they came.
>
> As soon as the Rebels caught sight of us they, with one exception, mounted their horses and commenced to move toward the town; this one threw his carbine over the saddle of his horse and fired at us, and I heard the bullet whistle past me...Three times he fired, but we were going down hill at a tremendous pace, and were close to him before he mounted, and then he flew away from us like the wind and was soon ahead of his comrades.
>
> We commenced to gain on them, and in another 100 yards I was within a horse's length of the hindmost. I shouted at him to "halt!" but he kept on. The boys behind me called to me to shoot him, which I could have done, as I was almost touching his horse. While on the dead run, I raised my pistol to fire, and as I did so, he turned in the saddle and disclosed the terror-stricken face of a half-grown boy. I

thrust my pistol into my blouse, and giving [my horse] an extra dig
with the spurs, I grasped the bridle of his horse and pulled him back
standing, snatching the pistol out of his hand.

...We were getting close to the town, when I discovered, right in
front of us, a party of twenty or thirty men, drawn up across the road,
holding up their hands and hats as if hailing us to stop, I saw that
they were not armed, but our blood was up, and we went through
them with a shout, scattering them like chaff. On into town we went,
the people flying in all directions, and in a few moments we were
in the center of the place, right in front of the post office.[3]

Despite this less-than-promising start, relations between
Palmer's men and the citizens of Salem proved to be quite un-
ruffled. Captain Weand's diary entry reveals how surprisingly
pleasant the whole occupation was:

April 10th...at 6 p.m. we reached Winston and Salem. Each has a
name of its own, but the two towns are really one. Here we met with
a most cordial reception, very different from the greetings we
usually receive. The ladies cheered us, and brought out bread, pies,
and cakes. The towns were settled by Moravians, from Bethlehem,
Pa. The people showed much enthusiasm at the sight of the flag we
carried, and many were the touching remarks made about it. Old
men wept like children and prominent citizens took off their hats and
bowed to it. Some women got to their knees, while we heard such
expressions as: "Look at the old flag!" "God bless it!" "Let me kiss
that flag!" ...there are plenty of stores here, and in the center of town
one of the finest seminaries we have seen in the South. It was a
charming place and they were good Union people, but we had no time
just then to do more than acknowledge it.[4]

Another eyewitness account, from the Moravian Archives of
Winston-Salem, confirms that the brief Federal occupation was
unexpectedly agreeable for all concerned:

In very great comparative silence about 3,000 cavalry passed
through our town, pitching their tents on the high ground beyond
the creek. Had it not been for the noise their horses and swords
made, it would have been hardly noticed that so large a number of
troops were passing through our streets. The strictest discipline was
enforced, guards rode up and down every street and very few...were
the violations of proper and becoming conduct on the part of the

soldiers...Fears were entertained by some, whether their good behavior would continue to last, and no doubt many a prayer ascended to the throne of a prayer hearing and answering God; and not in vain, for no outrages except the pressing of horses...were committed and even the cotton manufactory was spared by the Federals....[5]

As well-behaved as these Yankees were, the local citizens hedged their bets by hiding everything from horses to hamhocks until the bluecoats left town.

The 15th Pennsylvania did not have long to tarry in the pleasant surroundings of Winston and Salem. Stoneman had given Palmer orders to send out raiding parties from there to wreak all possible damage on the Greensboro-Danville railroad line, as well as the various factories and depots scattered through that part of the Piedmont.

An 86-man detachment headed for Florence and Jamestown. After a hard all-night ride, they reached that area on the morning of April 11. A 100-foot-long covered bridge over Deep River was burned, 40 or so men (including three officers) were taken, 60 horses and mules were captured, and an arms factory was demolished, along with 800 stand of finished rifles and 2,500 weapons in various stages of assembly. Another arms depot, at Florence, yielded 1,000 stand of arms, together with supplies of cotton, bacon, uniform cloth, flour, and salt. Everything was put to the torch, and the raiding party rejoined the regiment without losing a man, having ridden 52 miles and accomplished all that destruction in a mere 12 hours.

At the same time, another detachment of 100 men struck northeast. Its objective was the new Reedy Fork bridge, one of the most important links in the Greensboro-Danville line. The Reedy Fork structure proved unusually tough to bring down. It was new, built of unseasoned hardwood, and very strong. Two hours' work with axes and saws was required to prepare the bridge for burning, and during some of that time the raiding party was under long-range fire from a growing number of Confederate skirmishers and dismounted cavalry.

Shortly after they finally got the bridge blazing, the raiding detachment learned from some captured rebels that the train bearing Jefferson Davis and his entire Confederate cabinet had passed over the structure not one hour before the Pennsylvanians had started tearing it down.

With Palmer now in charge of a whole brigade, operational command of the 15th Pennsylvania had passed to one of his staff, Colonel Charles M. Betts. While Palmer's other raiding parties were "tearing up the pea patch" in that part of the Piedmont, Betts himself decided to lead a demonstration raid in the vicinity of Greensboro. Not far from that city, his scouts reported that there was a sizable body of rebel cavalry encamped only a mile away. This turned out to be the whole 3rd South Carolina cavalry regiment. Betts surprised them at breakfast with a hell-for-leather charge:

> The rebels fled to a neighboring meadow and took cover in a ditch, where they might have made a good defence and beaten us off, but our attack was so sudden that they never had time to get their second wind, and on demand they surrendered. The whole action and its results demonstrated what General Palmer had so often drilled into us, that a bold, dashing charge by a small body of good troops would overcome a much larger force.[6]

One of the Confederate prisoners, shaking his head in disbelief at the suddenness with which his entire outfit had been captured, asked his Pennsylvanian guard: "Do you fight this way all the time?"

"Yes," replied the Yankee trooper, "this is our style of fighting; how do you like it?" The Confederate's reply, if printable, was not recorded.

Another prisoner, an officer, disdainfully noted that, of the hundred or so rounds fired by the Pennsylvanians, none had hit anybody. "I congratulate you on your marksmanship," he sneered.

A Yankee officer, whose horse had been shot from under him during the charge (the only recorded casualty of the skirmish), angrily called back: "And the same to you, damn you!"

The breakfast which the South Carolinians had been fixing for themselves included a big chicken pie, still baking in a Dutch oven, and some peach brandy. Betts's men helped themselves to both. After what must have been a very satisfying meal, Betts sent a ten-man detachment further toward Greensboro — without much hope of seeing any of them again, he later admitted — under orders to burn the bridge over Buffalo Creek and chop down any telegraph wires they could find. When this detachment, commanded by a lieutenant named Wilson, reached the bridge, they apparently had to disperse a few Home Guard sentries. Federal accounts mention no fighting, so the skirmish must not have amounted to much. But modern-day Civil War buffs in Greensboro, using metal detectors, have dug up enough spent carbine rounds from the site of the old bridge to indicate that there must have been a fairly brisk exchange of fire.

Once his men were in control of the Buffalo Creek bridge, Wilson discovered a local farmer plowing his fields nearby. When Wilson approached the man, prepared to requisition an axe from him at gunpoint if need be, he was surprised to find the farmer quite willing to aid them. "I will help you, for I am as good a Union man as God let's live, but this is the first time I have dared say so."[7]

All of this raiding activity had the effect of drawing Confederate attention, and reserves, toward Greensboro. This enabled Stoneman to organize his move on Salisbury without any interference.

While Palmer's First Brigade was moving through Salem, Stoneman's Second and Third Brigades marched from German-town to Bethania. They dramatically interrupted some Easter Week religious services and ate everything in sight, but otherwise did little mischief. From Bethania, Stoneman headed back toward the Yadkin River, wresting Shallow Ford easily from a small party of Confederate pickets. From Shallow Ford, they marched southwest, toward Mocksville. The Mocksville Home Guard, a few dozen old men and boys, turned out for battle under the mistaken impression that the force reported on the outskirts of town was just another party of bushwhackers. They offered some resistance at Elisha Creek, but as soon as they realized the full strength of the Yankee force, they left the field. Stoneman burned down a cotton mill in Mocksville, and the citizens felt mightily put-upon at being ordered to prepare food for so many Yankees. Still, they got off lightly in terms of looting and rude behavior, as most of these towns did when Stoneman himself was present to keep an eye on discipline. Later, when Stoneman returned to Tennessee after completing his sack of Salisbury, tactical command reverted to General Gillem and the situation changed drastically.

At this time, Stoneman still was not aware that nearly all of the inmates of the notorious Salisbury prison camp had been evacuated in February, and that the last 500 or so men left there -- mostly those who had been too ill to leave with the earlier batch -- had been shipped to Charlotte at about the moment Stoneman was passing into Virginia.

No doubt Stoneman was disappointed over not being able to liberate the men personally, particularly in view of his good intentions and dismal failure on the Andersonville raid. But he had no doubts about the fact that, even without the prisoners, Salisbury was the most significant military objective left in North Carolina (with the exception of Jefferson Davis himself, of course). Governor Vance had sent sizable quantities of military stores down the rail line to Salisbury, both to keep them out of General Sherman's hands and to create a strategic stockpile in case General Johnston should fall back toward the mountains and try to maintain Confederate resistance for a while longer.

General Beauregard had ordered the Yadkin River bridge, eight miles northeast of Salisbury, fortified in late March. However, most of the troops who had been in the vicinity were pulled away by the raiding activity around Greensboro. On April 12, Beauregard received definite information that Stoneman was, in fact, at Shallow Ford, obviously making for Salisbury rather than Greensboro. He quickly ordered the troops who had been sent to Greensboro to turn around and hurry back to defend Salisbury. By that time, however, the railroads were so broken-down -- between what Palmer's men had done to them and four years of hard usage -- that no reinforcements arrived at Salisbury until after Stoneman had come and gone. When he attacked, the town lay virtually defenseless.

The residents of Salisbury were fearful, and rumors were flying from all directions. The general state of confused apprehension can be sampled from an item that appeared in the Salisbury newspaper, the *Daily Carolina Watchman*, on the morning of April 12 — the very day Stoneman struck:

Rumors were very abundant and extravagant yesterday morning on our streets. They produced a rather feverish state of the public mind throughout the day. We were gratified to learn from what seemed to be a reliable source, that there were no raiders in the mountains in sufficient force to justify much alarm from that direction. It is now said that the force seen at the Blue Ridge consists of deserters and tories about 400 in number.... [This was, in fact, Colonel Kirk's force, then busily fortifying the passes in Watauga County.]

There was also a rumor that Stoneman and his men were at Salem, or near there, on Monday, and not on the Yadkin in the more western counties. Indeed, we hear of Stoneman at several different points, making him rather ubiquitous for an ordinary being. Doubtless, he is hovering some where not very distant North of the railroad between this point and Danville, seeking an opportunity to cut it.

But the most extravagant of all the many rumors was that Gen. Lee and his staff had been captured.

P.S. Since the above was put in type, a train from the head of the Western road arrived [from Morganton] and brought a news report of the approach of raiders. We wish those about the head of the road would send us authentic news.

Also, we have a report that Stoneman has cut the N.C. Railroad at High Point. The telegraph is working no farther than Lexington, and the mail train due here at 2 o'clock has not yet arrived....[8]

On the morning of April 12, the senior Confederate officer in Salisbury was General W.M. Gardner. With the regular Confederate garrison off chasing wild geese around Greensboro, Gardner had only a scrappy collection of odds and ends with which to defend the city. The least reliable troops were 200 "Galvanized Irishmen" — immigrant Yankee draftees who had sworn allegiance to the Confederacy in order to get out of either the Salisbury or Andersonville prisoner-of-war camps. There were also about 100 Virginia troops and two batteries of artillery that happened to be in town on their way to join Joseph Johnston. The rest of Gardner's force consisted of some technicians and clerks from the Confederate government offices and factories in the area, some Junior Reserves barely old enough to shave, and some elderly Home Guardsmen.

Gardner positioned his men as best he could, covering the road from Mocksville behind a tributary of the Yadkin known as Grant's Creek. There were several possible fording points across this stream, in addition to the bridge from the Mocksville side, so he was spread very thin, with no more than 150 men at any given crossing point. Gardner concentrated his artillery near the bridge and had his men remove the planking from a large section of the deck to prevent Yankee horsemen from simply charging across.

Stoneman began his attack at dawn, but Gardner's cannon held him off until about eight o'clock -- although that implies more effective firepower than the defenders actually achieved. It probably just took Stoneman that long to make his preparations. The shelling from the Salisbury side of the river appears to have been desultory as well as not very dangerous. Stoneman sent detachments above and below the bridge, and some of Gillem's men from the 8th and 13th Tennessee regiments crawled out onto the structure and relaid the missing planks while a massive volume of covering fire was poured into Gardner's flimsy earthworks. The Tennesseans were able to get away with this stunt, under the snouts of at least eight enemy cannon, because the battery that covered the bridge was manned by Galvanized Irishmen who deliberately aimed over the heads of the attackers.

Some of the Irishmen elsewhere had already thrown down their guns and deserted. From them, Stoneman learned just how feeble the defenses of Salisbury really were. Gardner's main line of resistance, under heavy pressure at the bridge and easily outflanked both above and below it, collapsed by mid-morning.

There was still some spirited resistance in town, for a while. One Galvanized Irishman fought like a man possessed, sniping house-to-house at Stoneman's advance guard even after he had been shot through the lungs. Near death, he collapsed on the front porch of Mrs. M.E. Ramsey's house. As she bent over to drag him to shelter, she heard him whisper, in a voice phlegmy with blood, "They have killed me, but I die a brave man; I fought them as long as could stand." Astonishingly, the man not only survived, but was well enough to walk back to Mrs. Ramsey's house two weeks afterward and thank her for taking him to a hospital later that day.

One Confederate officer barricaded himself inside the town arsenal and fired at the Federals until they shot him down. Another Confederate straggler, an officer from Maryland named Stokes, was mounting his horse in front of the local Confederate headquarters when a squad of Stoneman's men came galloping into view. The Yankee officer leading the squad spotted Stokes and cried out, "There's a damned rebel — charge him!" and put spurs to his mount. Stokes coolly waited until the man was a horse's length away, then raised his revolver and shot the bluecoat in the torso, gravely wounding him. Stokes then spurred his own horse and galloped away, vigorously pursued. One Federal trooper, eager to run Stokes through with his saber, soon pulled far ahead of the others. Stokes employed a tactic familiar to modern-day fighter-jockeys: He "popped the brakes" on his horse, bringing the animal to a sudden halt. The pursuing Yankee flew by, of course, unable to check his momentum. Stokes calmly shot him in the back before wheeling around and making his own escape into the surrounding hill country.

All told, the Salisbury skirmish cost the Confederates about a dozen men killed and an equal number wounded. Stoneman left "several" dead at the creek and lost at least two more men killed inside the town itself. His total number of wounded cannot be stated with accuracy, but probably was not more than a dozen, if that many.

A few miles outside town, a passenger train fleeing the city was intercepted and halted by the 11th Kentucky. The Yankees fired a volley at the passenger cars, wounding several occupants. The bluecoats then relieved the passengers of such personal encumbrances as jewelry and luggage. Both the widow and the daughter of Confederate General Leonidas Polk were on this train, and they were robbed of some cherished family relics, including the general's sword and uniform. Remonstrances were made to Colonel Slater, commander of the Kentucky outfit, even by some of the Federals present, but he refused to return the purloined items to the Widow Polk, claiming that they were "captured on the battlefield" — a bald exaggeration, given the real circumstances.

General Stoneman now moved against one of the major objectives of his whole campaign: the strategically vital Yadkin River bridge. Here, however, he suffered the only significant tactical repulse of the entire raid. A force of more than a thousand men -- including several hundred Galvanized Irish, Home Guardsmen, and stragglers from regular units of every description, ably led by

General York from Louisiana -- had fortified a strong elevated position on the Davidson County side of the river, replete with several cannon. They were under strict orders from General Beauregard to deny the crossing to Stoneman at all costs, and deny it they did. The shooting began at about two in the afternoon and lasted until twilight. At about three, Stoneman's men moved up the guns they had captured earlier in the fight on the Mocksville Road and began firing from the opposite bank. This had little effect, thanks to the defenders' extensive earthworks.

By dusk, Stoneman called off the attack. He had seen and heard enough to conclude that he could not outflank the defenders easily — or quickly enough, since Beauregard was certain to be rushing reinforcements to Salisbury, now that he knew where Stoneman really was. Nor could Stoneman mount a frontal assault without suffering the sort of heavy losses he was under orders to avoid. Stoneman was no John B. Hood; he didn't like to see his men die in brave but bloody attacks, and so far, he had managed to inflict tremendous damage at a very low cost in lives. He wanted to keep it that way. He therefore withdrew back to Salisbury, leaving the vital bridge intact but guarded, and began destroying the vast quantity of military stores that had accumulated in the town.

Unaccustomed to the spunky resistance they had encountered, the Yankee raiders were ready to give Salisbury a rough time. The town was already infamous because of the horrors endured by the inmates of the now-abandoned prison camp. But Stoneman restrained his officers, especially Gillem, who was boasting loudly about how he wanted to make the inhabitants "think that all Hell had been let loose on them." While cooler heads were talking Gillem down from his fury, one bystander overheard him make a puzzling remark to the effect that, although he had been "born in Salisbury," he would be happy to incinerate the whole town. Mrs. Cornelia Philips Spencer, the first historian to write of Stoneman's raid -- and who interviewed numerous eyewitnesses only a year after the events -- passed this anecdote along without attribution. But she added, in an acidic footnote: "Is General Gillem a son of North Carolina?...If so, then we have only another proof that decency and good principles are not hereditary."[9]

By the time Stoneman's men had finished piling up the portable supplies, they had assembled a mountain of material about four blocks square. When it was set afire, the flames were visible 15 miles away. While the supplies burned and the ammunition flashed and banged, great amounts of food, clothing, and personal valuables were looted by the local Negroes and by Unionist "poor whites," many of whom had been living for months on the edge of starvation.

Eyewitnesses provided a contemporary chronicler with a vivid snapshot of the scene in Salisbury that night:

> On the night of the 12th-13th, the ordnance stores, arsenal, foundry, with much valuable machinery, the Government steam distillery, the depots and other buildings belonging to both the Central and Western [rail]roads and other public buildings were fired. The night being perfectly still, the sheets of flame rose steadily into the air...the incessant and distinct explosions of shells and fixed ammunition conveyed the impression to the anxious watchers, miles away in the adjoining counties, that a fierce battle was raging. There was no hallooing by the soldiers — no shouts — only the crackling of the flames and the bursting of the shells. Now and then a mounted troop swept through the streets, the horsemen in profound silence, the lurid flames from the distillery making their rough faces look ghastly enough, while the buttons and other mountings of their equipment sparkled in the firelight. No one thought of sleep that night, even the children.[10]

If General Johnston had been planning to fall back on Salisbury, the havoc wrought by Stoneman would have undone him, for Salisbury had become the main collection point for all military supplies in North Carolina, and Stoneman's troops were very thorough. Structures demolished included several Confederate government offices, ordnance warehouses, an arsenal, a foundry, a steam-powered government distillery, and all the railroad shops, whatever their original purpose. Here is the official tally of war material destroyed:

-- 10,000 stand of arms
-- 1,000,000 rounds of small-arms ammunition
-- 10,000 rounds of artillery ammunition
-- 6,000 pounds of gunpowder
-- 10,000 bushels of corn

-- 75,000 uniforms
-- 250,000 blankets (fine English wool, from the blockade-runners'
holds)
-- 20,000 pounds of leather
-- 6,000 pounds of bacon
-- 100,000 pounds of salt
-- 27,000 pounds of rice
-- 10,000 pounds of saltpeter
-- 50,000 bushels of wheat
-- 80 barrels of turpentine
-- $15 million in Confederate currency

-- Medical supplies valued at $100,000 in gold

After destroying this valuable hoard, Stoneman's column moved
out, toward Statesville, on the afternoon of April 13. Stoneman was
feeling ill and rode in a carriage. When they reached Statesville, the
Federals stayed only long enough to burn the railroad depot, a
modest quantity of military stores, and the printing office of the
passionately pro-Confederate *Iredell Express*. Stoneman, along
with the Second and Third Brigades, left Statesville on the morning
of April 14. But Palmer's hard-riding brigade stayed in town until
April 17, making preparations for yet another diversionary raid,
this time in the direction of Charlotte.

For General George Stoneman, the campaign was officially over.
He had done everything asked of him -- except liberate the Salisbury prisoners and burn the Yadkin River bridge — with a boldness, efficiency, and lack of bloodshed that reflected great credit to
his abilities as a leader and a tactician. The western third of North
Carolina, along with a large patch of southwestern Virginia, had
been ripped open by his columns, and Confederate war-making
capacity in the region had been devastated. The Virginia and
Tennessee Railroad had been completely disabled, materially contributing to Lee's decision to surrender at Appomattox. The
Greensboro-Danville line was also out of business, and vast
amounts of precious supplies had gone up in smoke. Worn out
from the sheer physical strain of the campaign, Stoneman was
ready to go back to Tennessee, accept the hard-earned plaudits of
his superiors, and prop up his feet.

Before he left the command, though, he organized its future

deployment. Palmer's brigade was to patrol and engage in railroad-busting in the Catawba River Valley, as far south as Charlotte, using Lincolnton as its headquarters. Meanwhile, General Gillem would take the larger part of Stoneman's force and make for Asheville. It was still possible that General Johnston would order his men to disperse into the mountains and wage guerrilla warfare, so Stoneman felt it was wise to maintain a Federal presence east of the Blue Ridge and near Asheville, the center of pro-Confederate sentiment in the western counties. Stoneman decided to accompany the Second and Third Brigades as far as Lenoir, and then, taking an escort large enough to guard the nearly 1,000 prisoners he had collected, he would head for Knoxville via the most direct route, through Boone and Blowing Rock.

Although Stoneman may have considered the campaign finished, General Gillem did not. He and his "Home Yankees" still had a few scores to settle in the mountains.

...AND BACK TO THE MOUNTAINS

Colonel Palmer's brigade left General Stoneman's main force on
April 14, took the Lenoir Road to Taylorsville, and then turned
south and passed through the tiny hamlet of Newton. There, they
paused just long enough to burn the jail and a Confederate commis-
sary building. On April 16 they reached Lincolnton, which was to
be their base for the next week.

Their entrance into town was not without incident. As Palmer
rode in, a shot was fired at him, the ball missing his head by mere
inches. An entire company peeled off and gave chase to the bushwhacker. When he was finally run down in an open field, he was
discovered to be a terrified boy of 15 or 16. Palmer gave the lad a
stern lecture, reminded him that he could have caused the deaths of
innocent townspeople, and then turned him over to his mother, who
promised to keep him on a tight leash.

Palmer's men enjoyed Lincolnton, a pretty little town of about
1,000 people, and found its inhabitants, though still unrepentant
rebels, to be decent, intelligent, and sensible. There was only one
nasty incident during the whole week: a bushwhacker from the
local countryside sneaked up and killed one of Palmer's pickets.
The victim was buried with full military honors in the Episcopal
churchyard, and some of the townspeople brought flowers.

Somewhere on the road between Lincolnton and Statesville,
Palmer's men intercepted a trunk filled with the personal valuables
and memorabilia of Mrs. Zebulon Vance, wife of the governor of
North Carolina. Palmer's men, of course, had a grand time rifling
through the personal effects of the famous rebel leader's wife, but

to his credit, Palmer ordered every trinket and bauble replaced. He then dispatched the trunk to Mrs. Vance, in Statesville, under an armed guard, with his compliments.

Such gentlemanly behavior contrasted strongly with the events that would mark General Gillem's erratic course back through the western counties. Gillem, no doubt stung by Stoneman's rebukes during the drunken "review" on the banks of the Yadkin River, had kept his men under tighter control during the Virginia and Piedmont raids. Now that they were heading back to home territory, where animosities boiled and seethed, and now that Stoneman was about to leave them and return to Tennessee, they reverted to the rough and brutal style they had always been known for.

During the march to Lenoir, Stoneman had ridden in his carriage near the head of the column; at the rear were the 900 to 1,000 prisoners he had accumulated, all under guard by some of Gillem's men. Gillem took sadistic pleasure in herding the prisoners along like cattle. Many of the captives were old or middle-aged men from the Home Guard, and many more were discharged Confederate veterans, often not fully recovered from serious wounds. Gillem allowed his men to drive these unfortunates hard, forcing some of them to march double-time along part of the route from Taylorsville to Lenoir. Gillem also whimsically withheld rations from the prisoners for 24 hours while they were confined in their impromptu prison camp — the grounds and buildings of Lenoir's St. James Episcopal Church. Several of the older or weaker men died.

Right about this time, a Confederate from Caldwell County, a veteran named Wilfong, had captured a straggler from one of Colonel Kirk's units. Wilfong brought the Yankee to Lenoir to turn him over to Confederate authorities -- or so he thought. Instead, Wilfong walked right into a Federal picket line and was taken prisoner himself. Freed, Kirk's guerrilla reported to General Gillem. The general thought it might be amusing to put Kirk's man in charge of his former captor. As a result, poor Wilfong never made it to the Tennessee border.

General Stoneman departed for Tennessee on April 17, taking the Confederate prisoners with him. Their march would still be rough -- and a number of them would die either from its rigors or from the conditions at Camp Chase, where they eventually ended up -- but with Gillem gone, and Stoneman riding with the column, the brutality was at least sporadic and furtive, rather than open and constant.

While Stoneman was sorting things out in Lenoir, Colonel Palmer's column was causing considerable alarm around Charlotte. The sparse Confederate forces still afield in the region offered no resistance to Palmer's men, who roamed as far and as wide as they willed, and they returned from their patrols convinced that there was not enough will to fight left in this part of the South for the feared guerrilla war to ever materialize. At one point, Palmer's 12th Ohio troopers skirmished — without known losses on either side — with a cavalry patrol sent out from Charlotte to Tuckasegee Ford, about ten miles west of the city. A day or two later, Palmer plunged down into South Carolina, just south of Charlotte, and burned a major railroad bridge over the Catawba River.

Gillem and his men stayed in Lenoir about 48 hours after Stoneman left. During their brief stay, they managed to make themselves thoroughly detested by the local population. However, not all of the men Gillem commanded liked or approved of his vindictive style of waging war, and most of the actions which have sullied Gillem's historical reputation were committed by east Tennesseans or North Carolina-born "Home Yankees" who bore some heavy grudges because of their own mistreatment. Officers who had not been caught up in the bitter sectional animosities of the mountain counties, or who had managed to rise above them during their service, tended to maintain tighter discipline and to look askance at some of the behavior Gillem permitted.

> Much depended on the personal character and disposition of the commanding officer of these detachments. If he happened to be a gentleman, the people were spared as much as possible; if he were simply a brute dressed in a little brief authority, every needless injury was inflicted, accompanied with true underbred malice and insolence. The privates always followed the lead of their commander.[1]

Gillem's men went out of their way to pillage the homes of known Confederate officers and Home Guard members. The womenfolk in these households were insulted, furniture was smashed, clothing ripped to shreds, and everything edible stolen. In one such house, belonging to a well-known and much-decorated Confederate hero, a pile of children's clothing was — to use the delicate phrase of a contemporary chronicler — "loathsomely polluted." Several women were beaten, and many more were verbally reviled and sexually harassed. Appeals were made to General Gillem, begging him to order a stop to such outrages, but he merely shrugged and turned his back on the supplicants, growling, "Well, there are bad men in every crowd." That same afternoon, the general himself was seen wearing on his uniform some bits of silk ribbon stolen from a Confederate lady. Some of Gillem's officers — young lieutenants, mostly — were shamed and disgusted by what was happening, and they ordered men under their personal control to guard some houses.

When Gillem's force rode out of Lenoir on April 17, no one was sorry to see him go. His next objective was Morganton, but he would not find his passage undisputed. In Morganton at that time was the experienced Confederate General McCown. Together with the local militia commanders, Colonel Walton and Colonel Tate — the latter officer still not recovered from a bad wound suffered in Virginia — he scraped together a force of Home Guard and stragglers variously estimated at 60 to 80 men, supported by one four-inch brass howitzer. This tiny force dug in at Rocky Ford on the Catawba River, a couple of miles outside Morganton.

Gillem's previous experiences had left him with nothing but contempt for the Home Guard, no matter what county or town they were from. These Guardsmen, however, were the same Burke County men who had bravely charged into the fire of Kirk's Spencers during the Camp Vance raid. When Gillem foolishly sought to brush them aside with a frontal attack across the ford, in the space of a few minutes he suffered some 20-25 casualties, including at least eight men killed. Gillem pulled back and found a ford some distance upstream which enabled him to outflank the steadfast defenders, forcing them to retire into the mountains.

Gillem was used to taking these little rebel villages without such opposition, and his men rode into Morganton in a bloody mood. They found the village deserted. Houses were shuttered and bolted, and the menfolk had gone into the hills. The angry disposition of Gillem's troops can be gauged from an incident that happened at the edge of town. Dozens of local slaves, eager to get a look at their liberators, crowded the rail fence alongside the stagecoach road. But Gillem's men were themselves mountaineers, and few, if any, were motivated by any deep abolitionist principles. As they rode past, returning the Negroes' cheers and waves with contemptuous sneers, one cruel Yankee sang out: "Hail Columbia, Happy Land! If I don't shoot a nigger, I'll be damned!" Then he raised his carbine and blew one of the waving onlookers off the fence. The rest of the crowd fled in terror -- wondering, no doubt, just what sort of "liberation" this was going to be.

Nearly every house within a radius of eight or ten miles around Morganton was broken into and ransacked. Some of the most brutal pillaging was done not by Gillem's men, but by hillbilly Unionists who came swarming out of the coves and hollows and helped themselves to the property of the better-off Confederate families: rugs, blankets, linens, silver, curtains, cooking utensils, books, clocks, and whatever else struck their fancy, whether they had any practical use for it or not. One unusually detailed eyewitness account of the looting leaves no doubt that a violent and long-repressed form of class hatred was being decanted, using the sanction of Gillem's rifles as both an excuse and a form of permission:

> [I will describe] the character of the lazy and disloyal elements that inhabit our "South Mountains," around the town of Morganton, that class of people, which you have no doubt heard of, [who are] an ignorant, illiterate, uncultivated set, untrue in every respect, false to their God and traitors to their country[.] [T]he circumstances actually occurred, and I give it without exaggeration.
>
> ...When the "Rear Guard"...nine robbers, entered the house [of R.C. Pearson] to plunder and pilfer, these women (the lazy class from the mountains) followed in, to reap their share of the spoils, they (the women) exceeded in number, the Yanks present on that occasion, after the house had been generally robbed, and the mountain women were laden with everything they could carry, such as...clothing, bedding, even dishes and such...A closet, the last unentered, attracted the eye and attention of the thieves, in a few moments the door was burst open with an axe, and the gang entered, ransacking it and scattering things in every direction, among the contents was a basket containing three or four bottles of "Champagne wine;" the basket was emptied and the spoils divided, an old woman

who stood near by waiting to receive her share, was handed a bottle. Another bottle opened, when the popping of the cork and the flashing of the wine, created such a panic, that the woman took flight and left the house almost instantly[;] the old woman who had received her bottle dropping it, and swearing that it was pizen, put there to kill them for nobody had ever seed liquor pop that way, she could not be prevailed upon to touch her bottle, nor would she taste the drink offered her by her Yankee friends; the same old hag was sharing the sweetmeats in the pantry, when a jar of citron was offered her, tasting it, she remarked that "watermelon rind was only fit for hogs," but that this was the sweetest rind she had ever seen....

The very day that the Federal command under Gillem entered and occupied the Town of Morganton, these women from the "South Mountains" swarmed our streets proclaiming their "jubilee," and rejoicing that the Yankees had arrived...these dishonest and traitorous hordes, of our own beautiful mountain clime....[2]

Some of the vandalism seemed not so much vicious as childish. At Pleasant Garden — in former days, a popular stopover on the stagecoach route to Asheville — General Gillem ordered a Mrs. Carson to cook a full dinner for himself and his staff. When the lady protested that the general's men had already stolen most of the victuals from the premises, and that the Negro cook had run off the day before, Gillem snarled at her: "You cook it yourself. I intend to have my supper, and if you don't get it, I will turn my men loose in your house." Mrs. Carson either could not or would not do as the general requested, so he opened the door and invited his men to do as they liked. After they had stolen whatever was left, they bashed open a keg of molasses and poured it all over the furniture.

Gillem's men also abused Mr. Carson, a colonel. One of the looters cornered Carson in his bedroom and demanded to be given a full change of clothes. Carson, with all the dignity he could muster, coldly informed the bummer that he had already been thoroughly looted; all he had left was, literally, the shirt on his back. "That'll do," replied the trooper, waving his pistol. Colonel Carson was forced to strip then and there.

By this time, April 18, word of Gillem's approach had reached Asheville, and General James Martin gathered all available Confederate forces and went out to stop him. Martin had nearly every organized Confederate company still in the field in that part of

North Carolina: Palmer's little brigade, and Love's regiment of Thomas's Legion. Martin chose Swannanoa Gap as the best place to make his stand. His men felled trees, blocking the road and its shoulders with a formidable abatis of sharpened limbs.

As the shrewdly observant Captain Weand of the 15th Pennsylvania had noted in his diary, Gillem's troops were too undisciplined to be much good against any kind of determined resistance. Gillem probed Martin's line of defense and everywhere found it too strong to assail frontally. Details of what actually happened at Swannanoa Gap are frustratingly few. Gillem made some sort of attack, not very energetically it would seem, and the Confederates "repulsed it easily." Casualty figures for this engagement, such as it was, do not seem to have been recorded by any of the few who wrote about it.

Checked in one direction, Gillem moved 40 miles south to Rutherfordton and made for Howard's Gap. General Martin had been expecting just such a maneuver and issued orders to Palmer's brigade to hurry there and fortify the pass. But Palmer's men refused to budge. Rumors had reached them of General Johnston's surrender to Sherman, and that, coming so soon on the heels of reliable news about Lee's capitulation, had convinced the mountaineers that the war was over. Nobody wanted to be the last man killed for a defunct cause.

While all this was happening, the 15th Pennsylvania had finished its business in the Catawba Valley and had been ordered to rejoin Gillem's column. As the Pennsylvanians passed along the same roads taken by Gillem's men earlier, they saw and heard increasing evidence of wanton pillage and vandalism. After the Pennsylvanians had entered Rutherfordton, on April 25, Captain Weand jotted in his diary:

> [This] is a very ordinary town, and the two days' stay of [Gillem's] Tennesseeans did it no good. They stole everything they could carry off, put pistols to the heads of the citizens, pursuaded them to give up their pocketbooks, and even took the rings from them ladies' fingers. The sympathy we used to feel for the loyal Tennesseeans is being rapidly transferred to their enemy.[3]

General Martin received official notification of the armistice between Sherman and Johnston on Saturday night, April 22. On Sunday morning, Colonel Palmer rode out of Asheville under a flag of truce; he encountered Gillem on the Hendersonville-Asheville Road, about six miles outside of town. It was agreed that a cease-fire should go into effect, and that General Martin would meet with General Gillem on the following day to discuss details.

By all accounts, that meeting was surprisingly cordial. Although Martin and Gillem had been in different classes at West Point, they had served together at several frontier outposts and apparently some embers of friendship still existed. They came to a straightforward arrangement: Gillem's men would be allowed to pass through Asheville and into Tennessee without resistance, and Martin would supply the column with 9,000 issues of Confederate rations. In return, Gillem agreed to keep his men in line and prevent them from "foraging" among the local population. General Martin described the events in a letter to Cornelia Philips Spencer, dated June 11, 1866:

> On Tuesday, the twenty-fifth of April, 1865, General Gillem passed through Asheville under a flag of truce and was furnished with nine thousand rations. Everything went off quietly and in order. The general and one Staff Officer dined with men and late in the evening when he was about to mount to join his command, I asked him if he would give me forty-eight hours notice provided for in the terms of the truce before...[resuming] hostilities, explaining to him at the same time that he would be several days nearer to General Sherman than I would be to General Johnston. He said certainly he would give me the notice.[4]

After picking up their rations in Asheville, Gillem's brigades continued on by different routes. Palmer's men were ordered to march by way of Waynesville, through Quallatown, and along the Little Tennessee River. Brown's and Miller's brigades were ordered to march straight through to Greeneville, Tennessee. Gillem himself, now that the war seemed truly over, decided it was time to resume the political career he had already chosen for himself, so he rode on to Tennessee with a small escort, where he obtained a leave of absence and headed for Nashville. The state legislature was assembling for its first postwar session, and Gillem wanted to be involved from the start.

His legacy of free-booting pillage remained with his Second and Third Brigades, however. When word reached them that the too-liberal truce agreement between Sherman and Johnston had been abrogated by the government in Washington, they took the news as blanket permission to do what they had been itching to do for several days: plunder Asheville. It seems likely they were under orders from Gillem to about-face and reoccupy the city, in case the Sherman-Johnston arrangement broke down. How they chose to behave was their business. They didn't give 48 hours' notice, either.

Nobody in Asheville was ready for what happened on the morning of April 26. Indeed, news had not yet even reached General Martin about the breakdown in the truce accords. The very same Yankee troops who had marched quietly through town 24 hours earlier, without a single unpleasant incident, were suddenly back. This time they came thundering into town with their swords flashing and pistols drawn, whooping and howling, riding onto front porches and smashing windows, firing wildly into houses, breaking down doors and stealing food, clothing, and valuables, smashing furniture and crockery, and beating up anyone who got in their way.

At the home of Judge Bailey, a gang of "villainous looking men" broke in, right after breakfast, and stole everything they could carry -- except for one slab of bacon, which they dropped after Mrs. Bailey pleaded with them. Shortly after the looters had left, an old Negro man who had known the Bailey family for many years came to the house, tears in his eyes, and apologized for having told the marauders where the judge lived. "I was scared to death, Jedge," he pleaded. "They said `Where does Jedge Bailey live — we want his watch!' and I said: `He ain't got no watch!' and they said: `Yes, he has — jedges always have watches, and if you don't show us the way, we'll shoot you!'"

When he learned about the sack of Asheville, Palmer of the First Brigade dispatched a letter of apology to General Martin, express-ing his professional disgust at the behavior of Gillem's men. Palmer characterized the incident as "unbecoming to the Honor of the United States."

Palmer's column started back to Tennessee on April 26. On the following day, they crossed the mountains' crests. Now that the fighting was over, Captain Weand and his men paused for a while to savor the scenery with the relaxed perceptions of men who are no longer in danger:

> April 26th. — Left at 2:30 p.m., but only marched ten miles, when we made camp. The next day we marched sixteen miles, to the top of Blue Ridge, on our way back to East Tennessee, wither we were ordered. Our march today was through the grandest scenery we have looked on during our term of service. We went up through Hickory Nut Gap...along the Broad River, up to its source. Towering above us, almost to the clouds, were the precipitous crags of Hickory Mountain, and at High Falls the water drops 380 feet from the summit. It was so imposing that the usual chat of the riders was hushed, as they gazed with awe at the sight. As we rode along we plucked the fragrant magnolia from the forest trees, and the wish of all was to stay longer with it, but that could not be done, and we went on up to the top, where plenty of forage was found. Our camp was at the entrance of the present "Biltmore" grounds, near Asheville....[5]

But the hard riding was not yet over for Palmer and his weary men. Before they could reach Tennessee, orders came for them to turn around yet again and head for Yorkville, South Carolina. Their mission: to intercept and arrest Confederate President Jefferson Davis. Palmer's men spent many more exhausting hours in the saddle before learning, to their great relief, that Davis and his escort had finally been bagged on May 15 at Irwin, Georgia.

Part 6:
Final Volleys

In his fainting, footsore marches, In his flight from the stricken fray

In the snare of the lonely ambush, The debts we owe him pay.

In God's hand alone is vengeance! But He strikes with the hands of men,

And His blight would wither our manhood, If we smite not the smiter again.

-- S. Teackle Wallis, "The Guerrillas: A Southern War Song," 1864.

THE 'BATTLE' OF ASHEVILLE

Asheville was the capital of secessionist sympathies in the mountain counties of North Carolina. Even in the final months of the war, when Confederate fortunes appeared doomed, some prominent local citizens agitated to make Asheville the new "capital of the Confederacy," should General Lee manage to unite the Army of Northern Virginia with General Johnston's Army of Tennessee and fall back to the Appalachians for a last stand. This implies that Asheville and Richmond had something in common, but in reality the two cities were nothing alike. Asheville in 1865 was a rough-hewn frontier town, lacking even basic amenities. It was still, in the words of one local historian, "a small country village...Its few streets were narrow, ungraded wagon roads without paving, crossings, bridges, culverts, side-drains, sidewalks or lights. The way to the Armory building was a very steep and narrow lane...a mere cul-de-sac. The town had no water supply, no sewer system, no public lights anywhere, no railroad, no telegraphic communication with any part of the outside world, no market, no municipal building, no public laundry...."[1]

The town had a prewar population of about 1,200. In its own modest way, it had become a military center — certainly, there was no other town in the mountain district that could boast a hospital and an arms factory. Some of the best Enfield-pattern muskets in the Confederate Army were manufactured in Asheville, weapons every bit as good as the authentic British Army models imported through the blockade. There were also two small training bases, Camp Patton and Camp Jeter. By April 1865, however, the camps were pretty much out of business, and after the fall of east Tennessee, the arms-making equipment had been shipped to South Carolina, where it was thought to be safer. Of course, that was before

General Sherman decided to march through South Carolina. Ironically, had the equipment been kept in Asheville, the factory would have been turning out weapons until the end of the war.

Due to its relative importance as a military objective, Asheville boasted more elaborate fortifications than any other town in the mountains. There were earthworks on Beaucatcher Mountain and on the crest of Stony Hill, and an earthwork battery -- mounting two bronze Napoleons -- overlooking the route into town beside the French Broad River. There were also some entrenchments within the town itself.

In addition to General Stoneman's raids, the Federal command sent some secondary probes across the border to keep the mountain defenders off-balance, and also to disrupt in advance any potential linkup with either Lee or Johnston. George Kirk's thrust at Waynesville was the first of these.

Another was launched on April 3. Orders were issued to Colonel Isaac M. Kirby of the 101st Ohio Infantry to "scout in the direction of Asheville, N.C." He departed Greeneville, Tennessee, with 900 regulars and another 200 or so Unionist partisans and deserters who had taken the oath of allegiance to the United States. He had two field guns, a wagon train, and seven days' worth of supplies. Kirby encamped, his first night, at Warm Springs, and there he decided to leave his cannon and his wagons under strong guard. With the infantry alone, he proceeded up the French Broad River toward Asheville.

On April 5, Kirby ordered his men to burn two bridges that gave access to the west bank of the river and could be used to cut him off. About ten miles north of town, Kirby's forces halted at the farm of Mrs. H.E. Sondley, widow of a prominent local citizen. They stole all of her horses, including a Shetland pony that belonged to her young son, Foster. The little pony couldn't keep up with the column, so one of Kirby's men shot it. Decades later, when Foster Sondley was a famous Asheville attorney as well as the author of a rich two-volume history of Buncombe County, he still wrote about the incident with obvious emotion.

There was one horse, described as an "inferior" animal, that Kirby either overlooked or deemed unworthy of stealing. As soon as the Yankees had moved on, Mrs. Sondley dispatched one of her servants on the horse. The servant passed along back trails un-known even to Kirby's turncoat guides and arrived in town in time to sound the alarm.

The ranking officer in Asheville on April 6 was Colonel George W. Clayton — General Martin and Colonel Palmer were both away in other threatened parts of the region. Clayton threw together a makeshift defense force around the town's Home Guard company, 44 men who called themselves the Silver Grays and whose ranks included a boy of 14 and a Baptist preacher of 70. Clayton had a hard time rounding up any more troops — several Confederate officers told him to forget it and declare Asheville an "open city," since the war was clearly winding down and nothing that happened in Asheville would make the slightest difference in the outcome.

It was the principle of the thing, Clayton insisted, and he bullied, argued, or shamed a total of 300 men into taking up arms that day — many of them convalescent soldiers who probably should have been in bed rather than in battle. The two little brass Napoleons were also hitched up for action. When he had this assemblage in some kind of order, Clayton marched them out of town to some rudimentary entrenchments covering the French Broad route, on top of Woodfin's Ridge.

The valiant defenders of Asheville found Kirby's men already in formation and waiting for them on wooded slopes about 600 yards away -- as though both forces had, by agreement, chosen this field in advance.

What followed was a very strange battle. No maneuvering took place at all: both sides just lined up and started banging lustily at each other. The shooting started at three in the afternoon and continued without letup until the light drained out of the sky at eight o'clock. At that point, some curious sort of panic seems to have swept the ranks of Kirby's force. His men retreated, en masse, pell-mell, down the same route they had come up earlier, leaving a surprising number of rifles, bayonets, canteens, and knapsacks strewn in their wake.

Kirby continued back to Tennessee without hindrance. In his after-action report, he advanced a number of not very convincing excuses as to why he did not overwhelm Clayton's little force. If any sense can be made out of these contradictory claims, it would seem that Kirby was under orders to keep his casualties to a minimum. He didn't like fighting in the mountains anyway, and he kept imagining phantom columns of rebels — perhaps some of Thomas's bloodthirsty redskins! — creeping through the woods on all sides of his force. Moreover, he knew the war was as good as over, or surely would be by the time he got back to Tennessee. The spirited (though not very deadly) resistance offered by Asheville's defenders had made him think twice about trying to capture the city. In effect, he seems to have said *To hell with it!*, and that is as close as the modern historian can come to explaining this curious engagement.

The Battle of Asheville was certainly as close to bloodless as a five-hour firefight can get. Both forces were just going through the motions. The defenders either suffered no casualties at all, or two slightly wounded, depending on which account you read. But the Asheville battery did hurl at least one cannon ball squarely into Kirby's position, for when the Confederates occupied the abandoned enemy positions early the next morning, they found "one leg in a boot."

THE
LAST WAR WHOOP

After General Gillem's unruly Yankees sacked Asheville on April 26, General Martin decided to move the headquarters of his Confederate command to Waynesville. This area, west of Asheville, offered the best defensive terrain, and it was the home ground of the last remaining organized Confederate unit in that part of North Carolina: Thomas's Legion. Colonel Palmer's brigade had simply evaporated, following his men's refusal to fight Gillem again after the skirmish at Swannanoa Gap on April 19. Only a small number of them had not deserted, and those that remained in uniform refused to obey any orders that would send them more than a few miles from their homes -- Colonel Kirk's Yankees were swarming all over the mountains north and east of Asheville, stealing and burning whatever they chose. Only the companies led by Will Thomas and James Love seemed willing to stick out the war to its end.

Love's men had been entrenched near Asheville on the morning when Gillem's troops suddenly reappeared and overran the city. Rather than surrender, Love had led his men through the town, just ahead of the Yankees, and through Pigeon Gap deep into the mountains.

After the Federals consolidated their hold on Asheville, they made plans to mop up. From Knoxville, General Stoneman sent orders to Kirk's Second North Carolina Mounted Regiment (led by Colonel William C. Bartlett) and to the Third North Carolina Mounted (led by Kirk himself), instructing them to scour the mountains both north and south of Asheville. Their mission was to prevent the formation of any large guerrilla bands either locally or from the Piedmont region, and to keep order...in their own special way.

From Waynesville, meanwhile, General Martin ordered Thomas's Indian battalion to leave Quallatown and link up with Love's regiment at Balsam Gap. This was accomplished about May 3. Love entrenched his 200 men at that passage, while Thomas detached a company of white mountaineer sharpshooters from Love and fortified Soco Gap, about 13 miles west of Waynesville. These were the last cards General Martin could play: five companies at Balsam Gap and five at Soco Gap — a grand total of just over 500 men. Within a day's march was an entire division's worth of Federals.

William Stringfield, now a lieutenant colonel, was not on hand for this final deployment. Instead, he had been sent on a special mission by General Martin. Stringfield was carrying a sealed dispatch, intended for General Stoneman at Knoxville, asking for official confirmation of the rumors that General Johnston had surrendered the Army of Tennessee at Greensboro. If the rumors were true, the message asked for a formal discussion of terms to bring about the end of the mountain fighting.

Stringfield left his Franklin headquarters with the sealed document on April 28, escorted by two dozen hand-picked Legion men. Ahead of them lay a four-day, 125-mile journey over some of the roughest terrain in eastern North America. Once across the border into Tennessee, Stringfield and his party were quickly surrounded by an 80-man patrol of Yankee cavalry. The Yankee commander accused them of being bushwhackers, insulted them in "vile" language, and wanted to disarm them — completely ignoring both the flag of truce and the stated purpose of Stringfield's mission. Matters grew very tense. At one point, Stringfield and his little band drew together, put hands on their sidearms and sabers, unthroated what Stringfield called "the last Rebel Yell I ever heard in the war," and prepared to fight it out with a force almost four times their size. Fortunately, another Federal officer, who outranked the hot-headed patrol leader, happened along just as things were straining to the edge of violence. He listened closely to Stringfield's explanation, then permitted him to continue on his way to Knoxville without having to fight a last-stand battle.

In Knoxville, the Confederate truce party encountered another hostile reception. The first Federal officer Stringfield tried to speak with seized the white flag from the soldier holding it, broke the staff in two over his knee, and stomped on the pieces. Then he pointed at Stringfield and told his men: "If this damn Rebel bats an eye, shoot his damn head off!" Stringfield did not back down. He glared toe-to-toe with the Yankee, called him a coward and a villain, and swore he could "whip a ten-acre field of such fellows."

Given Stringfield's condition by now, it is surprising that he finally managed to bluster his way in to see General Stoneman without being shot. But after bringing his message to Stoneman, he was coldly informed that, for all his pains in delivering it, there would be no reply. Stoneman saw no need to communicate with General Martin; Stoneman already controlled that part of North Carolina, through the instrument of Kirk's and Bartlett's commands, and he had reliable reports that Thomas's Legion had disbanded. That, Stringfield hotly told him, was a damned lie — only four days ago, the Legion had been digging in and was still full of fight.

Be that as it may, Stoneman said, the issue was moot, and the fighting capacity of the Legion not impressive. If Thomas's men hadn't been licked yet, they soon would be. He tossed Martin's dispatch aside and told Stringfield that the time had come for he and his men to take the oath of allegiance to the Union. Stringfield bridled — he had come here as an undefeated soldier, under a flag of truce. "Sir. I did not come here to take the oath!" he proclaimed. Stoneman suggested that a sojourn in the local hoosegow would perhaps change the colonel's feelings. And with that, William Stringfield was unceremoniously tossed into jail, where he was roughed up by a bunch of thuggish Union deserters who stole his coat, blanket, and spare underwear. Not until May 24 was Stringfield released, and that was only through the intervention of his old friend and recent sworn enemy, William G. Browlow, who had just been elected the reconstructionist governor of Tennessee.

General Martin rode to Stringfield's headquarters at Franklin on May 6 to learn if there had been any news of the truce party. By then, of course, Stringfield was behind bars, and Martin could only surmise that he had been killed or captured en route. He therefore gave command of Stringfield's troops to the remaining senior officer of the battalion, Captain Stephen Whitaker.

That same day, Bartlett's regiment of Yankees marched into Waynesville and occupied it without resistance. Will Thomas moved against him with a vigor he had not shown in months, taking the Indians and the company of sharpshooters. After concealing themselves in the steep forest about three miles from Waynesville, they dispatched a private in civilian clothes to spy out the situation. When this man got into town, he spread rumors that Thomas was coming with hundreds of bloodthirsty Indians. Meanwhile, Thomas also sent for Love's regiment, hoping to trap Bartlett within Waynesville. To fetch Love, he dispatched the sharpshooter company, commanded by a much-decorated veteran of General Jubal Early's raid on Washington, Lieutenant Robert T. Conley.

In order to reach Love's position as quickly as possible, Conley marched his tiny force — probably no more than 50 men — via White Sulphur Springs. In the middle of the forest, he ran smack into part of Bartlett's regiment. Although the Yankees outnumbered him about four to one, Conley reacted with the cool-headed courage that had made him one of Jubal Early's favorite young officers. He quickly formed his men into a battle line, unleashed a volley of accurate rifle fire, and followed up with a bayonet charge. The Federal detachment was routed.

One Yankee soldier was killed in this skirmish. His name was Arwood. He was, as far as anyone knows, the last regular soldier on either side, east of the Mississippi, to die in the Civil War. He lies buried today in the cemetery in Asheville.

Having scored this satisfying little victory en route, Conley now hastened on to Love's position at Balsam Gap. Love hurried his men toward Waynesville and rode ahead to find General Martin. It began to look as though the Confederates might turn the last battle of the mountain war into a substantial victory.

Colonel Bartlett, meanwhile, was wondering where the heck Colonel Kirk was. His scouts were bringing in reports of rebels, including those confounded Indians, closing in on him from all sides, and Kirk — who was supposed to be within easy supporting distance — was off somewhere stealing horses. Waynesville was not a good place to be surrounded. It was a tiny village with no more than 20 houses, and it was ringed and completely dominated by high mountains, all of which seemed to be in enemy hands.

On the night of May 6-7, Bartlett really started to get worried. Kirk still had not shown up, and Thomas had occupied two of the most commanding peaks near the town and had ordered his men to build hundreds of bonfires. Bartlett's men had the distinct impression of a noose closing around their necks as they watched that necklace of campfires spreading on all sides. The Indians contributed mightily to their discomfiture, filling the night with war whoops and giving vent to "hideous yells" that must have set Bartlett's men to nervously fingering their scalps.

The next morning, Bartlett sent out a flag of truce and asked for a parley. General Martin obliged, riding into town later with Colonel Love, Will Thomas, and Thomas's bodyguard of 20 bare-chested Cherokee warriors, all outfitted for the occasion with war paint, feathers, and gleaming tomahawks. Although junior to General Martin, it was Thomas who did most of the talking, and those who knew him thought he was on the verge of some kind of fit, so manic and emotional did he seem. He accused Bartlett of being a horse-thief and threatened, unless Bartlett surrendered, to turn his Indians loose on Waynesville to scalp every man in a blue uniform.

After Thomas finished this unusually melodramatic performance, a cooler discussion got under way inside the local resort hotel, ironically named Battle House. Bartlett admitted that Martin and Thomas seemed to have the drop on him, but pointed out that even the capture of an entire Yankee regiment, gratifying as it might be, would only postpone the inevitable and would almost surely summon massive, swift retaliation from Knoxville. And what would happen to Martin's little army then? Already, Martin had lost Palmer's force through massive desertion. Just how much longer could he realistically expect these men to fight, when all of them must be aware that the rest of the South had already laid down its arms?

Martin must have seen the validity of Bartlett's reasoning. Thomas did, too, now that his adrenalin had stopped flowing. What was the point of capturing, much less scalping, Bartlett's regiment? The next day, or the day after that, they would probably have to face Kirk's entire regiment, and if they managed to beat Kirk, they would have to deal with the regiments on their way to Asheville — a whole Yankee division, with another division or two just days away in Knoxville. If Martin would end hostilities now, Bartlett promised, he would prevail upon Kirk to stop ravaging the countryside, and he would try to obtain permission for the mountaineers to keep at least some of their arms and ammunition to protect their homes against bandits.

At last they agreed. On May 9, 1865, the mountaineers and their ever-faithful Cherokee comrades staged their final parade, signed their parole documents, and began drifting home to pick up the pieces of their lives.

The eastern Cherokees paid a heavy price for their loyalty to Will Thomas and to that strange white man's cause that he stood for. In addition to the men killed or disabled in Confederate service (not a large number in absolute terms, but painful enough to a tribe that had only about 400 able-bodied males to begin with), the Indians had suffered greatly from hunger during the last two years of the war. Considerable numbers of them had fled to Georgia and South Carolina, where the famine was not as acute. Some of the families that remained were forced, by the end of 1864, to eat weeds and tree bark. Thomas drew on his own dwindling resources to buy, often at grotesquely inflated speculators' prices, a little corn meal here, a little flour there, but it was not enough to relieve the Indians' suffering, and the gesture contributed materially to Thomas's financial ruin. On top of all that, not long after the shooting stopped the tribal enclaves were wracked by a smallpox epidemic that came close to exterminating several settlements.

After William Stringfield got out of jail on May 24, he went home to Strawberry Plains and tried to start up the family farming business again. But the hostility of his Unionist neighbors forced him to move to Rogersville. In 1871, after a decade of passionate, on-again, off-again courtship, he married Maria Love, the youngest sister of Will Thomas's wife Sarah. Then he turned his back on east Tennessee forever and moved to Waynesville. Stringfield became as ardent a North Carolinian as he had been a Confederate. He dabbled in regional politics in his middle years, once serving as secretary to Robert B. Vance when the latter was elected to the

U.S. Congress in 1872. Mostly, he acted as an agent for the Love family in their complicated but lucrative real estate dealings.

He and Maria enjoyed a squirely style of life as co-managers of the White Sulphur Springs Hotel, located on the site of the last Civil War battle fought in North Carolina. He served two terms in the state senate, in 1901 and 1905. In 1909, he wrote the chapter about Thomas's Legion which appeared in Walter Clark's *Histories of the Several Regiments and Battalions from North Carolina in the Great War, 1861-65* (and caused confusion among generations of historians by labeling the unit as the "69th North Carolina," a designation it was never known by during the war). His marriage to Maria was a strong union; they had seven children, and his heart was permanently wounded when she died in 1909.

Stringfield became intensely involved in Indian affairs, too, taking up the mantle of Will Thomas in that regard. There was usually a bunch of Cherokees hanging around the hotel, entertaining tourists with hairy war stories and posing for pictures. When the Indians went to conventions of Confederate veterans — where, you may be sure, they never failed to cause a stir — Stringfield went with them. He wrote glowingly about the Cherokees in numerous articles and speeches, and even authored a pioneering book about them in 1903. For their part, the Indians came to love Stringfield almost as much as they loved Thomas — and the word "love" is not chosen lightly. Stringfield was even inducted into the tribe and given a Cherokee name: "Cho-ga-See." His final years were comfortable. He died, a handsome and honored old warrior, at age 85, on March 6, 1923.

The last years of William Holland Thomas were pathetic. Declared *non compos mentis* in the spring of 1867, he was remanded to the state insane asylum in Raleigh, and there lived out much of the remainder of his life. His personal business empire crumbled almost more quickly than his mind, and his legal administrators (including James Love) were enmeshed for years in lawsuits of the most byzantine complexity, involving government, Indian, and personal claims, all mutually conflicting with one another. Many of Thomas's relatives and former friends were forced to bring suit against him, and in the end, every nickel and every acre went to pay off his creditors.

When Thomas's mental illness seemed in remission, he was allowed out of the asylum for some long stretches of time, and friends who visited him during those periods found him genial, lucid, and calm. After his wife's death in 1877, however, he became quite deranged and had to be recommitted for good. He spent his last years on an emotional roller-coaster, swinging from suicidal depressions to wild excitement, sinking for long periods into deep paranoid fantasies, and obsessively carrying on a raving, and at times incomprehensible, correspondence with numerous people, some of them total strangers, in different parts of the country.

Toward the end, there were long periods in which he lapsed completely into the Cherokee language, perhaps reliving in his mind those bold and vigorous days of his youth, up there in the high green valleys, where he had been the adopted son of a great chief. Thomas died, a hopeless lunatic, in 1893.

THE FALL
OF FORT HAMBY

The last "official" battle of the Civil War in North Carolina may have been Lieutenant Conley's engagement at White Sulphur Springs on May 6, but the violence did not stop there. A much bloodier battle took place in Wilkes County later that month. Fittingly, it did not involve regular troops of either side, but was fought between local citizens and a band of bushwhackers whose outrageous depredations had no military, or even quasi-military motivation, but were sheer banditry from first to last.

Like the Confederates, General Stoneman, too, had his share of deserters. Not many, but what they lacked in numbers, they made up in meanness. What drove them to act as they did is anybody's guess. From the pattern and timing of their deeds, it appears that they took a good look at the western counties through which they were marching, saw on every hand an undefended countryside open to pillage -- a countryside already partly overrun with brigands — and decided to help themselves.

Two of these deserters formed their own robber bands. Their names were Wade and Simmons. Little is known about Simmons. His gang made its headquarters in the Brushy Mountains, while Wade's men chose as their headquarters a hilltop house on the Yadkin River in Wilkes County. This "hideout" was in plain sight, almost defiantly so, and from its windows and loopholes their rifles could command the terrain for nearly a mile in all directions. Sometimes, the two bands operated together. When that happened, they could muster the equivalent of a company of infantry — about 50 men. When they operated separately, the number of men in each gang fluctuated between 20 and 30.

Wade's headquarters was on the east side of Lewis Fork Creek, a tributary of the Yadkin, and was within sight of the big river. From its elevation, the hilltop house commanded a clear view of the road

to Wilkesboro, and its occupants could unleash long-range rifle fire
on Holman's Ford, where the road crossed the Yadkin, not quite a
mile away. There was a local tradition that Daniel Boone himself
had once erected a fortified cabin on that same ground, so suitable
was it for defense, yet so close to both the river and the road.

"Fort Hamby," as the bandits christened their headquarters, was
an immensely stout two-story log structure, impervious to anything
smaller than a howitzer. Both floors had been loopholed, and from
the upstairs windows the occupants had superb fields of fire in a
360-degree radius. The name Hamby was derived from the names
of some ladies who had formerly occupied the house. Since every
contemporary chronicler describes these women as "disreputable,"
and since women were known to frequently come and go from the
place while it was occupied by Wade's marauders, it is possible
that Fort Hamby was originally nothing more than the biggest
whorehouse in Wilkes County.

Frustratingly little is known about Wade himself — none of the
men who dealt with him even recorded his first name. He claimed
to be from Michigan, and that at least meshes with the fact that a
Michigan regiment had galloped through that area with General
Stoneman.

What is puzzling about Wade is how long he thought he could
get away with his outrages. The war was all but over when he set
up his gang and began operations, and that corner of the state, by
the spring of 1865, offered slim pickin's in terms of lootable goods
and valuables. It would seem that Wade's leadership attracted men
who, having tasted the brigand's life, felt disinclined to give it up
for the more modest rewards of humdrum peacetime activity. In
other words, they were the wildest men in the mountains — men
who had been brutalized by years of hiding and fighting, and who
had grown to consider themselves beyond conventional morality as
well as the constraints of law and order. Wade himself appears to
have been one of those gang leaders who compels obedience
through the charisma that comes from being the most dangerous
and violent man among other violent men. He and a few others in
the band may also have been genuine psychopaths. On one occasion, they spotted a child climbing a fence near the river while the
youngster's mother was working the fields nearby. They decided to

polish their marksmanship by firing at this small target, and finally one of their rifle-balls blew the child off the fence rails, dead. On another occasion, again for no apparent reason but sadistic pleasure, they shot and mortally wounded a woman who was sitting in a wagon with her husband at Holman's Ford, almost a mile away — testimony to the power and accuracy of the weapons Wade had stashed inside Fort Hamby, along with several thousand rounds of ammunition.

Wade's and Simmons's gangs raided, alone or in concert, throughout Wilkes and Watauga counties, with occasional forays into Alexander and Caldwell counties. In a matter of weeks, they had spread a reign of terror over a big patch of western North Carolina. Unlike the furtive deserter and outlier bands, which usually preferred stealth to confrontation, Wade and Simmons operated blatantly, in broad daylight as often as at night, and showed utterly no regard for people or property. The Reverend William R. Gwaltney, of Alexander County — one of the men who later helped terminate the bandits' activities — described a typical day's work for Wade's pistoleros:

> They would ride into a man's yard, dismount, and several of them would enter his house and pointing loaded pistols at those inside would say: "If you open your mouth, we'll drop you in your tracks." While this was going on, others of the gang would be going through every drawer and trunk to be found, taking with them everything that suited them, together with every good horse on the place...All the people...lived in constant dread of them, and consequently were frightened at the mere barking of a dog or the rattle of leaves....[1]

On the side of law and order, there was a power vacuum. Confederate forces were officially no more, and the Home Guard in the region -- what was left of it after the shootout at Boone -- had been disbanded. There was as yet no Federal presence in the area, aside from a few small garrisons left in the wake of Stoneman's campaign. If Wade's depredations were to be stopped, it would be up to the mountaineers themselves to do it.

After a particularly brazen raid into Caldwell County on May 7, the local people made their first attempt to fight back. On the following Sunday night, Major Harvey Bingham — former commander of the Watauga County Home Guard, and the same Bingham who had been at the Battle of Beech Mountain — organized a party of men and led a well-planned attack on Fort Hamby.

When Bingham struck, Wade and his men were tuckered-out from their ride (and also, perhaps, from their dalliance with some of the "disreputable" ladies who had been seen coming and going from the fort). Bingham's men got the drop on the gang, and in fact were inside, with guns leveled, before Wade and his men could react.

Wade pleaded that they were helpless, and that they surrendered, and they would come peaceably, and so on — "Just give us time to dress, men." Major Bingham, gentleman that he was, obliged. The moment Wade's men sensed their captors' guard was down, they dove for their beds, where each man had hidden a carbine or a revolver, and came up blazing, some with pistols in both hands. Bingham and his men were almost pushed out of the door by the sudden wave of fire, and Bingham could do nothing to stop the rout, once it started. They left behind the bodies of two good men, named Henley and Clark, both from Caldwell County. Clark was the son of a respected Confederate general; both men were described by those who knew them as "young men of rare excellence of character."[2] Major Bingham himself had his clothes singed by several passing slugs. Some shots were fired in reply by the posse, but not a man in Wade's gang suffered so much as a scratch.

Emboldened to the point of arrogance now, Wade's men intensified their reign of terror. They singled out a wealthy gentleman farmer in Alexander County, Colonel McCurdy, believing he had hidden a quantity of gold on his land while Stoneman's men were passing through the region. McCurdy at first told them to go to hell, but changed his tune and showed them where the gold was hidden after Wade's men tied him to an apple tree and began skinning him with their Bowie knives.

While in Alexander County, Wade and his gang decided to hit the house of W.U. Green, a former Confederate officer. Green had heard they were in the area, though, and was ready for them. The bandits surrounded the house, and Wade approached the front door, dressed in a stolen Confederate uniform, and asked if he could come in for a bite to eat — he was, he explained, a paroled rebel soldier, on his way home, and powerful hungry.

"I know who you are," replied Green, "and if you come into this house, it will be over my dead body." Green meant what he said: Wade could see a pistol in one hand and a dirk in the other. Green had also armed his son and daughter and five of his servants. At about the time Green slammed the front door in Wade's face, one of the Negroes warned him that three of the desperadoes were trying to force the back door. Green ran through the house, bashed a hole in one of his windows, and opened fire, wounding one of the bandits and forcing the others to flee. Frustrated and angry, Wade decided the house was too well defended to storm, and led his men off into the night, back toward Fort Hamby.

By ten o'clock the next morning, he was being hotly pursued by 22 armed men, most of them Confederate veterans, led by Colonel Washington ("Wash") Sharpe. They tracked the outlaws all the way back to Holman's Ford, then divided their little force and approached the fortified house from two sides. They got to within 50 yards when Wade's men opened a devastating fire. Some of the bandits had three or four rifles loaded and lined up within reach.

An 18-year-old boy named Brown was killed with the first volley. Another brave lad, a 16-year-old named James Linney -- who was foolishly approaching the house on horseback -- took a Minie ball through the head, just below his right eye. The rest of the attackers, stunned, fell back in confusion. They fired dozens of shots at the fort, but their rounds merely chipped splinters out of the thick log walls. The mortally wounded 16-year-old took a long time to die; he lay where he had fallen, moaning and begging for water, until he finally expired on Monday evening. Wade's men ignored him.

Reverend Gwaltney was close by when Brown was hit. As their party neared the robbers' fort, Brown had turned in his saddle to savor the beauty of the valley, where the setting sun hung above the veiled undulations of the Blue Ridge. "What a beautiful Sunday to be engaged in work like this," the young man had mused. As soon as the firing started, Brown had seemed galvanized:

Brown hastily drawing his revolver, with flashing eye and face

307

> aflame, plunged forward into the fray, only a few steps were taken, only twice did his faithful revolver speak, when the fearful whack of the enemy bullet, as distinctly heard as the smiting together of the palms of the hands, indicated some one was struck. Brown suddenly reined in his horse, threw up his right hand from which his smoking revolver fell and exclaimed: "I'm shot, I'm killed." The hope was expressed that he was not seriously hurt. "Ah," he said, pointing to his bleeding leg from which the blood was flowing in a stream, "I shall be dead in five minutes." Then...he cried, "O, such a little time to prepare to die." These were the last words I heard him speak.[3]

The campaign to eradicate Wade and his men now became a community-wide effort. From Iredell County came a small company of veterans under Colonel Wallace Sharpe. The combined force of men from Alexander and Iredell counties began their march on Fort Hamby on the Tuesday following the attack in which Brown and Linney were slain. Just before they reached Moravian Falls, a man rode up to the column. He said he had been waylaid by one of the outlaws and was given a message, from Wade, to take to the assembled posse: "Come on. I am looking for you. I can whip a thousand of you."

Sharpe and his men held a conference and decided it would be best to send out a general call for assistance. Couriers were dispatched to Caldwell and Iredell counties, and to the Federal encampment at Lexington, asking aid from old comrades and former enemies alike. Then Colonel Sharpe's posse resumed its march. It was pitch dark when they reached Holman's Ford. A voice called out sharply: "Halt! Who comes there?"

"Men from Alexander," replied Sharpe. "And who are you?"

"Oxford's men from Caldwell. Advance!"

Thus augmented, the impromptu little army settled down for some sleep, well guarded by sentries at all points of the compass.

At daybreak, the 40 or so men broke camp and marched as far as the farm of a Mr. Tolbert. Inside Tolbert's house, a woman lay dying. She had been shot at the ford the day before, while crossing the stream in a wagon, sitting beside her husband. The shot had been fired from Fort Hamby. Tolbert, who had lived in fear of his life for weeks, was understandably agitated. He advised the men to go home and wait for heavy reinforcements. "You will not be able to take them with the small force that you have. They are on the lookout for you and have no doubt sent out for recruits...no sooner than you cross the top of yonder hill, you will be fired upon."

The matter was put to a vote. A number of men, including some of the bravest — men with the war records of heroes — were in favor of pulling back and waiting for more men. They were outvoted.

As the force neared Fort Hamby, Colonel Sharpe detailed the Reverend Gwaltney to take five men and get behind the fort, to the west. Gwaltney dutifully led his men off through a thicket of "old field pines" and cautiously inched his way uphill. "We had been in many places of danger during the war," he later wrote, "but never had our courage been tried as it was in our march through that thicket...we went single file, expecting every moment to be shot down."

At the edge of the woods, Gwaltney peered out. One of the outliers had come out of the fort and was bridling a fine-looking horse grazing in a field just below the building. Gwaltney moved off down the slope, toward Lewis Fork Creek, hoping to get a clear shot at the man — that would be one less defender to root out of the fort. By the time he got into position, however, the bandit had led the horse away.

Cursing his luck, Gwaltney suddenly heard the metallic snap of a misfire. Startled, he looked over his shoulder and saw one of his own men aiming at the creek behind him. Obviously, there was a bandit down there that Gwaltney could not see from his position, but that was clearly a danger to him. Several times, Gwaltney's comrade pulled, and each time his piece refused to shoot. In disgust, he turned back into the trees and borrowed a rifle from another man. This one worked. Gwaltney was in front of the weapon when it went off, although off to one side, of course; he thought he'd never heard a gun roar so loud. The intended target of this shot, now revealed by his sudden movements, was an outlaw who had been sitting on the side of the creek, presumably watching for the attackers. At the rifle's report and the sound of a Minie ball zipping past his ear, the man jumped into the creek and ran splashing toward the Yadkin River. No one ever saw him again.

At the shot, of course, the attackers abandoned all attempts at stealth. Inside the fortified house, Wade's men left their breakfast and manned their posts. They seemed deranged. Gwaltney had never heard a group of men make such a racket: "It was...like the howling of devils, cursing us with the most fearful oaths. They dared us to come on." Fire from the fort was so heavy and accurate that no one could leave cover and venture across open ground. The attackers kept behind trees and fallen logs, and both sides exchanged shots all day without effect. It was a stand-off.

Night fell, cloudy and moonless. Again, voices were heard among the attackers suggesting that the time had come to retreat and wait for reinforcements. Other voices, still the majority, expressed the feeling that the thing was well begun, and if they did not finish it, there might not be a second chance. Under cover of darkness, therefore, the attackers methodically laid siege to Fort Hamby, advancing under covering fire and throwing up breastworks to give themselves cover. One grizzled veteran, a man named Jim Connolly, remarked, "Well, my interest in Heaven may not be much, but such as it is, I would be willing to give it all for a piece of artillery...."[4]

Near dawn, Colonel Sharpe devised a plan for smoking out the bandits. He had spotted a small kitchen outbuilding near the fort, made from old dry pine logs and covered with boards. It was just near enough to the fort to make it worth burning. Barefooted, Sharpe crept up to the little shack, stuffed a handful of dry trash into one of the cracks in its walls, touched it with a match, and then sprinted back for the woods, accompanied by the crack of hostile rifle fire.

The kitchen went up like a pine-knot torch, throwing great gouts of blazing debris into the air and raining it down on the roof of Fort Hamby. Little fires began to spring up here and there, then began to combine and flow together into bigger fires. Pretty soon smoke could be seen gushing from the upstairs windows. The defenders now had only two choices: burn to death or face a quicker fate at the hands of their attackers. Someone yelled out for Wade and his men to surrender. One of the bandits asked what would happen to them if they did. Colonel Sharpe called back, "By God, we will kill every last one of you!"

But Wade was not finished yet. He led his men out with his

hands up, then, in the deceptive and flickering light of the fire, he broke away and "darted like an arrow" toward the river. Everybody who spotted him took a shot at him, but he passed unscathed through the hail of Minie balls, crossed the river at Holman's Ford, and was never caught.

He had left his men at the mercy of a force that was on the edge of turning into a mob. For a moment, it seemed as though Wade's men would be torn to pieces. But discipline was restored, and the victory was won with some formality and dignity.

Stakes were driven into the ground and the robbers bound to them. They begged for jail instead, but mountain justice was at work here, not "county seat justice." Colonel Sharpe told them that he would give them a little time to make their peace. "And don't pray to us," he growled, when several of them continued to beg for their lives. "Pray to God, for He alone can save you!"

Still, when some of the mountaineers began to jeer at the doomed men, Sharpe silenced them by ordering, "Men, we have given them time to repent and you shall not bother them." He commanded silence and asked Reverend Gwaltney to pray for them. Gwaltney declined, because "I feared to approach the Throne of Grace just then lest I might come into His Presence without sincere desires."

There was, rather amazingly, another preacher on hand for the battle, Isaac Oxford from Caldwell County, former captain of that county's Home Guard. He approached Gwaltney and said, "Here, hold my gun and I will pray for them." Oxford's "prayer" was simple and to the point: He thanked God for delivering the robbers into their hands and for sparing the lives of the attackers.

Somehow, to Gwaltney, that prayer didn't seem to cover every aspect of the situation. He caught Colonel Sharpe's attention and said, "I feel a desire to pray for them now." Permission was given, and "with all the earnestness in my soul," Gwaltney asked God to forgive and to save the souls of the men who were about to die. Then he stood up and took his place in the firing squad. "In a moment, the order to fire was given, and they were in eternity."[5]

That part of the night's business concluded, the victors extinguished the fire on the roof of Fort Hamby. Inside, they found a veritable pirate's trove of stolen goods, and, in the woods nearby,

20 fine horses, which were soon returned to their rightful owners. When everything of value had been removed, sometime after daybreak, it was set ablaze once more and burned to ashes.

Forty-eight hours after the burning of Fort Hamby, a detachment of 30 Federal cavalrymen arrived in response to the courier sent to Lexington. It was too late for them to help rid the countryside of Wade's band, but with the help of local guides, they proceeded to the Brushy Mountains and captured the other bandit chieftain, Simmons. Simmons was taken in chains to the jail at Lexington. But like Wade, he, too, escaped justice. Hidden in his clothing was a supply of stolen gold, and that night he bribed a guard and got away.

REVENGE AND REMEMBRANCE

A year or so after the war ended, there was a big construction project underway at Mars Hill College in Madison County. The work attracted a lot of local men who had been down on their luck since mustering-out of one army or the other.

One of these workers was a brick mason who loved to tell war stories to the younger men with whom he worked. He'd seen some hard soldiering as a Unionist guerrilla, and he had a lot of hairy yarns to spin. During the course of one of his tales, someone in the vicinity happened to bring up the by-now-famous incident of the killings at Nance Franklin's farm.

"I was there," boasted the brick mason. He went on to prove it by saying, "Usually, I can knock a squirrel out of a tree at 75 yards. Well, I done took squirrel-aim at that woman, almost close enough to touch her, and all I did was shoot off a piece of her hair."

One of the Mars Hill students who had been listening to the man's stories went home to Shelton Laurel that weekend and happened to relay the brick mason's account to a man named James Norton. Norton showed a lively interest in the tale, and offered the student a gold piece if he would introduce him to the bricklayer. The next week, Norton accompanied the student back to Mars Hill. After a little friendly prompting, the workman was glad to retell his story to Norton.

When he had finished, Norton said calmly: "That was my sister you shot the hair off of, and one of the boys you murdered was named after me." With that, he pulled a big Colt from beneath his coat and shot the brick mason in the stomach.

313

A jury eventually acquitted Norton, calling it "justifiable homicide." There was probably not a man in Madison County -- on either side, Confederate or Unionist -- who would have disputed the verdict.

During the trial, the prosecution lawyer tried to resurrect the once-common notion of the Nance boys as little more than cold-blooded bushwhackers, but the brutality of their deaths, and the ferocity with which they had defended themselves, undercut his case. At one point, he had Granny Franklin herself on the witness stand, and the judge asked her, "Madam, you tell us that you sent your young sons out to fight, and to kill or be killed. Did you bring them up for that sort of thing?"

Mrs. Franklin did not hesitate before replying. "I brought them up to be Christians, your Honor. I told them: Always be good boys, tell the truth, and be honest. But I also told them something else: If you've got to die, die like a damned dog — with your teeth in somebody's throat."

The legacy of the war took many other forms, too. On one of Colonel George Kirk's last raids into North Carolina, the Unionist raider, tired and hungry, stopped at the cabin of a man named John Franklin, near Pineola. Franklin didn't know his visitor was Kirk. So along with the food, Franklin served up some sociable conversation. At one point, he began to recount fearsome stories of the atrocities committed by Kirk. "Why if I had a few guns, I'd get a few other fellows and we'd kill the damned rascal!" Franklin bragged.

There was an angry scrape of chair on wooden planks as Kirk rose in a fury. "God damn you," he roared, "I am George Kirk!"

Franklin's wife fell to her knees, ashen-faced, and begged for her husband's life. Franklin seemed embarrassed by her behavior and stammered, "Mr. Kirk, I always knowed you wasn't half as mean as they all said you was...."

Evidently, Kirk wasn't -- at least not on this occasion. Seeing the rough humor in the situation, he grunted, reholstered his piece, and bade the Franklins a good day.

In gratitude, the Confederate family named their next child, a son, after the infamous George Kirk.

Many grand monuments and memorials have been erected since

the end of the Civil War, and some of them are located on major battlefields like Gettysburg and Antietam where they are visited by hundreds of thousands of tourists each year. But few of these monuments, perhaps, are as quietly eloquent as a pair of small granite markers placed by the inhabitants of Shelton Laurel. In 1968, a group of the Sheltons got together, pooled their resources, and commissioned the markers to memorialize their ancestors whose blood had nourished the land back in the iron-hard winter of 1863.

They could not possibly have done this in order to create a tourist attraction. Not one person in a thousand who drives by on the highway that has replaced the old French Broad Turnpike has even heard of what happened in Shelton Laurel during the Civil War. The granite markers are not set close to the road, but are on a green hillside at some distance from the passing cars. And there are no signs along the highway to tell anyone where the stones are.

But that's all right. The mountain people know where they are. Just as the mountain people still remember where the Civil War dead lie buried.

All around.

NOTES

CHAPTER 2: THE LAND AND ITS PEOPLE

1. Paludin, *Victims -- A True Story of the Civil War*, p. 23.

CHAPTER 3: THE ROOTS OF CLASS WARFARE

1. Quoted in Inscoe, John C., "Mountain Masters: Slaveholding in Western North Carolina," *North Carolina Historical Review*, April 1984, pp. 145-146.
2. Ibid, p. 158.
3. Ibid, p. 168.
4. Ibid, p. 172.

CHAPTER 4: 'WHEN THE WAR COME ALONG, I FELT MIGHTY SOUTHERN.'

1. Ambrose, Robert Paul, "A Critical Year (April 1860-April 1861): A Study of Unionist Sentiment in Western North Carolina During the Culminating Year of the Secession Movement," p. 15.
2. Ibid, p. 22.
3. Ibid.
4. Ibid, p. 33.
5. Sheppard, Muriel E., *Cabins in the Laurel*, p. 65.
6. Ambrose, p. 37.
7. Ibid, p. 42.
8. Dykeman, Wilma, *The French Broad*, p. 89.
9. Cotton, William D., "Appalachian North Carolina: A Political Study, 1860-1889," p. 101.
10. *Official Records*, Volume 18, pp. 810-811.

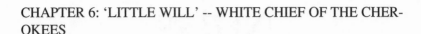

CHAPTER 6: 'LITTLE WILL' -- WHITE CHIEF OF THE CHER-
OKEES

1. Frome, Michael, *Strangers in High Places*, p. 89.
2. King, Duane H. (Edited), *The Cherokee Indian Nation*, p. 148.

CHAPTER 7: THE LEGION IN EAST TENNESSEE

1. Finger, John R., *The Eastern Band of Cherokees 1819-1900*, p.
85.
2. Russell, Mattie, "William Holland Thomas -- White Chief of the
Cherokees," pp. 360-361.
3. Thomas to his wife, Sarah Love Thomas, dated June 25, 1862;
quoted in Russell, pp. 363-364.
4. Crow, Vernon H., *Storm in the Mountains*, p. 12.
5. Ibid, p. 16.
6. Ibid.
7. Campbell, James B., "East Tennessee During the Federal
Occupation, 1863-1865," pp. 66-67.
8. Finger, p. 90.
9. *Official Records*, Volume 20/ii/p. 395.
10. Crow, p. 40.

CHAPTER 8: THE CHEROKEES ON GUARD

1. *Official Records*, Volume 30/iii/p. 474.

CHAPTER 9: CONVENTIONAL OPERATIONS, SEPTEMBER
1863 - JUNE 1864

1. *Official Records*, Volume 29/ii/pp. 836-837.
2. Finger, *The Eastern Band of Cherokees*, p. 90.
3. Ellis, Daniel, *Thrilling Adventures of Daniel Ellis, Scout*, p. 426.
4. Kirk, Charles E. (editor), *History of the 15th Pennsylvania
Cavalry*, pp. 332-333.
5. Ibid, pp. 345-346.

6. Ibid, pp. 348-349.
7. Ibid, p. 337.
8. Ibid, p. 353.
9. Ibid.
10. Mrs. M.B. Moore to Zebulon Vance, February 16, 1863, quoted in Barrett, John G., *The Civil War in North Carolina*, p. 186.
11. Crow, Vernon H., *Storm in the Mountains*, p. 58.
12. Barrett, p. 233.
13. *Official Records*, Volume 53/i/p. 324.

CHAPTER 10: LIGHTNING OUT OF TENNESSEE -- KIRK'S RAID ON MORGANTON

1. *Official Records*, Volume 52/i/p. 517.
2. Williams, Dewey E., *Burke County's Camp Vance*, p. 11.

CHAPTER 11: THE LEGION IN DECLINE

1. Crow, Vernon H., (editor), "The Justness of Our Cause: The Civil War Diaries of William W. Stringfield," Nos. 56-57, 1980-81, p. 99.
2. Ibid.
3. Clark, Walter (editor), *Histories of the Several Regiments and Battalions from North Carolina in the Great War, 1861-65*, Volume IV, p. 756.
4. Ibid.
5. *Official Records*, Volume 39/i/p. 854.
6. Ibid, Volume 42/iii/1253-1254.

CHAPTER 13: 'THE COUNTY HAS GONE UP....'

1. Paludin, Phillip Shaw, *Victims -- A True Story of the Civil War*, p. 71.
2. Castel, Albert (editor), "The Guerrilla War" — special issue of *Civil War Times Illustrated*, October 1974, p. 34.

3. Cotton, William D., "Appalachian North Carolina: A Political Study, 1860-1889," p. 112.
4. Ibid, p. 113.
5. Sheppard, Muriel E., *Cabins in the Laurel*, p. 64.
6. *Official Records*, Volume 53/supplement/pp. 326-327.

CHAPTER 14: THE 'BONNIE AND CLYDE' OF WATAUGA COUNTY

1. Arthur, John Preston, *Western North Carolina, A History from 1730 to 1913*, p. 168-169.

CHAPTER 15: THE LAST HOG

1. Hannum, Alberta Pierson, *Look Back in Love*, p. 138.

CHAPTER 16: SHOOT-OUT ON BEECH MOUNTAIN

1. Dugger, Shepherd M., *War Trails of the Blue Ridge*, p. 114-117.
2. Ibid, pp. 117-118.

CHAPTER 17: THE QUILT OF VIOLENCE

1. Paludin, Phillip Shaw, *Victims -- A True Story of the Civil War*, p. 77.
2. Sheppard, Muriel E., *Cabins in the Laurel*, pp. 52-54.
3. Arthur, John Preston, *A History of Watauga County*, p. 172.
4. Dugger, Shepherd M., *War Trails of the Blue Ridge*, pp. 122-123.

CHAPTER 18: ESCAPES AND ENCOUNTERS

1. Hadley, J.V., *Seven Months a Prisoner*, p. 149.
2. Ibid, p. 175.
3. Ibid, pp. 206-207.
4. Ibid, p. 202.
5. Ibid, p. 212.

6. Ibid, p. 221.
7. Ibid, pp. 227-228.
8. Ibid, p. 233.
9. Ibid, pp. 237-238.
10. Ibid, p. 246.
11. Richardson, Albert D., *The Secret Service -- The Field, the Dungeon, and the Escape*, p. 452.
12. Ibid, p. 458.
13. Ibid, pp. 463-464.
14. Ibid, p. 465.
15. Ibid, pp. 466-467.
16. Ibid, p. 469.
17. Ibid, pp. 185-188.

CHAPTER 19: 'BLOODY MADISON'

1. Paludin, Phillip Shaw, *Victims -- A True Story of the Civil War*, p. 29.
2. Ibid, p. 61.
3. Clark, Walter (editor), *Histories of the Several Regiments and Battalions from North Carolina in the Great War, 1861-65*, Volume III, p. 661.
4. Ibid, pp. 664-665.
5. Ibid, pp. 668-669.
6. Ibid, pp. 661.

CHAPTER 21: THE KILLING

1. Paludin, Phillip Shaw, *Victims -- A True Story of the Civil War*, p. 94.
2. Ibid, pp. 95-96.

CHAPTER 22: WINTER 1865 -- THINGS FALL APART

1. Stringfield, William W., "North Carolina Cherokees," *The North Carolina Booklet*, Volume III, No. 2, July 1903, p. 12.

2. Clark, Walter (editor), *Histories of the Several Regiments and Battalions from North Carolina in the Great War, 1861-65*, Volume IV, p. 759.

3. Ibid.

4. Dugger, Shepherd M., *War Trails of the Blue Ridge*, p. 120.

5. Crow, Vernon H., *Storm in the Mountains*.

6. *Official Records*, Volume 47/iii/pp. 730-731.

CHAPTER 23: ERUPTION FROM TENNESSEE

1. *Official Records*, Volume 45/i/p. 1074.

2. Captain Weand's narrative in Kirk, Charles E., (editor), *History of the Fifteenth Pennsylvania Cavalry*, p. 507.

3. *Official Records*, Volume 49/i/p. 810.

4. Weand in Kirk, p. 493.

5. Ibid, p. 524.

6. van Noppen, Ina W., *Stoneman's Last Raid*, p. 29.

CHAPTER 24: INTO THE PIEDMONT

1. Kirk, Charles E., (editor), *History of the Fifteenth Pennsylvania Cavalry*, p. 496.

2. Ibid, p. 500.

3. Ibid, pp. 539-540.

4. Ibid, p. 501.

5. van Noppen, Ina W., *Stoneman's Last Raid*, pp. 40-41.

6. Kirk, p. 543.

7. Ibid, pp. 545-546.

8. van Noppen, p. 61.

9. Spencer, Cornelia Phillips, *The Last Ninety Days of the War in North Carolina*, p. 202.

10. Ibid, pp. 205-206.

CHAPTER 25: ...AND BACK TO THE MOUNTAINS

1. Spencer, Cornelia Phillips, *The Last Ninety Days of the War in*

North Carolina, pp. 196-197.

2. van Noppen, Ina W., *Stoneman's Last Raid*, pp. 78-79.

3. Kirk, Charles E., (editor), *History of the Fifteenth Pennsylvania Cavalry*, pp. 507-508.

4. van Noppen, p. 85.

5. Kirk, p. 508.

CHAPTER 26: THE 'BATTLE' OF ASHEVILLE

1. Sondley, F.A., *A History of Buncombe County, N.C.*, p. 691.

CHAPTER 28: THE FALL OF FORT HAMBY

1. Pittard, Pen L., *Prologue -- A History of Alexander County*, p. 42.

2. Clark, Walter (editor), *Histories of the Several Regiments and Battalions from North Carolina in the Great War, 1861-65*, Volume V, p. 287.

3. Ibid, p. 291.

4. Ibid, p. 293.

5. Pittard, p. 43.

BIBLIOGRAPHY

Sources relevant to the trilogy as a whole:

Ashe, Samuel A'Court, *History of North Carolina*, Volume II, The Reprint Press, Spartinburg, 1971.

Barrett, John G., *The Civil War in North Carolina*, University of North Carolina Press, Chapel Hill, 1963.

Barrett, John G., and Yearns, W. Buck, *North Carolina Civil War Documentary*, University of North Carolina Press, Chapel Hill, 1980.

Butler, Lindley S., and Watson, Alan D., *The North Carolina Experience -- An Interpretive and Documentary History*, University of North Carolina Press, Chapel Hill, 1984.

Clark, Walter (editor), *Histories of the Several Regiments and Battalions from North Carolina in the Great War, 1861-65*, Published by the State of North Carolina, Goldsboro, 1901 (four volumes).

Commager, Henry Steele (editor), *The Official Atlas of the Civil War*, Thomas Yoseloff Inc., New York, 1958.

Corbitt, D.L. (editor), *Pictures of the Civil War Period in North Carolina*, North Carolina Department of Archives and History, Raleigh, 1958.

Esposito, Vincent J. (editor), *The West Point Atlas of American Wars*, Frederick Praeger, New York, 1960 edition.

Gilham, William, *Manual of Instruction for the Volunteers and Militia*, West and Johnson, Richmond, Virginia, 1861.

Johnson, Robert Underwood, and Buel, Clarence Clough (editors), *Battles and Leaders of the Civil War*, Commemorative Edition in four volumes, Thomas Yoseloff, Inc., New York, 1956.

Jordan, Weymouth T. (editor), *North Carolina Troops, 1861-65*, in ten volumes, North Carolina Department of Archives and History, Raleigh, 1981.

Lefler, Hugh T., and Newsome, Albert R. (editors), *North Carolina -- The History of a Southern State*, University of North Carolina Press, Chapel Hill, 1963 and 1975 editions.

McPherson, James M., *Battle Cry of Freedom*, Oxford University Press, New York, 1988.

McWhiney, Grady, and Jamieson, Perry, *Attack and Die -- Civil War Tactics and the Southern Heritage*, University of Alabama Press, 1982.

Mitchell, Joseph R., *Military Leaders of the Civil War*, G. P. Putnam's Sons, New York, 1972.

Official Records, The War of the Rebellion, Volume LXVII, "Operations in the Carolinas," Thomas Settle, 1865.

Tucker, Glenn, *Front Rank*, North Carolina Confederate Centennial Commission, Raleigh, 1962.

Sources relevant to Volume Two, "The Mountains":

Allen, W.C., *Annals of Haywood County*, privately printed, 1935.

Ambrose, Robert Paul, "A Critical Year (April 1860-April 1861): A Study of Unionist Sentiment in Western North Carolina During the Culminating Year of the Secession Movement," master's thesis, University of North Carolina at Greensboro, 1975.

Arthur, John Preston, *A History of Watauga County*, Everett Waddey Co., Richmond, Virginia, 1915.

Arthur, John Preston, *Western North Carolina, A History from 1730 to 1913*, Raleigh, North Carolina, 1914.

Brewer, Alberta, *Valley So Wild*, East Tennessee Historical Society, Knoxville, 1975.

Bryan, Charles Faulkner, "The Civil War in East Tennessee, a Social, Political, and Economic Study," Ph.D thesis, University of Tennessee, Knoxville, 1978.

Callahan, North, *Smoky Mountain Country*, Duell, Sloan & Pearce, New York, 1952.

Campbell, James B., "East Tennessee During the Federal Occupation, 1863-1865," Publications of the East Tennessee Historical Society, No. 19, 1947.

Carpenter, Clarence A., *The Walton War and Other Tales of the Great Smoky Mountains*, Copple House Books, Lakemont, Georgia, 1979.

Castel, Albert (editor), "The Guerrilla War" — special issue of *Civil War Times Illustrated*, October 1974.

Clark, Walter (editor), *Histories of the Several Regiments and Battalions from North Carolina in the Great War, 1861-65*, Published by the State of North Carolina, Goldsboro, 1901 (four volumes).

Cotton, William D., "Appalachian North Carolina: A Political Study, 1860-1889," Ph.D thesis, University of North Carolina, Chapel Hill, 1954.

Crow, Vernon H., (editor), "The Justness of Our Cause: The Civil War Diaries of William W. Stringfield," Publications of the East Tennessee Historical Society, Nos. 56-57, 1980-81.

Crow, Vernon H., *Storm in the Mountains*, Museum of the Cherokee Indian, Cherokee, North Carolina, 1982.

Dykeman, Wilma, *The French Broad*, Rinehart & Co., New York, 1955.

Dugger, Shepherd M., *War Trails of the Blue Ridge*, privately printed, Banner Elk, North Carolina, 1932.

Ellis, Daniel, *Thrilling Adventures of Daniel Ellis, Scout*, Haper and Brothers, New York, 1867.

Fain, James T., *A Partial History of Henderson County*, Arno Press, New York, 1980.

Finger, John R., *The Eastern Band of Cherokees, 1819-1900*, University of Tennessee Press, Knoxville, 1984.

Fink, Harold S., "The East Tennessee Campaign and the Battle of Knoxville in 1863," Publications of the East Tennessee Historical Society, Knoxville, No. 29, 1957.

FitzSimmons, Frank L., *From the Banks of the Oklawaha*, Golden Glow Publishing Co., Hendersonville, North Carolina, 1976.

Fletcher, Arthur L., *Ashe County: A History*, Ashe County Research Association, Jefferson, North Carolina, 1963.

Frome, Michael, *Strangers in High Places*, Doubleday & Co., New York, 1966.

Hadley, J.V., *Seven Months a Prisoner*, Scribners & Sons, 1898.

Hannum, Alberta Pierson, *Look Back in Love*, Vanguard Press, New York, 1969.

Hayes, Johnson J., *The Land of Wilkes*, Wilkes County Histrorical Society, Wilkesboro, North Carolina, 1962.

Hickerson, Thomas F., *Echoes of Happy Valley*, privately printed, Chapel Hill, North Carolina, 1962.

Inscoe, John C., "Mountain Masters: Slaveholding in Western North Carolina," *North Carolina Historical Review*, April 1984.

King, Duane H. (editor), *The Cherokee Indian Nation*, University of Tennessee Press, Knoxville, 1979.

Kirk, Charles E., (editor), *History of the Fifteenth Pennsylvania Cavalry*, Philadelphia, 1906.

Madden, David, "Unionist Resistance to Confederate Occupation: The Bridge Burners of East Tennessee," Publications of the East Tennessee Historical Society, Nos. 52-53, 1980-81.

McLeod, John Angus, *From These Stones -- The First Hundred Years of Mars Hill College*, Mars Hill, North Carolina, 1955.

Medford, Clark, *The Early History of Haywood County*, privately published, Waynesville, North Carolina, 1961.

Medford, Clark, *Mountain Times, Mountain People*, privately published, Waynesville, North Carolina, 1963.

van Noppen, Ina W., "The Significance of Stoneman's Last Raid," *North Carolina Historical Review*, January-October 1961.

van Noppen, Ina W., *Stoneman's Last Raid*, North Carolina State University Print Shop, Raleigh, 1966.

van Noppen, Ina W., John J., *Western North Carolina Since the Civil War*, Appalachian Consortium Press, Boone, North Carolina, 1973.

Paludin, Phillip Shaw, *Victims -- A True Story of the Civil War*, University of Tennessee Press, Knoxville, 1981.

Phifer, Edward W., *Burke -- The History of a North Carolina County, 1777-1920*, privately published, Morganton, North Carolina, 1977.

Pittard, Pen L., *Prologue -- A History of Alexander County*, privately published, Taylorsville, North Carolina, 1958.

Richardson, Albert D., *The Secret Service -- The Field, the Dungeon, and the Escape*, American Publishing Co., Hartford, Connecticut, 1865.

Russell, Mattie, "William Holland Thomas — White Chief of the Cherokees," Ph.D thesis, Duke University, Durham, North Carolina, 1956.

Sheppard, Muriel E., *Cabins in the Laurel*, University of North Carolina Press, Chapel Hill, 1935.

Siler, Leon M., "My Lai Controversy Recalls 1863 Tragedy on the Shelton Laurel," *The State Magazine*.

Sondley, F.A., *A History of Buncombe County, N.C.*, Advocate Printing Co., Asheville, North Carolina, 1930.

Southern Historical Society Papers, Volume XXI, pp. 294-296, "A Modern Horatius," Richmond, Virginia, 1893.

Spencer, Cornelia Phillips, *The Last Ninety Days of the War in North Carolina*, Watchman Publishing Co., New York, 1866.

Stringfield, William W., "North Carolina Cherokees," *The North Carolina Booklet*, Volume III, No. 2, July 1903.

Wellman, Manly Wade, *The Kingdom of Madison*, University of North Carolina Press, Chapel Hill, 1973.

Wharton, H.M. (editor), *War Songs and Poems of the Southern Confederacy*, Philadelphia, Pennsylvania, 1904.

Williams, Dewey E., *Burke County's Camp Vance*, privately printed in Morganton, North Carolina, 1976.

INDEX

Henderson County, 21, 26, 29, 37, 170, 174-176, 185

Hendersonville, 28, 37, 182, 184, 286

Hendersonville Times, 35

Heroes of America, 116, 196-197, 242

Heth, General Henry, 44, 219, 223-224, 231

Hillsville, 261

Home Guard, 2, 47-49, 99, 107, 118, 122, 141, 145, 154, 161-163, 168-169, 172-176, 178, 181, 184, 191, 193, 197, 199-200, 202, 236-237, 240-242, 247, 252, 254-255, 261, 269, 271, 280-282, 293, 305-306, 311

Hood, General John B., 246, 248, 274

Hooker, General Joseph, 245-246

I

Iredell County, 310

Iredell Express, 278

J

Jackson County, 21, 29, 93, 125, 129

Jackson, General Alfred C. ("Old Mudwall"), 84-87, 111-112

Jackson, General Stonewall, 84, 245

Jamestown, 267

Jefferson, 29, 241

Johnston, General Joseph E., 105, 110, 175, 246, 248-249, 270-271, 275, 277, 285-287, 291-292, 296

Johnstone, Andrew, 176-178

Junior Reserves, 271

K

Keelan, James, 78-79

Keith, Colonel James A., 219, 223, 225-227, 229-231

Kirby-Smith, General Edmund, 62-63, 70-71, 223

Kirk, Colonel George W., 74, 98-99, 109, 113-119, 130-131, 135-136, 144-145, 150, 152, 157, 161-162, 166, 178, 201, 203, 232, 237-239, 241, 256, 271, 280, 282, 292, 295, 297-300, 314

Kirkland, "Bushwacker," 171

Kirkland, "Turkey Trot," 171

Knoxville, 22, 38, 44, 65-67, 70-72, 76-77, 84-89, 95-96, 99, 102-103, 107-108, 119, 168, 186, 188, 190-191, 194-195, 201-202, 217, 229, 253, 277, 295-296, 299-300

L

Laurel Valley, 209, 214, 224-226

Lee, General Robert E., 44, 124, 127, 157-158, 171, 175, 197, 223, 245-246, 248-251, 260-263, 271, 276, 285, 291-292

Lenoir, 41, 256, 277, 279-282

Levi, John T., 84-85

Lincolnites, 10, 77, 204, 215-216

Lincolnton, 277, 279

Linville, 174

Longstreet, General James, 44, 87, 102, 104, 111, 143, 146

Love, James Robert, 71, 84, 86-88, 110-112, 124-125, 235, 237, 285, 295-296, 298-299, 301

Love, Matthew, 71, 127-128

Lumbee Indians, 60

Lynchburg, 68, 260, 262-264

M

Macon County, 21, 29, 70, 108, 125

Madison County, 5, 9, 11-12, 21, 26, 34, 37, 44, 83, 89, 114, 116, 135, 142, 157, 178, 209, 213-216, 219, 221, 225, 231, 232, 313-314

Mars Hill, 115, 145, 210, 313

Mars Hill College, 145, 313

Marshall, 9-11, 83, 98-99, 210, 218-219, 222, 225, 227-228

Seddon, James A. (Confederate Secretary of War), 129, 146
Sevier, 15
Sevier County, 61, 78
Sevierville, 89-90, 99, 102-103
Shallow Ford, 269-270
Sharpe, Colonel Washington, 307
Shelby Eagle, 35
Shelton, 15
Shelton Laurel, 3, 9, 44, 83, 135, 178, 209-212, 219, 223, 227, 229, 231, 313, 315
Sherman, General William Tecumseh, 4, 45, 78, 119, 246-251, 270, 285-287, 292
Simmons, 303, 305, 312
Smoky Mountains (see also "Great Smoky Mountains"), 14, 56, 58, 86, 89-90, 96-97, 102-104, 130, 176, 209, 226, 237
Soco Gap, 238, 296
Spencer repeating rifles, 115, 117-119, 136, 163, 202, 237, 252, 282

Statesville, 196-197, 276, 279-280
Stoneman, General George, 128, 130, 245-262, 264-265, 267, 269-277, 279-281, 292, 295-297, 303-306
Strawberry Plains, 67-69, 71, 73, 78, 81, 83, 86, 89, 121, 235, 300
Stringfield, William W., 69-70, 74, 78-79, 121, 123-126, 128, 130-131, 235-239, 296-297, 300-301
Sugar Grove, 240, 253
Surry County, 21, 37, 143, 169, 261
Swannanoa Gap, 22, 285, 295

T

Tait, Colonel George, 242
Teague, Captain Robert, 178-179
Terrell, James W., 65-66, 69, 71, 73-74
"The Grooms Tune," 179
Third North Carolina Mounted Infantry Regiment (Union Army), 114, 295
Thomas, William Holland, 27-29, 54-63, 65-73, 80-86, 88-90, 92, 95-96, 98-111, 121-127, 129, 131, 171, 218, 225, 235-238, 242, 252, 294-302
Thomas's Highland Legion, 3-4, 54, 62-63, 65, 67-69, 71-72, 74-75, 78, 80, 82-88, 92, 96-97, 99, 101, 103, 107, 109-112, 116, 121-124, 127-130, 170, 192, 203, 235, 285, 295-297, 301
Transylvania County, 37, 170, 218

V

Valle Crucis, 240-241
Vance, Brigadier General Robert B., 27, 95, 102-106, 110, 129, 131, 152, 251-252, 300
Vance, Jack, 187-192, 194-195
Vance, Zebulon Baird, 27, 33-35, 37, 44, 54, 58, 95, 98, 106-107, 111, 126, 129, 138-139, 143-146, 148-149, 225, 231, 242, 270
Vaughn, John C., 128
Vicksburg, Battle of, 142

W

Wade, 303-308, 310-312
Walker, William C., 70, 72, 84, 86-88, 92-93, 106, 128, 170
Warm Springs, 98, 102, 129-131, 225, 292
Watauga County, 5, 21, 26, 29, 140-141, 143, 152-153, 157, 161, 164, 171-173, 240-241, 253-255, 271, 305-306
Waynesville, 54, 71, 170, 237-239, 286, 292, 295-296, 298-300
Weand, Captain, 252-253, 265-266, 285, 288
West, Captain John, 47-49
Wheeler, General Joseph, 247, 264
White Sulphur Springs, 298, 301
Wilkes County, 5, 21, 33, 37, 139, 143, 196-197, 203, 258, 303-305